Social Justice and Islamic Economics

T0298883

Under the current economic order, social injustice is ever-increasing. Issues such as poverty, inhumane working conditions, inadequate wages, social insecurity and an unhealthy labor market continue to persist. Many nations are also unable to produce policies capable of resolving these problems. The characteristics of the capitalist system currently render it unable to provide social justice. In fact, on the contrary, the system reinforces these injustices and prevents economic and social welfare from reaching the masses. Many Muslim scholars have analyzed and, indeed, criticized this system for years.

This book argues that an alternative and more equitable theoretical and practical economical order can be developed within the framework of Islamic principles. On the other hand, the experiences of societies under the rule of Muslim governments do not always seem to hold great promise for an alternative understanding of social justice. In addition, the behaviors of Muslim individuals within their economic lives are mostly shaped by the necessities of daily economic conditions rather than by the tenets of Islam that stand with social justice. Until the 1990s, studies of Islamic economics made connections between finance and the notion of social justice, but work conducted more recently has neglected this issue.

It is therefore evident that the topic of social justice needs to be revisited in a more in-depth manner. Filling an important gap in existing literature, the book uniquely connects social justice and Islamic finance and economics on this topic. Theory, practice and key issues are presented simultaneously throughout this book, which is based on the writings of a number of eminent scholars.

Toseef Azid is Professor of Economics at the College of Business and Economics, Qassim University, Saudi Arabia.

Lutfi Sunar is Associate Professor of Sociology at the Istanbul Medeniyet University, Turkey.

Islamic Business and Finance Series
Series Editor: Ishaq Bhatti

There is an increasing need for western politicians, financiers, bankers and indeed the western business community in general to have access to high quality and authoritative texts on Islamic financial and business practices. Drawing on expertise from across the Islamic world, this new series will provide carefully chosen and focused monographs and collections, each authored/edited by an expert in their respective field all over the world.

The series will be pitched at a level to appeal to middle and senior management in both the western and the Islamic business communities. For the manager with a western background the series will provide detailed and up-to-date briefings on important topics; for the academics, postgraduates, business communities, manager with western and an Islamic background the series will provide a guide to best practice in business in Islamic communities around the world, including Muslim minorities in the west and majorities in the rest of the world.

Dilemmas and Challenges in Islamic Finance
Looking at Equity and Microfinance
Edited by Yasushi Suzuki and Mohammad Dulal Miah

Islamic Social Finance
Entrepreneurship, Cooperation and the Sharing Economy
Edited by Valentino Cattelan

Rethinking Islamic Finance
Markets, Regulations and Islamic Law
Ayesha Bhatti and Saad Azmat

Social Justice and Islamic Economics
Theory, Issues and Practice
Edited by Toseef Azid and Lutfi Sunar

For more information about this series, please visit www.routledge.com/Islamic-Business-and-Finance-Series/book-series/ISLAMICFINANCE

Social Justice and Islamic Economics

Theory, Issues and Practice

Edited by Toseef Azid and Lutfi Sunar

Routledge
Taylor & Francis Group

LONDON AND NEW YORK

First published 2019 by Routledge

2 Park Square, Milton Park, Abingdon, Oxfordshire OX14 4RN
52 Vanderbilt Avenue, New York, NY 10017

Routledge is an imprint of the Taylor & Francis Group, an informa business

First issued in paperback 2020

British Library Cataloguing-in-Publication Data
A catalogue record for this book is available from the British Library

Library of Congress Cataloging-in-Publication Data
Names: Azid, Toseef, editor. | Sunar, Lèutfi, editor.
Title: Social justice and Islamic economics : theory, issues and practice / edited by Toseef Azid and Lutfi Sunar.
Description: Abingdon, Oxon ; New York, NY : Routledge, 2019. | Series: Islamic business and finance series | Includes index.
Subjects: LCSH: Social justice--Religious aspects--Islam. | Economics--Religious aspects--Islam. | Social justice--Islamic countries. | Economics--Islamic countries.
Classification: LCC BP173.43 .S63 2019 | DDC 297.2/73--dc23
LC record available at https://lccn.loc.gov/2018051656

ISBN: 978-1-138-55881-6 (hbk)
ISBN: 978-0-367-66047-5 (pbk)

Typeset in Times New Roman
by Integra Software Services Pvt. Ltd.

Contents

vi   *Contents*

Figures

Tables

Contributors

Qazi Masood Ahmed, PhD, Professor and Director, Centre for Business and Economic Research, Institute of Business Administration (IBA), earlier he also served the institute as the Chairperson, Centre for Executive Education (CEE). Other current assignment includes member Tax Advisory Council, the Federal Board of Revenue, Government of Pakistan. Dr. Qazi also served Government of Sindh as its Chief Economist for two years. His research and teaching experience is spread over 25 years and he has published over 50 papers in international and national journals. Additionally, he also served the Social Policy and Development Centre for more than seven years as its Technical Adviser.

Toseef Azid, PhD, is Professor of Economics at the College of Business and Economics, Qassim University, Saudi Arabia and International Visiting Research Scholar of Economics Department, Wayne State University, USA. He holds a PhD in Economics from the University College of Wales, Aberystwyth, UK (1993), a Master's in Economics from Quaid-i-Azam University (1979). He received a COT Scholarship from the government of Pakistan to study at UCW, an Overseas Research Scholarship from British government, and a Fulbright Award Scholar in Residence (2006) where he worked on a research project on "Economics of Middle Eastern Countries." He was a visiting Fellow at the Markfield Institute of Higher Education UK (2005–2006 and 2007). He has taught in Pakistan, Brunei, UK, USA and Saudi Arabia. His research focuses on technological change, development Economics, labor economics, Islamic economics and Islamic finance. He has published more than 60 papers in local and international journals. He has participated in several conferences held in Iran, Saudi Arabia, Turkey, Canada, Australia, Indonesia, Malaysia, Bahrain, Qatar and Pakistan. One of his most recent books has been published by Routledge, UK (*Labor in an Islamic Setting: Theory and Practice*).

Valentino Cattelan, PhD, is currently a fellow at the Käte Hamburger Kolleg "Recht als Kultur," University of Bonn. His research focuses on classical fiqh and its contemporary application in the market of Islamic finance. His work intersects law, economics and religion, with a particular emphasis on the comparison between fiqh and law as distinct normative disciplines, their underlying rationales, their distinct property rights theory and the conceptualization of the market in Islamic economics. Since the completion of his PhD in Law and Economics (Siena), Dr. Cattelan has held research positions at the University of Rome Tor Vergata, the Oxford Centre for Islamic Studies, IE Business School in Madrid and the Max Planck Institute for Social Anthropology in Halle. He is the author of several articles in Islamic contract and commercial law, and the editor of the volumes *Islamic Finance in Europe: Towards a Plural Financial System* (2013, Edward Elgar), and *Islamic Social Finance: Entrepreneurship, Cooperation and the Sharing Economy* (forthcoming, Routledge).

Muhammad Omer Chaudhry, PhD, is Associate Professor at Bahauddin Zakariya University, Multan, Pakistan and holds a PhD in Logistics/ Supply Chain Management with a specialization in Transport Economics from Molde University College, Norway, MSc in Logistics from the same College, MPhil from BZU, Multan. He has published a number of academic papers in national and international journals. He presented many papers at peer-reviewed conferences all over the globe. He has also conducted some significant research in Islamic economics.

Masudul Alam Choudhury, PhD, is Visiting Professor at the Department of *Shari'ah* and Economics, Academy of Islamic Studies, University of Malaya and International Chair, Postgraduate Program in Islamic Economics and Finance (IEF), Faculty of Economics, Trisakti University, Jakarta, Indonesia. He served as professor at School of Business Administration, Cape Breton University Sydney, Nova Scotia, Canada (1985–2006), Department of Economics and Finance, College of Economics and Political Science, Sultan Qaboos University, Muscat, Oman (2006–2014), Professorial Chair of Islamic Finance, Institute of Islamic Banking and Finance, International Islamic University Malaysia Kuala Lumpur, Malaysia (2014), Visiting Foreign Professor, Institute of Agricultural and Resource Economics, University of Agriculture Faisalabad, Pakistan (Appointed by Higher Education Commission Pakistan, 2016), Visiting Professor, Social Economy Centre, Ontario Institute for Studies in Education, University of Toronto, Canada (2014–2015; 2017 July–Aug on Research Leave from APIUM). He earned his PhD (Political Economy) from University of Toronto in 1977, Master of Economics from University of Toronto in 1973, MPhil Mathematical Statistics from University of Islamabad, Pakistan in 1969, MSc Pure and Applied Mathematics, University of Islamabad in 1968 and BSc Hons. Pure Mathematics from University of Dhaka, in 1967. He is Editor-in-Chief and founder of the SCOPUS-listed, journal *Humanomics: International Journal of Systems & Ethics*. He has more than 20 books to his credit and many academic papers published in renowned international journals. He has also won notable international awards, i.e. COMCEC 30th Anniversary Academic Award for Islamic Economics & Finance, Global Award in Islamic Humanities, Visiting Fellow, Oxford Centre for Islamic Studies, Rockefeller Fellow in Bellagio Study and Conference Center, Sultan Qaboos University (National University of Oman) Distinguished Research Awards and King Fahd University of Petroleum and Minerals (Saudi Arabia) Educational Service Award.

Mehmet Tarik Eraslan is currently a PhD student in Yıldırım Beyazıt University department of Social Policies. He is an economics graduate from Ankara University, Turkey and holds a Master's degree in European Studies from Middle East Technical University and a Master's degree in Economics from North Carolina State University, USA.

Ben Jedidia Khoutem, PhD, is Associate Professor of economics at The High Institute of Accounting (ISCAE), Tunisia. She completed her undergraduate studies at the Faculty of Economics and Management of Sfax in 1993 and subsequently taught there. She has received an honorary Presidential Prize in Economics. Then, she received a Master's degree of Advanced Studies in Money, Finance and Banks from University Lumière Lyon II, France in 1994, and completed her PhD in Economics at University Lumière Lyon II in 1998. Her first academic job was as an Assistant Professor on the Faculty of Economics and Management of Sfax, 1999–2004. Dr. Ben Jedidia's publications and research areas pertain to Islamic banking, financial intermediation, financial development. She has published in *Journal of Policy Modeling, Journal of Religious Ethics, Etudes en Economie Islamique, International Journal of Islamic and Middle Eastern Finance and Management, Journal of Islamic Accounting and Business Research*, among others.

Ozan Maraşli is a research assistant at the Department of Islamic Economics and Finance, Istanbul Sabahattin Zaim University, Turkey. He holds his BSc in Business Administration from Bilkent University, Ankara, Turkey (2014) and is currently studying for a Master's in Economics at Istanbul Technical University, Turkey. He is also a member of the Research Center for Islamic Economics (IKAM), which contributes to the knowledge of Islamic economics and raises awareness about the field both at the national and international levels.

Osamah Hussein Al Rawashdeh, PhD, is currently an Assistant Professor at University of Qassim College of Business and Economics and Director of AACSB Office (CBE). He earned his Bachelor's degree at Poona University (1994, India), his Master's degree at M.S. Baroda University (1996, India) and PhD at University of Rajasthan (2001, India). He has more than 13 academic research publications and has also given invited international conference talks. His interest research is funded by the corporate finance, credit management and banking and non-banking systems. He possesses a wealth of knowledge in the financial theory of teaching and applications in college classroom, acquired by attending seminars and workshops. He is the Director of the AACSB Office in CBE and serves in many committees (Director of the Financial Program, and Director of the Curriculum Development Committee, and Revising and Developing Curriculum etc.) He has published in national and international peer-reviewed journals also serving as international advisor of academic journals.

Yulizar D. Sanrego, PhD, is currently director of Centre of Islamic Economic & Finance Pesantren (CIEFP)—University of Darussalam Gontor and Economic Advisor to Saudi Arabia Monetary Authority (SAMA). His holds PhD in Islamic Economics from Syarif Hidayatullah—State Islamic University, Indonesia with the thesis title on "The Effect of Social Capital on Loan Repayment Behavior: A Study on Group Lending Model (GLM) Application in Islamic Microfinance Institution." Part of the dissertation was awarded the Best Research Paper at the 2nd Sharia Banking Research Forum (FRPS)—Central Bank of Indonesia. He is doing some research, particularly in the field of Islamic Economics, Finance and Fiqh Muamalah issues. He used to become fellow researcher for two years (2006–2008) in Central Bank of Indonesia. He is the recipient of IRTI-IDB Research Grant in the field of Islamic Microfinance and The Ministry of Religious Affairs Research Grant in the issue of Corporate Sukuk Development. He appointed Working Group of The Committee of Islamic Financial Services Development (KPJKS)—Finance Services Authority (FSA), Republic of Indonesia since 2014.

Salman Ahmed Shaikh, PhD, is a scholar in Economics at National University of Malaysia. He did BBA Finance from Bahria University, MS Finance from SZABIST and a Master's in Economics from Institute of Business Administration. He has published several peer-reviewed papers and book chapters in the field of Islamic Economics and Finance. He has presented his research in conferences held in Turkey, Indonesia, Malaysia, Brunei and Pakistan. He has also taught in Pakistan at the Institute of Business Administration Karachi and SZABIST.

Lutfi Sunar, PhD, is currently Associate Professor in the Department of Sociology in Istanbul Medeniyet University, Turkey. His major research interests are classical sociological theory, orientalism, modernization, social change and political economy. He has published various articles in international journals around this field. Among his recent books are *Marx and Weber on Oriental Societies* (2014), *Türkiye'de Toplumsal Değişim* (as editor, 2014), and *Eurocentrism at the Margins: Encounters, Critics and Going Beyond* (as editor, 2016), *Debates on Civilization in the Muslim World: Critical Perspectives on Islam and Modernity* (as editor, 2016).

Omer Faruk Tekdogan, is currently Deputy Head of Department at Under-secretariat of Treasury—Republic of Turkey. He worked as a Policy Analyst at Development Co-Operation Directorate in Organisation for Economic Co-Operation and Development (2016–2017) where his main research areas were Official Development Finance for infrastructure, investment, private sector development and regional connectivity. He is a PhD candidate in Islamic Economics and Finance in Istanbul University and he holds a Master's in Economics from North Carolina State University. His past and present research fields cover Islamic economics, Islamic finance, monetary economics, banking and development economics.

Husnu Tekin got his Bachelor's degree from Erciyes University in Economics and a Master's degree in International Development Policy from Duke University. He is currently a PhD student at the Department of Islamic Economics and Finance in Istanbul University. He has completed his coursework and taken the PhD proficiency exam and is currently writing his dissertation on the topic of "Economic Institutions in Islamic Civilizations and Their Role in Income Inequality." He has successfully defended at two thesis monitoring committees and is expected to be awarded his PhD in the first half of 2018. He is currently working for the Turkish Treasury as Vice Chairmen in the Directorate of Administrative and Financial Affairs. His main research interests are Islamic economics and finance, poverty & inequality, structural reforms and labor market. As well as English (advance) he knows Arabic (intermediate).

Aimatul Yumna, PhD, is a lecturer and researcher at Faculty of Economics Padang State University Indonesia. She holds a PhD in Microfinance from Deakin University Australia and a Master's in Finance from the University of New South Wales, Australia. She was awarded the Australian Development Scholarship (2005) and DIKTI Scholarship from government of Indonesia (2010). She was a research Fellow at the Financial Services Authority of Indonesia (Otoritas Jasa Keuangan) where she worked on the issue of Islamic banking product development. Her major research interests are on microfinance, Islamic charity, Islamic economics, and Islamic finance. She contributed several books chapters to the *Handbook of Research on Development and Religion and Islam and Development*. She also participated in several reputable conferences held in Qatar, Turkey and Indonesia.

Foreword

Social justice is an aspiration throughout the world but all too often outcomes are disappointing with increasing wealth and income disparities. Many of the young find themselves excluded from economic activity as they face futures of lengthy unemployment. Selfish behavior by high earners manifests itself through corruption at the expense of the poor. Markets clearly are not working in many economies resulting in social and economic injustice.

To ensure greater social justice moral guidance is needed, and this is more likely to succeed if it is underpinned by religious teaching. This newly edited volume demonstrates that social justice is inherent to Islamic teaching. The approach is multifaceted with the potential for different areas of economic and financial activity to be governed by the theory of justice in Islam. Believers have direct responsibility to the Almighty for how they manage the resources under their control. The privilege of ownership bestows social obligations and should be seen as an opportunity by the economically active to serve their Creator.

The contributors cover a wide range of institutional topics, including whether Islamic banks can contribute to social justice through their allocation of finance. Institutions such as *waqf* and *Zakat* are examined in depth, as these are of crucial importance to how Islam approaches social justice. An insightful contribution on how micro-*takaful* can assist those in the informal economy breaks new ground. In summary this book is a very welcome addition to the literature on Islamic economics and finance. It is also a valuable contribution to the extensive literature on social justice which deserves to be widely read.

Rodney Wilson,
Emeritus Professor,
Durham University, UK

Preface

Under the rule of the dominating economical order, income injustice increases every passing day; poverty has become a universal problem; inhumane working conditions, inadequate wages, social insecurity and an unhealthy labor market have all continued to persist till this day. Many states are also unable to produce policies capable of meeting these demands. Characteristics of the current capitalist policies that make it unable to provide social justice, which, on the contrary, are reinforcing this injustice and preventing the economic and social welfare from reaching the large masses have been criticized by Muslim scholars for years. Claims that an alternative theoretical and practical economical order has been developed within the framework of Islamic principles follow these criticisms.

On the other hand, the experiences obtained in societies under the rule of Muslim governors do not seem to promise an alternative social justice understanding. In addition, the behaviors of Muslim individuals within their economic life are mostly shaped by the necessities of the daily economic conditions rather than by the conducts of Islam that stand with social justice. At this point, when we take into consideration the aim of the studies produced under the topic of Islamic economics in the 1960s and its close relation to the notion of social justice, that is, despite the studies that were conducted in the later years which were more interested in the area of finance, it becomes clearer that the topic of social justice needs to be discussed again in a more well-founded manner.

In this context, the fourth Islamic Economics Workshop aims at holding discussions that approach issues closely related to social justice from the perspective of Islamic economics. The objective is to gather academics from various parts of the world conducting studies in this area to examine the causes of the current social and economic injustice in an in-depth and realistic manner. Also, they are gathered to conduct a collective study on how to form a theoretical basis for a social justice understanding based on Islamic principles for which alternative mechanisms are to be included, in addition to the kind of concrete solutions that are to be developed within this understanding.

The fourth Islamic Economics Workshop was held by the Association for Science, Culture, and Education (ILKE), the Scientific Studies Association (ILEM) and the Turkish Entrepreneurship and Business Ethics Association (IGIAD) in Istanbul from April 2–3, 2016. The topic of the workshop was "Social Justice from the Perspective of Islamic Economy." This workshop was hosted by Istanbul University, papers discussed social justice and relative subjects from the perspective of Islamic Economics. This current volume has some selected papers from the fourth Islamic Economics Workshop.

Editors

Toseef Azid and Lutfi Sunar

1 Social justice in Islam

An introduction

Toseef Azid and Lutfi Sunar

The literature on social justice and Islam is limited. Mostly this literature is composed of religious sources and interpretation of the texts. However, the problem of social inequality is rising today all over the world because of neoliberal economic policies. For that reason, the issue should have been analyzed from a factual and social viewpoint. In this volume, we aimed to discuss the theoretical and practical solutions to the current problems related to the inequality and social justice.

One of the hottest topics of the contemporary social theory is justice. In the last 50 years, a deep and disseminated discussion is going on between liberals, socialists and communitarians, which has been started and extended by John Rawls, Alasdair McIntyre, Robert Nozick, Amartya Sen and many other prominent social theoreticians. The main focus of these discussions is the rising inequalities and diminishing social justice in the world capitalist order.

On the other hand, the issue keeps its importance for the non-Western world under the conditions of unequal global development. It does not only have economic meaning but also much political and theological significance because of the ruins of the colonization. In modern times, many Islamic scholars alongside political thinkers and social activists have responded to the very hot topic of social justice. It was the main theme of Muslim social theory for many years. However, in the last 20 years, the issue did not take up too much attention but has now found its way back on the lists of current debates. This is an interesting contradiction. While the problem of inequality is rising permanently, the decline of the issue of social justice needs a convincing explanation. In this volume, we are trying to open new debates around the issue of inequality and social justice.

Establishing the social justice in Islam

The basic model of any system of Islam is based on the unity of God (*Tawheed*). There is no deity except Allah, he is the creator of the universe and the ruler of this universe; he is the owner of each and everything; he is the supreme authority, sovereignty is only for him and every human being is accountable to him for his actions. Social justice makes up a significant part of Islamic studies. However, for studying social justice one has to examine Islam's philosophy related to the universe and humankind. It observes from the teaching of Islam that unjust behavior, wrongdoing and mischief are not accepted whatever the situation and also these are against the moral and ethical values of Islam. It observes that after reviewing the different commandments of the religion of Islam that the social issue cannot be resolved in isolation, because all the issues are closely interrelated to each other. From the Islamic point of view, social justice cannot be established if people worship something other than Allah. Allah alone is worthy of worship. According to Muslim scholars, we cannot achieve a just society without worshipping Allah. This is the vertical axis of the understanding of Islamic social justice.

According to the teaching of Islam, a just society can be achieved through the mutual cooperation among the different social/economic agents and members of the society. Seyyid Qutb (1952, 1980, 1982, 1992a, 1992b, 1993a, 1993b, 1993c, 1993d, 1994a, 1994b), Abul Ala Mawdudi (1967, 1974, 1980, 1985, 1986, 1989) and Ali Shariati (2006, 2010) the great contemporary Muslim scholars of the past century, they stated in their writings that it is the responsibility of all mankind to establish justice. In their opinion, when people ignore the commands of Allah then the outcome will be oppression, tyranny and an unjust society. They stated that under an Islamic system absolute justice is required (*al-adl al-mutlaq*). Justice will be maintained in society if people do not abuse their powers and as a result people will have a peaceful, kind and cooperative society. The old Muslim jurists like Ibn Khaldun, al-Azraq and al-Ghazali share the opinion that injustice is the outcome whenever any society ignores the laws which are provided by Allah. According to all Muslim scholars justice is an inevitable thing for maintaining the peace in any society. According to Qutb, Mawdudi and Shariati, true justice can only be achieved when we are following the orders of Allah and not following people's own selfish desires and interests.

However, one cannot ignore the role of the state in establishing justice in a society. This is the horizontal axis of the understanding of social justice. We have several examples in Islamic history that the Islamic state has played a very important and successful role in establishing justice. There is a consensus among Muslim jurists that this is the responsibility and duty of the Islamic state to provide basic necessities to all of its citizens. On the other hand, this is the duty of all members of a society to work hard for their livelihood and to earn lawful (*halal*) earnings. Due to certain reasons, if they are not able to provide the basic needs to their family then this is the duty of the Islamic state and Islamic society to help them from the government treasury or from voluntary funds, i.e. *Zakat* and charity.

The concept of justice in Islam is originated from the *Tawheed* (unity) of God. It has certain characteristics such as humans being equal and free, everyone having equal opportunities, everyone having the responsibility to serve society and increase its welfare, undue pressure should not be placed by authority on anyone, there should be a close relationship between the individuals and society, however, all these should be according to the laws of Allah. It implies that the theory of justice is practically applicable to Islamic society. According to Qutb and Mawdudi, under the Islamic system, social justice has following three foundations:

(i)   *Absolute freedom of conscience*: no association with God, worldly orders have no value if they are conflicting with the orders of Allah, enslaving men is not acceptable and there should be freedom from materialism.
(ii) *The complete equality of all human beings*: all humans are a servant of God, everyone has the same rights and responsibilities, everyone has the same opportunities, no discrimination among races, color or gender, the only preference is for God-fearing people.
(iii) *Social solidarity*: it is based on social cooperation, mercy, love, no self-ishness, mutual social responsibility, no one is allowed to live in isola-tion, brotherhood among the believers, trust and respect among the members of the Islamic society, maintaining the peace and stability.

It is concluded from the above discussion that faith (*iman*) is the most important element of human life. Faith provides the moral and ethical train-ing to humans, it creates love among the members of the society/commu-nity, good deeds and conduct are the outcome of that life which is spent under the umbrella of faith, it enables humans to differentiate between moral and immoral, good and evil and so on.

In this framework, Islam guides the human being and emphasizes that how we will be able to reduce the conflict among the different social agents, how to minimize the social disparities and how to create the justice in the human society. It is also important that citizens have the right to live peace-fully, they have the property right to own property and no one can misuse or exploit the property owned by others.

Social justice under the political system of Islam

Under the Islamic system, the state plays a very important role in estab-lishing social justice. According to al-Ghazali, the Islamic state and laws of *shari'ah* are highly correlated, i.e. *shari'ah* is the foundation and the state is the responsible for following the laws of *shari'ah*. Al-Mawardi and Ibn Taymiyyah also emphasized that without justice the state cannot perform its duty in an optimal way. According to them, it is the duty of the state to protect the religion as well as look after the worldly affairs of all of its citizens. They are of the opinion that the community also has the same responsibility as the state, and the state has to perform the duty to enjoin good and prohibit evil. al-Banna, Qutb and Mawdudi share the

same opinion. According to them, a state without strong faith is not able
to perform its role in establishing social justice. Furthermore the state,
with its political power, can achieve the targets of justice in a society.
Qutb and Mawdudi stated that if the state or a community are not following the laws of *shari'ah* it means they have rejected the laws of Allah
and they will be considered to be unbelievers. They emphasized that it is
the duty of the state or community to provide the basic necessities to
society and provide the proper training to the workers so they will be
able to get gainful employment. He also stated that this is the responsibility of the government to maintain the peace, enjoin good and forbid evil.
They further elaborated two types of states, i.e. Dar al-Islam (where the
government follows the laws of *shari'ah*, it does not matter what the percentage of Muslims is) and Dar al-Harb (where the government does not
follow the laws of *shari'ah*, it does not matter what the percentage of
Muslims is). Some Muslim scholars have the opinion that the authority
of the state is not absolute, its role is just as a trustee and should follow
the laws of *shari'ah*. The state should be governed by pious people
because the different duties of the state cannot be performed if the rulers
are not morally strong and do not obey the orders of Allah. So obeying
the laws of *shari'ah* is a necessary and sufficient condition for establishing
social justice in a society. However, a number of scholars explained that
in the system of Islam, a state without religion is not able to determine
its role for maintaining political and social affairs. They emphasized that
Islam assures a balance between religion and politics (Lewis, 1981; von
Grunebaum, 1962).

In the view of Muslim scholars, the political system should be based on
a belief in Allah and justice should be carried out by the administration,
shari'ah laws should be implemented in their pure form, there should be no
discrimination among different citizens based on ethno-religious groups.
This is the duty of the Muslim ruler as a vicegerent to Allah to establish
justice, keep peace and harmony among the different members and segments
of society. If he is unable to do that then he has to leave the position. On
the other hand, this is the religious duty of the believers to cooperate with
the government in establishing justice, the environment of brotherhood and
equality in society. According to Muslim scholars this can be done only if
there is the implementation of *shari'ah* laws. It is also emphasized that the
laws of *shari'ah* are superior to family relations, the personal interest of the
individuals and worldly activities. It is also assumed that under an Islamic
state the evils, wrongdoings, vices will not take place and they will be eradi-
cated due to the blessings of this system. As a result, the state will have
more time for the well-being of its citizens. It is also assumed that believers
have absolute ownership over their lives and wealth and their role is as
a trustee to Allah. They have to live their lives according to the orders of
Allah, in this way they are able to establish justice in their social lives. As
Ibn Taymiyya said:

The aim of commissioning the Prophets and of revealing the Books, therefore, is to have people administer justice in the cause of God and in the rights of His creatures. Thus he who deviates from the book shall be corrected by iron (force of arms).

(Ibn Taymiyya, n.d, p. 41)

Social justice in the economic system of Islam

Islam, because of its unique characteristics, has the ability to solve the different economic crises which are being faced by humankind. Under this system, entrepreneurs have freedom and can produce whatever they want, however, Islam has drawn a line between permitted (*halal*) and unpermitted (*haram*) economic activities. All these activities have their own moral and ethical boundaries, no one is allowed to cross these boundaries. Islam does not appreciate immoral actions, for example, greed, selfishness, vices, extravagant, injustice, corruption and wickedness. The circulation of wealth only among rich people is not allowed. Wealth, which is in actual terms created by Allah, should be spent on the welfare of the whole community and especially for the Muslim *ummah*. The first priority should be given to one's own family members and then to the community. Consequently, it has an impact on all humankind. In all of the affairs of this world, the role of the man is a trustee and he should spend this wealth according to the teaching of the *Qur'an* and *Sunnah*.

Islam also provides guidance to believers on how they should spend their income and wealth and in return what reward they will receive from Allah. Their utility is not only based on a reward in this world but also depends on the reward in the life hereafter. As the *Qur'an* says in Chapter 2 of the *Qur'an*:

> The likeness of those who spend their wealth in the way of Allah is as the likeness of a grain (of corn); it grows seven ears, and each ear has a hundred grains. Allah gives manifold increase to who He wills. And Allah is All-Sufficient for His creature's needs, All-Knower. Those who spend their wealth in the Cause of Allah, and do not follow up their gifts with reminders of their generosity or with injury, their reward is with their Lord. On them shall be no fear, nor shall they grieve.
>
> (Qur'an, 2: 261–262)

However, the reward of the spending is dependent on the intention of the believers. If their spending is only for the sake of Allah, then they will receive a reward from Allah otherwise they do not receive a reward. For example, if they spend their money on the poor of society and their intention is to gain public fame, then it has no value in the eyes of Allah. However, under the Islamic system the disbursement of charity has a positive, significant impact on philanthropists and beneficiaries, i.e. the philanthropists become more generous, become free from greed and self-ishness. It supports beneficiaries and provides them with their subsistence. As a result, it creates a just society in an environment of unity and soli-darity. It also purifies the heart of both parties from greed, jealousy, envy, selfishness, etc. Similarly, the class struggle and warfare is not the norm of a society under an umbrella of faith in Allah. It means man has to spend his money in the right way and will receive a reward from Allah. If he spends even a single penny in the wrong way, then he will be assumed to be a spendthrift and will be liable for punishment. The man-agement of wealth is another issue which the *Qur'an* has mentioned in a very precise way:

> Do not give your wealth, which Allah has made a means of support of you, to the weak minded, but feed and clothe them from it and speak to them words of kindness.
>
> (4:5)

Islam always tries to create a just society in all spheres of life. There is a strict prohibition on the exploitation and oppression among members of an Islamic society. All the transactions should be in accordance with the laws which are given by Allah. Everyone has the same opportunity to earn wealth and it should not be circulated among groups of rich people. Islamic instruments like *zakah*, the interest-free system and the law of inheritance have their unique implications in establishing social justice under the Islamic system. Due to these instruments the degree of prosperity will enhance the Islamic economy and society. Furthermore, those who are performing their duties towards their fellow Muslim brothers will get the reward from their lord. Especially when they disburse charity, it provides social assurance, guarantee and insurance to the recipients particularly in a vulnerable envir-onment and unexpected circumstances. It is believed that if the state and community are following the rules and regulations which are given by Allah then a just and sound society could be established.

Different dimensions of social justice

In the fourth Islamic Economic Workshop (IEW) in 2016, a number of papers were presented in English as well in Turkish. All of these papers dis-cussed social justice in the system of Islam. Different dimensions related to social justice were reviewed, for example, the theory of justice under the umbrella of Islam, behavior of the market, the role and policies of the gov-ernment, contractual freedom, the role of Islamic financial institutions, social aid and its impact on the labor market, Islamic institutions like *waqf*, *Zakat*, Islamic insurance (*takaful*), an interest-free economy and their role in establishing social justice and decreasing the amount of poverty, etc. All of the papers discussed the significance of social justice in the framework of Islamic economics.

In the second chapter in this volume, Choudhury applied the *Tawhidi* methodology, he derives the meaning and subtleties of the theory of justice as the balance of complementarities between the life-sustaining elements and socio-scientific systems with which the human order interacts. The balance of the wider scope of social justice thus derived ontologically from the monotheistic law (*Tawhid*) is shown to acquire a socioscientific analytical explanation. Upon this generalized theory of universal complementarities, the theory of justice as balance rests. It is thereby applied in methodological and applied ways to every particularity of the generalized theory. The particular embedding of the theory of justice within its generalized theory of the unity of knowledge can establish a comparative field of social contract and constitutional economic applications. According to Choudhury, the substantive analytical theory then emerges from the primal ontological foundation of the *Qur'anic* law of oneness of God (monotheism: *Tawhid*). It is functionally understood in terms of the episteme of the unity of knowledge. An example relating to justice and peace is given to explain the contrasting meanings of the opposing theories of justice in *Qur'anic* and from a rationalist methodological viewpoint. This chapter also presents contemporary debates on social justice (such as Rawls and Dworkin) and its relationship to Islamic economics.

In the third chapter, Azid, Al Rawashdeh and Chaudhry discuss whether existing laws and social understandings broadly benefit everyone or only work well for the wealthy and powerful segment of society. Furthermore, it discusses which institutions work efficiently in the given social, cultural and religious environment, i.e., market, society or government. Another issue which is related to the government and society—either a strong society produces a strong government or vice versa. How do these two pillars work in a just society and how it is possible for them to create a just environment? How do the members of a society consider the rights of the deprived segment of that society? Is it possible for the market, government and society to promote the voluntary sector to fill the gap and how does this voluntary sector help achieve a higher degree of social justice?

In the next chapter, Cattelan raised a number of questions, such as: What is the role of human freedom in the Islamic conceptualization of the market? To what extent is the free market economy compatible with the notion of social justice in Islam? Which instruments can enhance wealth redistribution in an Islamic economy? This chapter aims at providing a reply to these intertwined issues moving from an Islamic understanding of contractual freedom as the performance of God–man's agency relationship (*khilafah*) to consequent policymaking inputs in order to promote social justice according to Islamic values. This chapter also considers the current practice of Islamic finance at a global level and its distance from the community dimension that the real free market, as a place of sharing and cooperation. It is also highlights the role of political economy tools, in order to fully realize the welfare derived from the "invisible hand" of *khilafah*.

In Chapter 5, Jadedia discusses the role of Islamic financial institutions in the improvement of the state of social justice. Since Islamic finance is unsuitable for usury, debt rescheduling, speculative transfers, gambling or waste and other purely monetary activities, it seems to be an effective avenue for justice and social well-being. It can be associated with other initiatives of Islamic redistributive mechanisms such as *Zakat, Sadaqat* and *Waqf* all of which aim to enhance social justice. In a nutshell, this chapter discusses the relationship between the principles of Islamic banking system and social justice with the reference to equality of access to finance and protection of the weak against economic hardships

In Chapter 6, Tekdogan and Eraslan try to explore how social aids affect people's willingness to work and whether they are useful for maintaining social justice. Within this context, this chapter describes social aid measures with some historical background and tries to evaluate their contribution to social welfare. And also a theory of wage determination and well-being in the context of a social contract of Islamic theory of justice is presented. This chapter covers the different types of social assistance programs in Turkey, social assistance and motivation to work, prospects of social aid (*zakah, sadaqa, waqf*) and their productive utilization in the system of Islam.

Chapter 7 covers the concepts of *waqf* and its role in reducing poverty and inequality to provide social justice in societies. Tekin emphasizes that *waqf* institutions may be reconsidered as a tool for fighting against poverty in today's world just as they were in the past by redesigning them according to the needs of the modern economy. In particular, given the feature of sustainability in *waqf* institutions it seems noteworthy to reconsider these institutions in terms of poverty alleviation in today's world. This chapter also discusses the theory of social justice with the objective of well-being (*maslaha*). This chapter covers the different issues related to poverty especially in the Muslim countries and institution of *waqf* as an instrument for the eradication of poverty especially its role in the premodern Islamic world.

Interest, as its prohibited by Allah, has a remarkable impact on social justice. In the next chapter, the effect of interest on social justice is analyzed in the context of the real interest rate and income inequality. Income inequality is a well-known phenomenon which arises when there is an unequal distribution of assets, income and wealth among society. The unequal distribution of income, generally, leads to the division of society, as the bottom of the society suffers from this division, while the top of the society reaps the benefits from it. Changes in the real interest rate lead to distortions in income equality and thereby social justice. In this chapter, it is found out that both low and high-interest rates may have an unequalizing impact on income. Hence, the thing that produces the inequalities is not the increasing or decreasing interest; rather it is interest itself. Marasli further discusses the intercausal relations between (all) interest rates, trade, and balanced distribution of the social contract of well-being.

Productive *Zakat* is a mechanism whereby *Zakat* is utilized to help eligible recipients generate income and use *Zakat* funds for productive activities. Disbursing Zakat in the traditional way by providing cash payments to recipients basically has little impact on the welfare of the recipients since the poor tend to have high propensity to consume. Productive *Zakat* has been suggested as a better mechanism than "direct *Zakat* funds" in reducing income inequality and increasing social justice. Chapter 9 explores the use of productive *Zakat* as a social justice mechanism in Indonesia. Data was collected from three *Zakat* institutions and *Zakat* recipients using semi-structured interviews and questionnaires. Data was then triangulated and analyzed using case study approach. This chapter found some challenges related to low participation of the poor in the programs. This low participation is unexpected since *Zakat* is supposed to be given to the poor. Yumna argues in this chapter that society's cultural norms and values, particularly those norms related to the marginalization of the poor that inevitably lead to self-exclusion by the poor from a productive *Zakat* program.

Sheikh and Ahmad estimate the potential *Zakat* collectible in 17 OIC countries for overcoming the poverty gap as measured by poverty the headcount ratio and poverty gap index in Chapter 10. They find that the *Zakat* to GDP ratio exceeds Poverty Gap Index to GDP (PGI-GDP) ratio in all countries except in Bangladesh, Mozambique and Nigeria where the *Zakat* to GDP ratio is less than the PGI–GDP ratio with the poverty line defined at $1.25 a day. We also discover that the *Zakat* to GDP ratio exceeds PGI–GDP ratio in all countries except in Bangladesh, Mozambique, Nigeria and Pakistan where the *Zakat* to GDP ratio is less than PGI–GDP ratio with the poverty line defined at $2.00 a day. In their estimation results, they also show the comparison of *Zakat* to GDP ratio against the poverty headcount ratio. We have discovered that the *Zakat* to GDP ratio exceeds the poverty head count ratio to GDP (PHCR–GDP) in all countries except in Bangladesh, Mozambique, Nigeria, Pakistan and Tajikistan with the poverty line defined at $1.25 a day. They also found that the *Zakat* to GDP ratio exceeds PHCR–GDP ratio in all countries except in Bangladesh, Indonesia, Kyrgyz Republic, Mozambique, Nigeria, Pakistan and Tajikistan with the poverty line defined at $2.00 a day. Therefore, they saw that the institution of *Zakat* has significant potential to contribute towards poverty alleviation. Finally, they showed that the aggregate resources pooled together from the potential *Zakat* collection in 17 OIC countries will be enough to fund resources for poverty alleviation in all 17 OIC countries combined. Hence, there is an important role to be played by OIC in collaborating with member countries and transferring the necessary resources from the *Zakat* surplus regions to the *Zakat* deficit regions.

Islamic micro-*takaful* with its Community-Based Insurance (CBI) is an emerging concept for providing financial protection, particularly for credit life and credit disability against the cost of illness, accidents, fires and improving access to quality health services for low-income rural households that are excluded from formal insurance (*takaful*). The overall objective of Chapter 11 is to review the recent practice of BMT (*Baitul Mal Wattamwil*) Union of Indonesia (PBMT Indonesia) as Islamic micro-*takaful* provider that addresses the link between CBI and social capital in pursuing social justice for community members. Sanrego, also discusses the theory of social justice in an endogenous relationship with the economic reasoning in the context of *takaful*.

In the end, editors present the economic reasoning of the idea of balance and equality in Islamic Economics and the theory of justice and its endogenous intercausality with economic reasoning will be presented in the conclusion. At the end, a review of the previous chapters will be presented and also recommendations for further research opportunities. This chapter will also suggest some further policy implications based on the previous chapters.

All of the abovementioned chapters suggest that social justice should be the main ingredient of Islamic society. Islamic injunction and its different institutions (like *waqf, Zakat,* charity, interest-free economy) are providing the significant support for establishing social justice. The teaching of the *Qur'an* and the practices of the Prophet (*sunnah*) and Islamic traditions and historical experiences guide us in how to create an environment of justice, brotherhood, honesty, fairness, selflessness, equity and morality in all the spheres of life. It has also been observed from the conclusion of the different chapters included in this book that Islam tries to maintain a balance in all of its aspects. And this balance is supportive in establishing social justice. It has also been observed that it is not possible to establish social justice in its true spirit without the support of authorities, state as well as with the help of the community. For establishing social justice, state and community are complements to each other. In nutshell, we reach this conclusion that community and state are both strong pillars that are able to maintain all the moral norms of society.

References

Ibn Taymiyya, A. I. A. A.-H. (n.d.). *al-Siyasat al-Shar'iyya fi Islah al-Rai wa'l-R-aiyya.* Alexandria: Dar al-Iman.
Lewis, B. (1981). The Return of Islam. In M. Curtis (Ed.), *Religion and Politic in the Middle East* (pp. 9–29). Boulder, CO: Westview Press.
Mawdudi, A. A. (1967). *Islamic Law and Constitution,* trans. by K. Ahmad. Lahore: Islamic Publications.
Mawdudi, A. A. (1974). *First Principles of the Islamic State,* trans. by K. Ahmad. Lahore: Islamic Publication Limited.

Mawdudi, A. A. (1980). *Towards Understanding of Islam.* London: U.K. Islamic Mission.

Mawdudi, A. A. (1985). *al-Nazariyat al-Islam al-Siyasiyya.* Jedda: al-Dar al-Saudiyya (Arabic).

Mawdudi, A. A. (1986). *Islamic State,* trans. by M. Siddiqi. Karachi: Islamic Research Academy.

Mawdudi, A. A. (1989). *Four Basic Quranic Terms,* trans. by A. Asad. Lahore: Islamic Publication Ltd.

Qutb, S. (1952). *al-Adala al-Ijtimia fil Islam.* Cairo: Matba'aa Dar al-Kitab al-Arabi (Arabic).

Qutb, S. (1980). *Ma'alim fil Tariq.* Cairo: Dar al-Shuruq (Arabic).

Qutb, S. (1982). *Khasais al-Tasawwur al-Islami.* Beirut: Dar al-Shuruq (Arabic).

Qutb, S. (1992a). *Fi Zilal al-Qur'an.* Cairo: Dar al-Shuruq (Arabic).

Qutb, S. (1992b). *Islam the Religion of the Future* (al-Mustaqbal li Hadha al-Din). Kuwait: al-Fanal Press.

Qutb, S. (1993a). *Nahw Mujtama Islami.* Beirut: Dar al-Shuruq (Arabic).

Qutb, S. (1993b). *Mashahid al-Qiyama fil-Qur'an.* Cairo: Dar al-Shuruq.

Qutb, S. (1993c). *Marakat al-Islam wa'1-Rasmaliyyaya.* Cairo: Där al-Shuruq (Arabic).

Qutb, S. (1993d). *Islam and Universal Peace* (al-Salam al-Alami wal-Islam). Indian-apolis, IN: American Trust Publication.

Qutb, S. (1994a). *al-Taswir al-Fanni fi'l-Qur'an.* Cairo: Dar al-Ma`ärif (Arabic).

Qutb, S. (1994b). *This Religion of Islam* (Hadha al-Din). Riyadh: International Islamic Publishing House.

Shariati, A. (2006). *Man & Islam,* trans. by F. Marjani. North Haledon, NJ: Islamic Publications International.

Shariati, A. (2010). *The Hajj,* trans. by M. al-'Asi. Kuala Lumpur: Islamic Book Trust.

von Grunebaum, G. E. (1962). *The Search for Culture Identity.* Los Angeles, CA: University of California Press.

2 A theory of justice in Islam

Masudul Alam Choudhury

Background

In the Islamic literature on social justice one cannot find a single citation dealing with the precise definition of social justice in Islam. Most works done on the topic of an Islamic meaning of social justice end up characterizing this sublime precept with a range of its values with which social justice is related, such as equality, fairness, charitable distribution and a balance of conscious actions to sustain a good social order (Kamali, 1989, 1991). Such a vector of values does not end up. Consequently, a precise definition of social justice in terms of its endless number of attributes cannot be derived. Nonetheless, a critical value like social justice, which the *Qur'an* elevates to high importance,[1] needs to be well defined. This moral and social requirement is also the case with all other critical objective values.

The aggregation of all such values arising from the *Qur'an* and the *sunnah* form the good values of life, the truth. Contrarily, the aggregation of the opposing characterized practices and beliefs comprise falsehood, the bad. Truth and falsehood are distinctly separable beliefs and practices, except when some such practices remain temporarily indeterminate (*mutashabihat*), but only to become well-determined with the advance of knowledge that is foundationally premised on the ontology of monotheism, *Tawhid* as Law. *Tawhid* is the cardinal foundation of Islamic belief as the unity of knowledge separating truth from falsehood, with the advance of human knowledge known as *fitra*. But the idea of balance as a systemic precept of the unity of knowledge extends to the nature of unity of the world-system. The world-system is induced by the unraveling of systemic unity even as human knowledge advances to understand and reconstruct the essence of complementary organic unity of being and becoming.[2]

The theme of social justice although spoken highly by Muslim scholars yet has failed to be defined precisely. Thereby, the implications of its high altar of human and global concept remains verbose and murky. The *Qur'an* has laid down the important elements of social justice as Balance. Balance (*mizan*) is the reflection of the design, scope, objective and purpose of the primal ontological law of *Tawhid* that God has bestowed in "everything" with which individuals and the social and global order interact to establish social, global and socio-scientific contractarian systems.

Comparatively with Occidental epistemological contexts as well, the theory of justice is only partially addressed; yet again, only according to rationalist inclination. Consequently, various theories of justice, as given by Occidental social and scientific philosophers, remain ingrained in rationalist philosophy having no trace of monotheism in them. The precept of Balance and Moderation in terms of the unity of knowledge by complementarities between the variables representing the good things in life (life-fulfillment needs, Truth) remains undefined both among Muslim and Occidental scholars. Hence a precise theory of justice as Balance and Moderation that spans the universal and particulars of "everything" remains absent.

Objective

This chapter will derive the meaning and subtleties of the theory of justice as the balance of complementarities between the life-sustaining elements and socio-scientific systems with which the human order interacts. The balance of the wider scope of social justice thus derived ontologically from the monotheistic law (*Tawhid*) is shown to acquire a socio-scientific analytical explanation. Upon this generalized theory of universal complementarities, the theory of justice as balance rests. It is thereby applied in methodological and applied ways to every particularity of the generalized theory. The particular embedding of the theory of justice within its generalized theory of the unity of knowledge can establish a comparative field of social contract and constitutional economic applications.

A substantive analytical theory then emerges from the primal ontological foundation of the *Qur'anic* law of oneness of God (monotheism: *Tawhid*). It is functionally understood in terms of the episteme of the unity of knowledge. An example relating to Justice and Peace is given to explain the contrasting and opposing meanings of the theory of justice in *Qur'anic* and in the rationalist methodological viewpoint.

A brief discourse on social justice

The goal in this chapter is to define what, in reference to the *Qur'an*, can be derived as the definition of justice and social justice. A comparative technical approach is adopted. We start with a limiting approach to the large vector of elevated values attributed to the topic of Social Justice, as pointed out above. We reduce such a large vector by functional symbolism and its analytics as follows:

Let, $\mathbf{X}(\theta)$ denote the vector of all such an inexhaustible number of attributes of Social Justice reduced to this symbol. The vector of values is induced by knowledge-flow parameters denoted by "θ"-values.

The primal ontological sense of the central Law of *Tawhid* is denoted by Ω. It is mapped by the mathematical well-defined, continuous and complete function (Maddox, 1970) of the sunnah, "S". We write, the total ontological origin as, $\Omega \to_S$: (Ω, S).

$\{\theta\}$ are continuous and compact sequences of knowledge-flows that are derived from the ontological premise as epistemological consequences of the unity of knowledge embodying the world-system of general and particular themes, denoted by f1.

We write $\Omega \to_S$: $(\Omega, S) \to_{f1} \{\theta\}$.

The nature of the unity of knowledge as universally characterized by the primal ontology of the *Tawhidi* Law and carried through the epistemology of knowledge-flows emanating from the primal ontology induces the theoretical abstraction and its formal applications in the world-system under study. Thus we have the vector of knowledge-embedded variables (equally matrices and tensors) denoted by $X(\theta)$.

We write, $\Omega \to_S$: $(\Omega, S) \to_{f1} \{\theta\} \to_{f2} \{X(\theta)\}$.

Since all of the variables and functionals in S,f1,f2 are continuous and well-defined non-null, and mathematically compact in a neighborhood, so we can write any positive monotonic functional of the mentioned function to have the same ontological and epistemological properties as of the rest (Friedman, 1982). Thus, let such a sequence of functionals be denoted by,

$\{W(X(\theta)\}$ mapped on $\{\theta, X(\theta)\}$ by "w",
such that, $\Omega \to_S$: $(\Omega, S) \to_{f1} \{\theta\} \to_{f2} \{X(\theta)\} \to w\{W(X(\theta)\}$.

Now the properties of the ontological and epistemological unity of knowledge extend over the domain, $\{\theta, X(\theta)\}$. The principal property is displayed by continuous intervariable complementarities. This result also implies inter-causality between the variables comprising the vector $\{X(\theta)\}$. The result of the intercausal relations are organismic in terms of the unity of knowledge between the variables spanning the domain, $\{\theta, X(\theta)\}$.

The above properties are summarized in the evaluation of the well-being functions, $\{W(X(\theta)\}$. We write the result in terms of the *Tawhidi* String Relations as shown in Figure 2.1.

Critical definitions of concepts

In Figure 2.1 some important definitions need to be given to define Justice and Social Justice according to the *Tawhidi* methodological worldview applied to Justice as the grand theme. The most important of the entities to define is the well-being function (*maslaha*) as the singular objective function underlying Figure 2.1. As the formal form of evaluation of the well-being objective criterion in Figure 2.1 points out, the nature of this functional criterion is to conceptually and quantitatively evaluate (estimation and simulation) according to the methodology emanating from the ontological and epistemological parts. Because the methodology impinges on the formulation of the well-being model, its evaluation reflects the methodical nature of appraising the degree to which intervariable endogenous and intercausal relations in complementarities exist.

Well-being criterion in terms of the Tawhidi *unity of knowledge*

The well-being function is therefore the objective criterion of measuring and explaining the degree of intervariable complementarities found to exist for the specific problem under study. Such complementarities between the good things in life as can be deduced by discourse in reference to the *Tawhidi* ontological law, and not necessarily in reference to the so-called objective and purpose of the term coined as *"shari'ah-*compliance" is a sure sign of the unity of knowledge between the good things of life that otherwise configure the *Tawhidi* unified world-system of both non-physical and physical entities of truth.

The phenomenology of the entire *Tawhidi* String Relation of Figure 2.1 encompasses the fullness of the methodological level of its *Qur'anic* derivation and the empirical manifestation yielded by the quantitative application of the science of consciousness to the particular issues and problems under study. In this regard, Kaku (2015) defines consciousness in the following way: "Consciousness is the process of creating a model of the world using multiple feedback loops in various parameters (e.g. in temperatures, space, time and in relation to others), in order to accomplish a goal (e.g. find mates, food, shelter)."

Balance and moderation in the *Tawhidi* methodological worldview

Principle of pervasive complementarities

The principle of pervasive complementarities permanently negates marginalizm, and thereby the axioms of economic rationality as a particular derivation from the domain of rationalism. Thereby there is a logical negation of mainstream axioms of resource scarcity, optimality, steady-state equilibriums and a marginal rate of substitution (opportunity cost) between competing alternatives. All these are logical results in the face of knowledge-flows that make choices between the good things in life undeterred by the continuous resource generation in respect of the unity of knowledge along the IIE (Interactive, Integrative, Evolutionary)-learning processes. Such properties of the well-being function and its circular causation relations between the endogenous variable by intercausality are thereby logical consequences on methodological and mathematical grounds. Hence the concomitant results arising from mathematical analysis form universal truth. Therefore, the *Tawhidi* Law with its yielding of the unity of knowledge in "everything" is a universal truth. This arises from the underlying mathematical logicalness. The resulting consequences are also unique, because the organic relational definition of ethics in socio-scientific and moral values are embedded and explainable enumerable phenomena. All such consequences are not to be found in any of the mainstream theories and so-called *shari'ah-*compliance treatments.

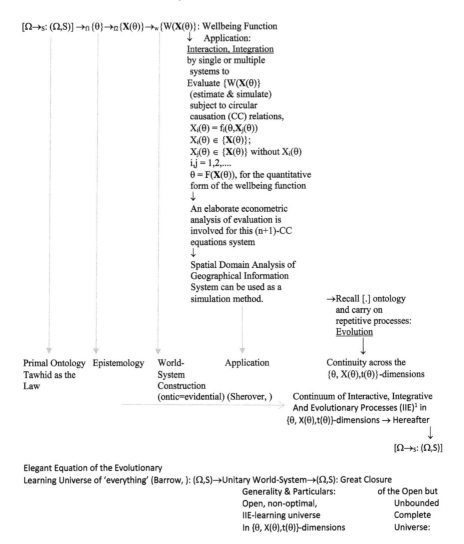

$[\Omega \to_S: (\Omega,S)] \to_{f1}\{\theta\} \to_{f2}\{X(\theta)\} \to_w\{W(X(\theta)\}$: Wellbeing Function

Figure 2.1 The topography of the *Tawhidi* methodological worldview in the unity of knowledge and the induced world-system

Balance and moderation in terms of the Tawhidi *methodological worldview*

The concept of balance and moderation (*mizan* and *wasatiyyah*) is derived from the property of pervasive choices of intervariable complementarities with scope for a simulation of the well-being function, subject to circular causation relations to create a better integrated world-system on particular issues in the light of the *Tawhidi* unity of knowledge. Thus three kinds of choices arise: There is the choice according to permissible goods and services in material and conceptual forms (*halal*). Then there are those choices that are categorically forbidden (*haram*). These are rejected in the choice set. Because they form a falsehood, they contradict Truth. These two disparate worldviews do not both follow the IIE-learning rule of the unity of knowledge as explained in Figure 2.1. The characterizing variables of the two opposites do not interrelate in the same basket according to the *Tawhidi* rule of the unity of knowledge. But they separately follow the same procedure of the *Tawhidi* String Relations with their opposite characteristics. These characteristics are the permanent the unity of knowledge caused by continuous resource regeneration in the Good basket (Truth). The equilibriums of the evolutionary learning set of Good-variables are characterized by what is referred to as Evolutionary Convergence. This means a permanent property of convergence in response to the evaluated (estimated followed by simulated) degrees of attained complementarities between variables in the well-being function. Nonetheless, the possibility of improvement is attributed to the resulting evolutionary equilibriums of punctuated form (Grandmont, 1989) under the impact of the IIE-learning processes occurring in the $\{\theta, X(\theta), t(\theta)\}$ dimensions. "$t(\theta)$" is a time variable induced by knowledge-flows over the event domain of $\{\theta, X(\theta), t(\theta)\}$. The implication of $t(\theta)$ is that change, observation and evidences are created by knowledge, not by time taken absolutely. Time records such events; knowledge causes them to occur.

Contrarily, the variables of the Bad-basket (Falsehood) have the property of dialectical bifurcations (Popper, 1998; Wallerstein, 1998) or stead-state equilibrium. In the latter case, no further learning processes abide. Resources are not endogenously generated. They must be injected exogenously to jump-start the evolution of inter-variable relations. These are the properties of the Solow model of economic growth (Solow, 1980). In the endogenous case of dialectics with bifurcations there is also the case of Romer's Endogenous Growth Model (Romer, 1986). In both of these two cases, the economy and society face social differentiation between the variables of the Bad-set. Examples are of the most irreconcilable context between labor and capital, between God and rationalism in capitalism and liberal economy and society. These comprise the case of methodological individualism as the permanent feature of mainstream economics and social contract Buchanan (1999).

The *Tawhidi* methodology represented in Figure 2.1 applies to both of the cases of monotheistic unity of knowledge and social differentiation, but in the separated Truth and Falsehood worldviews of social choices. There are substantive issues here pertaining to the nature of monotheism versus rationalism (Ghazali, 1997; Choudhury, 2014). The attributes of Balance and Moderation in society at large, including as well as the cosmic order having a relationship with human existence are principally endowed by the unity of knowledge of being and becoming. The implication of these knowledge-induced values is in the testing and reconstruction of the unity of knowledge explained by pervasive complementarities between the good things of life. Contrary to such values are the properties of methodological individualism and social differentiation in the Bad-set (Falsehood). The effect of such a property is described by the cessation of evolutionary learning with convergence in dialectical processes; or the end of learning in any state of steady-state equilibrium. Scarcity, competition, marginalizm and the end of the novelty of learning are the properties of economic rationality with the occurrence of steady-state equilibriums (Shackle, 1971).

The principle of Balance and Moderation interconnects between the human world-system, the ecological world-system and the cosmological world-system. This extension of the universal principle of Balance and Moderation complements all subsystems of the human, nonphysical and physical order concerning self and other in the broadest meaning of this grand social relations in a world-system (*'alameen*).

Consistency of reasoning

Consistency of reasoning in the *Tawhidi* String Relation is defined by its elegant equation (Figure 2.1): *Tawhid* as Law mapping into the world-system forms neighborhood openness in the small scale conscious universes with evolutionary convergences. This process of knowledge regeneration and induction of the emergent world-systems accumulates to the Closure and Final Optimal unraveling of *Tawhid* as Law in the Hereafter. This formal pattern repeats itself across the continuum of $\{\theta, X(\theta), t(\theta)\}$-dimensions. Events in such evolutionary and learning continuum form intersystemic history (Burstein, 1991; Hawking & Mlodinow, 2010). Consequently, every event attains itself purposefully according to the phenomenological completeness of the *Tawhidi* String Relations. This historist evolutionary property yields the universal and unique nature of the multiverse of *Tawhidi* continuum. Its existence is proved by the Fixed-Point Theorem in non-compact neighborhoods of evolutionary learning systems. Consequently, the continuum property of End and the Beginning[3] of the *Tawhidi* Law establishes the consistency of the *Tawhidi* methodological worldview.

Social justice in Islam according to *Tawhidi* methodological worldview

The high pedestal of Justice holds critical importance in Islam as a central design of the conscious universe in its totality. This comprises a particular way of understanding the generality of universal purpose comprehending all forms of interrelations. The *Qur'an* (2:143) declares "Thus have we made of you an Ummah justly balanced, that you might be witnesses over the nations and the Apostle a witness over yourselves ..." At the order of complementary intersystem linkages in diversity, including ecological and cosmological orders, the *Qur'an* (55:7) declares: "And the Firmament has

He raised high and He has set up the balance (of Justice)." The countless subsystemic orders that complement each other according to the organic relations of the unity of knowledge bestowed by *Tawhid* in its explanatory and evidential sense conveyed by the monotheistic Law, altogether comprise the Signs of *Allah*. In these Signs the most critical conceptual and explanatory evidence is found to rest on the principle of universal complementarities between the good things of life (Truth), and the contrariness and avoidance of Falsehood.

The essence of complementarities that centers the meaning of balance and purpose in the universe also conveys the grandest meaning of Justice as Balance. The *Qur'an* brings out this intercausal nature of diversity in the good things of life in the following verses:

> And it is He who spread the earth and placed therein firmly set mountains and rivers; and from all of the fruits He made therein two mates; He causes the night to cover the day. Indeed in that are signs for a people who give thought.
>
> *Qur'an*, (13:3-4)

Thus while the *Tawhidi* methodological worldview yields the model of generality and particular of issues and problems of diverse but interlinked complementary systems, a most important particular example is that of Justice (Social Justice). The *Qur'an* (4:135) declares:

> O you who have believed, be persistently standing firm in justice, witnesses for *Allah*, even if it be against yourselves or parents and relatives. Whether one is rich or poor, *Allah* is more worthy of both. So follow not [personal] inclination, lest you not be just. And if you distort [your testimony] or refuse [to give it], then indeed *Allah* is ever, with what you do, Acquainted.
>
> *Qur'an*, (4:135)

Indeed, the principle of Balance and Moderation to be discovered in terms of the grandest systemic meaning of organic unity establishes the highest order of Justice according to the *Tawhidi* Law (Bayrakli, 1992). The same principle grounds the mind of metascience. If humanity does not cast mercy and purpose on the ecological order, it will destroy the very order and purpose of existence. If the cosmological order does not enter the equation of existence, human beings will end up being a thoughtless creature, devoid of the subtle meaning of existence. Thus what the *Qur'an* establishes as the ultimate worldview of unity of organic relations by the Law of *Tawhid* prevailing in the order of Justice as the total Balance between nonphysical and physical entities as Signs of Allah, has been taken up by the good thinking minds of universal generality. The fact that the *Qur'an* conveys such a grand meaning of Justice in terms of intersystemic complementarities by the ontology of the unity of knowledge, *Tawhid* as Law, makes this law of Justice universal. The same would fail to be the universal law if only social justice concerning human relations was the narrow bound of Justice.

Said Nursi wrote beautifully on the theme of the organic intercausal impact of the unity of the *Tawhidi* Law on the generality and particulars of things. Among the critical particularity is the theme of Balance as Justice. Said Nursi wrote: "The *Qur'an*, throughout all of its verses, aims mainly to establish and confirm four basic, universal truths: the existence and Oneness of the Maker of the universe; Prophethood; bodily Resurrection; and worship and justice"[4]

Likewise, on the theme of universal Balance through purposive complementarities between the good and cosmic entirety of events, Kant (1949, p. 261) wrote:

> Two things fill the mind with ever new and increasing awe and admiration the more frequently and continuously reflection is occupied with them; the starred heaven above me and the moral law within me. I ought not to seek either outside my field of vision, as though they were either shrouded in obscurity or were visionary. I see them confronting me and link them immediately with the consciousness of my existence.
>
> (Kant, 1949, p. 261)

Justice as free good for well-being

This is a well-known precept across history and civilization leading to the ultimate rise of Truth over Falsehood. Yet the distribution of resources to realize justice has faltered severely even at the highest levels of development institutions and multilateral development agreements. The International Monetary Fund has always listened to the commanding voices of its major member countries to bar extensions of resource allocations to various developing countries under its conditionality requirements. It is likewise true of the World Bank's punishment of developing countries by its structural adjustment conditions (Helleiner, 1986). Thus even at the expected highest levels of fair distribution of development resources to meet the ideals of justice, this principle of Social Justice globally remains unattained as a free good. In the reasoning of economic theory, the central assumption of scarcity in its marginalist meaning denies a continuous flow of resources by complementarities between social justice and economic efficiency. The goal of maximization of economic and financial objectives has caused the powerful market players to deny the social good to all. Examples here are of poverty alleviation per unit of resource distribution to poor enterprises. This is a reality most evidently seen in the case of Muslim countries. Statistically, it is estimated that one third of Muslims live on less than USD2 a day. Besides, poverty disempowers the poor from participating in one's own choice of destiny and future. Thus poverty raises multidimensional features of dysfunction (Sen, 2010).

With all this evidence on the precept of poverty alleviation so often evoked using precious words, we would discredit this information as being unreliable. Instead, we make the following measure to explain the attainment of poverty alleviation out of resource distribution. Resource distribution in turn is a measure of distributive equity as a measure of Social Justice. We will continue to hold to our intersystemic complementary understanding of the meaning of Justice in terms of the unity of knowledge across the knowledge, space and time dimensions $[\{\theta, X(\theta), t(\theta)\}]$.

Let, $R(\theta)$ denote resource generation and allocation for the target group of the poor $P(\theta)$.

$r(\theta) = (R(\theta)/P(\theta))$ denotes per capita allocation of resources per unit of the target group.

$t(\theta)$ denotes intertemporal development planning time horizon.

$(1+r(\theta))^{t(\theta)}$ denotes increment of resources by the incidence of $r(\theta)$ over $t(\theta)$ time period.

Each of these variables is induced by θ-parameter by virtue of specific discursive effects represented by θ-parameter, Islamic or other in terms of the different formulas that arise, respectively.

For the non-Islamic case, $t(\theta)$ runs from 1 to ∞.

For the Islamic case, event-specific points in history causes $t(\theta)$ to be finite. Muslim mathematicians in the classical period of Islam preferred to use finite horizon modeling. A similar mathematical preference was upheld by Hilbert (1967).

We write the binomial expansion (by suppressing the "θ" symbol) in other than Islamic case of resource regeneration and allocation over time,

$$(1 + r)^t = 1 + t^*r + t(t - 1)/2^*r^2 + \ldots + r^*t,$$ for finite t-value or continue on the series to ∞.

For a steady-state measurement of resource generation and per-capita resource allocation, $r < 1$ for the series to be convergent. The goal of distributive equity is defeated in an endogenous scale of development planning. Exogenous injection of resources at transaction cost can abide.

For the Islamic case, existence of a steady-state equilibrium is replaced by evolutionary equilibriums. Now simulated complementary cases of evaluation of the well-being function, subject to circular causation relations (Figure 2.1), result in a complementary relationship between $R(\theta)$ and $P(\theta)$. Thus, $r\uparrow \Rightarrow$ binomial series are evaluated in finite time to yield finite results in accordance with evolutionary learning processes in $\{\theta, r(\theta), t(\theta)$-dimensions.

Hence, the systemic IIE-learning properties according to the *Tawhidi* methodology and its application in terms of the substantive meaning of the unity of knowledge causes Social Justice to be a freely available, hence endogenous system element in the well-being function. This result also implies that, resources are generated according to increasing returns to scale in the endogenous development process. Such a development process is characterized by life-fulfillment regimes. They are the kinds that meet the needs of Justice in its totality (Levine, 1988; Streeten, 1981).[5] The presence of life-fulfilling regimes of endogenous socioeconomic development based on intervariable complementarities between the good things of life and avoidance of the contrary type of Bad encompass the totality of the universe of Justice in Islam.

Elements of justice in Islam

We mentioned above that the correct way to define Justice in Islam is not by enumerating the many blessed elements it has, for these are inexhaustible. The way to define Justice, and thereby Social Justice in Islam in a precise way is to represent it by an analytical symbolism. This approach is then placed in the *Tawhidi* methodological framework with its applications to the particular theme of Justice (Social Justice). It is at the application stage that we can identify the particular elements comprising Justice and study Social Justice in Islam. Thereby, the specific inhering elements of the Justice precept can be studied by the generalized methodological worldview of *Tawhid* as the Primal Ontological Law. The nontechnical way of understanding the precise definition is to resort to the obvious meaning arising from the analytical approach.

Among the inexhaustible blessed elements of Justice that comprehend every good possibility in the universe we name a few here: fairness, equality, distributive equity, justice with compassion, liberty, freedom, trustworthiness, judgement, etc. These and an inexhaustible number of blessed elements of the precept of Justice apply to the individual in relation to the self and others; and to collectivities such as institutions, governments, the wider scope of governance, the global order and intellectual formalism comprising nonphysical and physical entities and everything between the heavens and the earth that relate to the well-being (*maslaha*) of all in its entirety.

For reason of well definition of the high precept of Justice including social justice in it, this chapter has adopted the *Tawhidi* methodological framework along with the explanatory, analytical, and applied perspectives that arise therefrom. This was explained as the unique and universal way of explaining anything and everything of experience that can be identified for specific study and intellectual inquiry.

Such a universality and unique way of premising the definition of Justice and Social Justice in the *Tawhidi* methodological worldview of the unity of knowledge and its induced world-system, presents a challenge in Islamic intellection that has not been readily noted. The primacy of the *Tawhidi* Law (Ω,S) in Figure 2.1; and the appearance of the *shari'ah* with its epistemological composition in $(\theta,\mathbf{X}(\theta))$ relegates the *shari'ah* to the Primal Ontology of *Tawhid* as the true Law of everything. It is therefore the *Tawhid* alone and not the *shari'ah* that must be referred to as the foundation of Islamic permanence of Law. Within this is the belief, thought and scope with a global and extended domain of intellection.

The *shari'ah* is a set of derived rules (*ahqam*) from the *Tawhidi* Law; but also, by references to interpretations of rules by various scholars and between them. These latter ones are not necessarily all in reference to the *Qur'an* in the first instance. Such *shari'ah* derivations run the danger of erroneous interpretations,[6] as it has happened with the various Muslim sects (*madhabs*). For instance, a very central issue of a just generation and distribution of resources is the avoidance of interest and interest-like valuation rates. Yet almost all of *shari'ah* financial instruments today are debt-ridden like rentals (*ijara*). The financial rate of renting any kind of resource, financial or real in today's so-called "*shari'ah*-compliant" instruments are not determined in the face of unknown risk and return in a perpetual probabilistic resource distribution situation. This problem of debt capitalization is true as *shari'ah*-compliant financing instruments not only for mark-up pricing (*murabaha*) as a primary instrument, but also for other primary and secondary financing instruments as well. Hence the problem of injustice caused by such modes of debt-financing in the form of interest-like shadow rate prevails in *shari'ah*-compliant financing instruments (Choudhury, 2017). The same is not true of the *Tawhidi* methodological approach in the case of its organic unity of relationship between money, spending and the real economy (Choudhury & Asmak, 2017).

In the case of the generalized methodology of intersystemic circular causation organic relations of the unity of knowledge to evaluate well-being criterion function no perspective of *shari'ah*-compliance idea has any directive. Likewise, the purpose and objective of the *shari'ah* called *maqasid as-shari'ah* has no role to input. The implication thus is that, overwhelmingly human-engineered perceptions among Islamic groupings have the predominant role in setting *shari'ah* rules and limits. This feature of the development has been true in the history of *shari'ah*. Consequently, there have never arisen profound properties of the type of *Tawhidi* unity of knowledge across diverse multiverse systems. The *shari'ah* remained constricted to the mundane world of worldly affairs (*muamalat*) (Choudhury, 2015).

The other principle of Tawhid as the ontological Law is to identify and avoid Falsehood in the face of Truth. The *Qur'an* (7:13)[7] declares against the nature of arrogance as falsehood being contrary to Justice as Good and blessed. Likewise, there is the verse of the *Qur'an* (17:37)[8] on arrogance as being contrary to Justice. In reference to Figure 2.1 the differentiation between Truth and Falsehood is singularly premised on the principle of the unity of knowledge and its induction of the world-system of the good things of life. Likewise, the same generalized methodology also points out the phenomenon of systemic and intervariable differentiation as the proof of Falsehood in the world-system of the Bad things of life (Falsehood) (*mafasid*) by way of methodological individualism and social differentiation.

It is for the above reasons of universality and uniqueness of *Tawhid* as the primal ontological Law contrary to the fabrication of *shari'ah*-compliance, that it is appropriate to accept such rules of the *shari'ah* that refer to the *Tawhidi* Law alone (*Qur'an* and *sunnah*). The same direct reference to *Tawhid* as the Law also applies to the practice of juristic interpretation (*fiqh*). We thereby refer to such a pure category of *shari'ah* rules related to the full phenomenology of the *Tawhidi* Law as "*shari'ah al-Tawhid*" and "*maqasid as-shari'ah al-Tawhid*".

Thus in the end, four functions are necessary for defining and establishing a wider field of intellection comprising Justice as Balance and Moderation in the light of *Tawhidi* unity of knowledge and the generality and particulars of the world-system. Included in this wide field of Justice is Social Justice, which is merely confined to worldly affairs (*muamalat*) in terms of the traditional scope of *shari'ah*-compliance. The four functions for well definition of the *Tawhidi* impact on Justice are, (1) the submission by belief and reason to the Primal Ontological Law of *Tawhid*; (2) the righteous deeds in the world according to the *Tawhidi* Law; (3) avoidance of false and illogical deeds; (4) belief in the Great Event of the Hereafter as the reality of the complete manifestation of *Tawhid* at the End as it is in the Beginning of creation. This final reality on which Justice and Truth are premised and Falsehood shunned is explained by the Elegant Equation of the Total Universe given in Figure 2.1.

An application of the theory of justice to states of peace caused by varying degrees of stability in complementary interrelations

Peace and peaceful coexistence, conflict resolution and interdependence are some of the characteristics of stable relations via participation. Sustainability of the state of participation explains the nature of complementarities between diverse agencies. Such a state of participative understanding is thereby derived from the *Tawhidi* Law premised in the organic unity of knowledge involving discourse and mutual contracts. The theme of Justice (Social Justice) is thereby invoked. The theme of peace in the complementary state of coexistence by the unity of knowledge is explained in Figure 2.2.

Let $\mathbf{x}(\theta)$ denote states of Justice; $\mathbf{y}(\theta)$ denote states of Peace corresponding to their complementarities. Thus, $\{\mathbf{x}(\theta)\} \Leftrightarrow \{\mathbf{y}(\theta)\}$. All the variables are induced by probabilistic $\{\theta\}$-values along the IIE-paths. Thereby, $\theta = \text{plim}$ $\cup_I^{\text{Interactions}} \cap_I^{\text{Integration}} \{\theta_{II}\}$; $d\theta/dt > 0$; $t = t(\theta)$.

Figure 2.2 can be adapted to the case of those episteme that marginally, yet unsuccessfully, voice the importance of the moral imperative in historical consciousness (Lucaks, 1968; Kant, see Infeld, 1963; Bhaskar, 2002; Aquinas, see Torrell, 2005).[9] The dividing H-line between Justice (a priori) and Peace (a posteriori) represents nonsymbiotic thinking caused by the absence of probability limit in attaining unity of knowledge. The shifting of the H-line represents the varying depth of the marginalist thinking, opposing the principle of complementarities. The states $\{\mathbf{x}(\theta), \mathbf{y}(\theta)\}$ allow for some degree of thinking in the methodology of consilience. Yet this

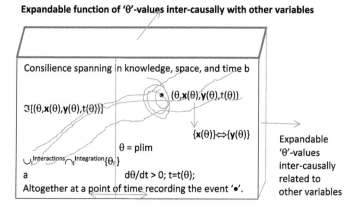

Figure 2.2 Consilience, unity of knowledge between justice and peace across knowledge, space and time dimensions

allowance remains distanced from the evolutionary learning framework of IIE-processes on gaining the unity of knowledge. The marginalist divide remains permanent between a priori and a posteriori reasoning despite the voice of Justice and Peace. There was no discovery of the universally generalized methodological abstract-empirical worldview towards explaining the imminent nature of complementarities between the diversely unified world-system of $\{\mathbf{x}(\theta),\mathbf{y}(\theta)\}$.

With allowance for evolutionary learning processes in the unity of knowledge and the knowledge-induced world-system (Figure 2.1) as shown by the solid expanding Edgeworth-Bowley Box of Figure 2.2, the meeting point of the diverse social indifference curves establish the Peace point. It lies within an evolutionary learning domain of $\{\theta,\mathbf{X}(\theta),t(\theta)\}$, that marks all event points of the trajectory of History (ab), as shown. In respect of such evolutionary learning dynamics, Justice as Balance and Moderation induced by *Tawhidi* ontology of the unity of knowledge and sustainability by the continuity property, is explained by $\Im[(\theta,\mathbf{x}(\theta),\mathbf{y}(\theta),t(\theta))]$. The transformation $(\Im)$ of Peace explains the multiple states of stability in the events of conscious History (ab).

Contrasting theories of justice (social justice)

Theories of Justice in western intellection have been prominent in the works of Hume (1988), Kant (1964), Rawls (1971) and Nozick (1973). One can identify a specific place of social justice in the theories of social choice by Arrow (1951) and deontological economics by Sen (1990). In the constitutional theory of liberty of Hayek (1967), and intertemporal theory of Justice in Dworkin one can read particular ways of defining Social Justice. Certain

specific trends of thought can be found in all these works that have contributed in contrasting ways to different schools of thought on moral values
and the epistemic foundations of reasoning.

The ontological foundations of knowledge regarding existential experience
are thereby differently constructed. Among these it remains a debatable
intellectual problem to identify which foundational ontology of being and
becoming of the experiential world-system arises in an endogenous way—
that is without enforcement and loss of will. Any loss of freedom caused by
the enforcement of a certain ontological law by any form of self, market,
institutional inflicting and compulsion, as between religion and freedom,
constitutes a problem of heteronomy. The problem of heteronomy divides
the reality of the free acceptance of God as a priori reasoning of being,
from its partitioning off of the a posteriori reasoning constricted by sheer
evidential cognition. The result is equivalent to the separation of a priori
reasoning from a posteriori reasoning caused by the equivalent separation
between deductive and inductive reasoning and the like.

The question remains to be asked: according to the rationalist nature of
reasoning why has God and monotheistic reality fallen off from all of physical and social sciences? The cause is attributable to the problematique of
heteronomy in the following way: in all of socio-scientific thought, God and
monotheism have been interpreted as an enforced reality upon free will of
human choice. Free will predominates. Thus the absence of God does not
affect the materialistic way of socio-scientific reasoning emanating from the
world as it is rationally perceived. Rationalism is the ontology of separating
reasoning between the a priori and a posteriori. The moral imperative is
necessary, but it is unnecessarily enforced in human will. Consequential
rationalist applications follow.

The problem then is the absence of identifying a continuous and meaningful mapping interrelating the a priori and the a posteriori domains and
freely sustaining this continuous interdependence across the entire generality
and particularities of the world-system issues and problems under investigation. Such a problem has remained unresolved because of the absence in
rationalism, and thereby the existence of the problematique of heteronomy,
of the of continuous mapping of rationalist reasoning and its evidences in
the diverse world-systems. Equivalently, this is the problem of failing to
interconnect ontology with epistemology so as to thereby yield the total
seamless meaning of phenomenology of reasoning and the positivistic construct of the relationship between God and the world-system. Any resolution in Occidental thought of the God–World divide being enforced on
human will to choose becomes heteronomous in nature,

Along such lines of predominance of heteronomy in rationalism as primal
ontology of Occidentalism, Kant was unable to unify the a priori and the a
posteriori despite his deep emphasis on moral imperative. Kant was thus a
rationalist deductive reasoner who had to give up the moral imperative arising from the monotheistic foundation and cast the moral imperative to the a

posteriori world-system. With Kant along the same trend of reasoning there is Rawls. Rawls improvised on justice as fairness; but implicated exogenous institutions and policies to correct the inequality caused by his idea of Original Position and an enforced Difference Principle, both to enforce equality of a state of moral decadence. Popper was a deductive dialectical thinker. For him, like Wallerstein, the dialectical world-system of capitalism was permanently in its states of bifurcation of dialectical processes without any need for a self-governed and intuited consilience of the unity of knowledge. Arrow was a deductive reasoner. In his social choice theory, the impossibility theorem of well defining a social welfare function, and thereby allocation of social choice preferences, were attained by a dictatorial agent. Thereby the axiom of "irrelevant preferences" prevailed, causing a loss of freedom. Sen (1990) is a deductive reasoner with deep concern for the moral foundation of duty-bound social construction. This is his deontological economics applying moral and ethical values to social choices.

In Hume the ontology of intercausality of relations was confined to the a posteriori world-system as the foundation of epistemic reasoning. That was because of the assumption that, causality in terms of an explainable inter-relationship cannot exist at the realm of God, Hence God and the world-system cannot be intercausal in the sensate way of Hume's thought. It is difficult to identify Hayek, but his roots in Austrian School of Economics were deeply epistemological in nature, makes him a likely deductive reasoner having an evolutionary relationship with inductive reasoning. Thereby, deductive and inductive reasoning were of an integrative nature in his economic reasoning. Just as Rawls was a modern Kant, so also Nozick is a modern Hume. Nozick's causality in favor of the market process puts him at the level of a neoclassical reasoner. He appraises the right of self-interest and original entitlement of hunter-gatherer type as an original right. Any interruption of such entitlement claims, such as by way of imposition of tax levy, even though for the common good, was argued to be morally abhorring.

Dworkin treated the topic of social justice as a relational issue over time. Thus he argues that, social justice and fairness abide only at the point of occurrence of a relationship between living entities at given points of time within a generation. Dworkin most likely is an inductive reasoner, as he observes the fact of existing relational possibility to deduce on the state of fairness and social justice in intertemporal conditions of social contract.

Conclusion

The definition of Justice in Islam in its extended meaning, and within which is the definition of Social Justice is of the relational organic unity of knowledge derived from the *Tawhid* as the primal ontological Law and then applied to the generality and particulars of the world-system. The consequence of such a relational organism between entities is coexistence between the good things of life and avoiding falsehood. The evaluation of the degree of Justice across systems of existences and for the common unified good is measured by the intervariable participative complementarities in the well-being function. The well-being objective criterion is evaluated subject to intercausal relations between the complementary variables while negating the marginalist variables of social differentiation. Justice is therefore essentially a relational worldview of interentity symbiosis in the good things of life (Truth).

The meaning of Justice so defined breaks down the problematique of heteronomy between God and the world-system by the presence of the continuous mapping given by the guidance of Prophetic teaching (*sunnah*). While the liberty of free choice is bestowed on mankind, man has been instructed with reasoned arguments to acquire the goodness of the unity of knowledge (*Tawhid*) as the Truth and avoid Falsehood. The sustainability of such a continuous learning is shown to exist in the unity of knowledge across continuum. Sustainability of the evolutionary learning processes continue across systemic continuums until the moment of the Great Event, the Hereafter.

Indeed, in the whole of socioscientific inquiry the principle of the unity of knowledge derived from the primal ontological Law of *Tawhid*, monotheism stands out as the ultimate search of metascience (Barrow, 1991). Justice is explained by Balance and Moderation of the *Tawhidi* Law. Within this generality is the particular case of Balance and Moderation of the specific inquiry in the world-system. This latter case of the particular derived from the generality constitutes Social Justice. All attributes of Justice and Social Justice can be taken up within the generality and its particulars, respectively.

Thus Justice and Social Justice are defined by the application of the generalized worldview of unity to the particular. On the other hand, the definition cannot be completed by enumerating the inexhaustible particular attributes to reach the generality of Justice. The *Qur'an* (31:27) declares:

> And if all the trees on earth were pens and the ocean (were ink), with seven oceans behind it to add to its (supply), yet would not the words of Allah be exhausted (in the writing): for Allah is Exalted in Power, full of Wisdom.
>
> (*Qur'an*, 31:27)

On the ultimate relational creative order of unity Whitehead (1979, p.57) writes:

> The creative action is the universe always becoming one in a particular unity of self-experience, and thereby adding to the multiplicity which is the universe as many. This insistent concrescence into unity is the outcome of the ultimate self-identity of each entity. No entity—be it 'universal' or 'particular'—can play disjoined roles. Self-identity requires

that every entity has one conjoined, self-consistent function, whatever be the complexity of that function.

(Whitehead, 1979, p. 57)

Agius (1990, pp. 82–83) succinctly summarizes the intergenerational process idea of sustainability in the functional ontological sense. Within such a model of social contract finds Justice and Social Justice find their resting abode:

> Whitehead's philosophical understanding of the universe as an inter-connected web of relations, as well as the ontological nature of the relational self offer a new paradigm of human society. In contrast to the individualism of the liberal tradition, process philosophy defines human society as a relational structure of experience. … "The present holds within itself the complete sum of existence, backwards and forwards".
>
> (Agius, 1990, pp. 82–83)

Notes

1 *Qur'an* (4,135):

> you who have believed, be persistently standing firm in justice, witnesses for *Allah*, even if it be against yourselves or parents and relatives. Whether one is rich or poor, *Allah* is more worthy of both. So follow not [personal] inclin-ation, lest you not be just. And if you distort [your testimony] or refuse [to give it], then indeed *Allah* is ever, with what you do, Acquainted.

2 *Qur'an* (36:36): Exalted is He who created all pairs—from what the earth grows and from themselves and from that which they do not know. This verse is also explained by the evolutionary dynamics of the following interrelationship: *Haqq ul-Yaqin* (primal ontology = *Tawhid*); *Ilm ul-Yaqin* (epistemology); *Ayn ul-Yaqin* (observations and evidences = ontic).

3 *Qur'an* (57:3): "He is the First and the Last, the Outermost and the Innermost and He has full knowledge of all things."

4 (www.brainyquote.com/quotes/said_nursi_778038, accessed on 15-12-2018).

5 Imam Shatibi (Masud, 1994) characterized such a life-fulfilling basket as comprising basic needs (*dururiyath*), comforts of life (*hajiyath*), and refinements of life (*tahsa-niyath*). By our inter-causal organic unity of relations the Shatibi basket is not inde-pendently comprised of the three categories. Rather, these categories are complemented according to the process of dynamic basic-needs regimes of development.

6 Muiniddin Ibn al-Arabi wrote in regards to the obfuscations that external inter-pretations can make to the *Tawhidi* singular truth and avoidance of falsehood. Chittick (1989) translates Ibn Al-Arabi in this regard:

> Useless knowledge is that which is disconnected from its source and origin, i.e. from the divine reality. Any knowledge outside of *tawhid* leads away from *Allah*, not toward Him. But knowledge within the context of *tawhid* allows its posses-sor to grasp the interconnectedness of all things through a vast web whose centre is the divine. All existent things come from *Allah* and go back to Him.

7 *Qur'an* (7:13): (*Allah*) said: "(O *Iblis*) get down from this (Paradise), it is not for you to be arrogant here. Get out, for you are of those humiliated and disgraced."
8 *Qur'an* (17:37): "And do not walk upon the earth exultantly. Indeed, you will never tear the earth [apart], and you will never reach the mountains in height."
9 Torrell (2005) explains: The circular plan, as of circular causation, remained a worldly process in the *Summa*. The divine law, just as in Kantian heteronomy, remained numinous for the world-system. On the circular plan of religion and the world-system, Thomas Aquinas' idea of circular causation in *Summa* is explained by Torrell (Choudhury, M. A. 2014, p. 155)

> The work (*Summa*) is in fact constructed according to a circular plan that draws the reader into the "going-out-from-returning-to" (*exitus-reditus*) movement, which is that of the entire universe coming from God to creation and returning to him as its final end.

References

Agius, I. (1990). Towards a Relational Theory of Intergenerational Ethics. In S. Busuttil, E. Agius, P. S. Inglott, & T. Macelli (Eds.), *Our Responsibilities Towards Future Generations* (pp. 73–93). Malta: The Foundation for International Studies in Cooperation with UNESCO.

Arrow, K. J. (1951). *Social Choice and Individual Values*. New York, NY: John Wiley & Sons.

Barrow, J. D. (1991). Laws. In his *Theories of Everything, the Quest for Ultimate Explanation* (pp. 12–30). Oxford, England: Oxford University Press.

Bayrakli, B. (1992). The Concept of Justice (*Adl*) in the Philosophy of Al-Farabi. *Hamdard Islamicus*, XV(3), pp. 21–31.

Bhaskar, R. (2002). *Reflections on Meta-Reality, Transcendence, Emancipation and Everyday Life* (p. 146). New Delhi: Sage Foundation.

Buchanan, J. M. (1999). The Domain of Constitutional Economics. In his *The Logical Foundations of Constitutional Liberty*. Indianapolis, IN: Liberty Fund.

Burstein, M. (1991). History versus Equilibrium: Joan Robinson and Time in Economics. In I. H. Rima (Ed.), *The Joan Robinson Legacy* (pp. 49–61). Armonk, NY: M.E. Sharpe, Inc.

Chittick, W. C. (1989). *Sufi Path of Knowledge*. Albany, NY: State University of New York Press.

Choudhury, M. A. (2014). *Tawhidi Epistemology and Its Applications (Economics, Finance, Science, and Society)*. Cambridge, UK: Cambridge Scholars Publishing.

Choudhury, M. A. (2015). Res extensa et res cogitans de maqasid as-shari'ah. *International Journal of Law and Management*, 57(6), 662–693.

Choudhury, M. A. (2017). The Ontological Law of Tawhid Contra 'shari'ah-compliance' in Islamic Portfolio Finance. *International Journal of Law and Management*, 63(6), 413–434.

Choudhury, M. A., & Asmak, A. B. R. (2017). Micro-Money, Finance, and Real Economy Interrelationship in the Framework of Islamic Ontology of Unity of Knowledge and the World-System of Social Economy. *International Journal of Social Economics*, 45(2), 445–462.

Friedman, A. (1982). *Foundations of Modern Analysis*. New York: Dover Publications, Inc.

(Imam) Ghazzali, A. H. trans. by Marmura, M.E. (1997). *The Incoherence of the Philosophers*. Provo, UT: Brigham Young University Press.

Grandmont, J.-M. (1989). Temporary Equilibrium. In J. Eatwell, M. Milgate, & P. Newman (Eds.), *New Palgrave: General Equilibrium* (pp. 164–185). New York, NY: W.W. Norton.

Hawking, S. W., & Mlodinow, L. (2010). *The Grand Design*. New York, NY: Bantam Books.

Hayek, F. A. (1967). *Studies in Philosophy, Politics and Economics*. Chicago, IL: The University of Chicago Press.

Helleiner, G. (May 1986). The Question of Conditionality. In C. Lancaster & J. Williamson (Eds.), *African Debt and Financing* (pp. 63–104). Washington, DC: Institute for International Economics, Special Report No. 5.

Hilbert, D. (1967). On the Infinite. trans. by S. Bauer-Mengelberg. In J. van Heijenoort (Ed.), *From Frege to Godel: A Source Book in Mathematical* Logic, *1879–1931* (pp. 367–392). Cambridge, MA: Harvard University Press.

Hume, D. (1988). *An Enquiry Concerning Human Understanding*. Buffalo, NY: Prometheus Books.

Kaku, M. (2015). Consciousness – A Physicist's Viewpoint. In his *The Future of the Mind*, Chapter 2. New York, NY: Anchor Book.

Kamali, M. H. (1989). *Siyasah shari'ah. The American Journal of Islamic Social Sciences*, 6(1), 59–81.

Kamali, M. H. (1991). *Principles of Islamic Jurisprudence*. Cambridge, UK: Islamic Texts Society.

Kant, I. trans. by C. J. Friedrich (1949). Religion within the Limits of Reason Alone. In C. J. Friedrich (Ed.), *The Philosophy of Kant* (pp. 365–411). New York, NY: Modern Library.

Kant, I. trans. by L. Infeld (1963). The General Principle of Morality. In L. Denis & O. Sensen (Ed.), *Kant's Lectures on Ethics. A critical guide*. Indianapolis, IN: Hackett Publishing Co.

Kant, I. (1964). *Groundwork of the Metaphysics of Morals*, trans. by H. J. Paton. New York, NY: Harper & Row Publishers.

Levine, D. (1988). *Needs, Rights, and the Market*. Boulder, CO: Lynne Rienner.

Lucaks, J. (1968). *Historical Consciousness*. New York, NY: Harper & Row Publishers.

Maddox, I. J. (1970). *Elements of Functional Analysis*. Cambridge, UK: Cambridge University Press.

Masud, M. K. (1994). *Shatibi's Theory of Meaning*. Islamabad, Pakistan: Islamic Research Institute, International Islamic University.

Nozick, R. (1973). Distributive Justice. *Philosophy and Public Affairs*, 3(1), 45–126.

Popper, K. (1998). *Conjectures and Refutations: The Growth of Scientific Knowledge*. London, UK: Routledge & Kegan Paul.

Rawls, J. (1971). *A Theory of Justice*. Cambridge, MA: Harvard University Press.

Romer, P. M. (1986). Increasing Returns and Long-Run Growth. *Journal of Political Economy*, 94, 1002–1037.

Sen, A. (1990). Freedom and Consequences. In A. Sen (Ed), *On Ethics and Economics* (pp. 58–88). Oxford, UK: Basil Blackwell.

Sen, A. (2010). *Commodities and Capabilities*. Oxford, UK: Oxford University Press.

32 *Masudul Alam Choudhury*

Shackle, G. L. S. (1971). *Epistemics & Economics*. Cambridge, UK: Cambridge University Press.

Solow, R. (1980). *Growth Theory, an Exposition*. Oxford, UK: Oxford University Press.

Streeten, P. (1981). From Growth to Basic Needs. In his *Development Perspectives*. New York, NY: St. Martin's Press.

Torrell, J. P. trans. by B. M. Gueven (2005). A Circular Plan. In J.-P. Torrell *Aquinas' SUMMA, Background, Structure, and Reception* (pp. 27–36). Washington, DC: The Catholic University of America Press.

Wallerstein, I. (1998). Spacetime as the Basis of Knowledge. In O. F. Bordo (Ed.), *People's Participation, Challenges Ahead* (pp. 43–62). New York, NY: Apex Press.

Whitehead, A. N., Griffin, D. R., & Sherburne, D. W. Eds. (1979). Fact and Form. In his *Process and Reality*. New York, NY: The Free Press.

3 Social justice, market, society and government

An Islamic perspective

Toseef Azid, Osamah Hussain Al Rawashdeh and Muhammad Omer Chaudhry

It is assumed that in a conventional economic system the market can distribute resources in an efficient way. However, in real terms, it is not possible for this market mechanism to work in a proper manner due to its imperfections. In most cases the market is unable to reduce the inequality and poverty in society. On the one hand, policymakers suggest a strong and legal system for the just distribution of resources whereas on the other hand academics propose a strong and moral society for achieving social justice. Most of them are of the opinion that the success of the system is dependent on the functioning of the market within the framework of the strong legal foundations of the state and a solid moral society.

It is generally assumed that social justice is mainly concerned with the redistribution of resources. The question which is always faces experts is whether social arrangements benefit the whole community or not. Do the laws and social understandings broadly benefit everyone or do they only work well for the wealthy and powerful segment of the society? Which institutions work efficiently in the given social, cultural and religious environment (i.e., market, society or government)?

Another issue which is simultaneously related to the government as well as to the society, either a strong society produces a strong government or vice versa. How these two pillars are work in a just society and how can they create a just environment? How do the members of society consider the rights of the deprived segment of society? Is it possible for market, government and society to promote the voluntary sector to fill the gap and how is this voluntary sector helpful in achieving of a higher degree of social justice?

In this chapter an effort will be made to reply the above mentioned questions within the framework of Islam. An appropriate model will be developed which will help us understand how, within the universal set of Islam, these three subsets (society, market and government) are working as a complementary set to one another. And how are these three subsets able to achieve the Pareto optimality? And it will also be discussed in the present chapter how the objective of public interest (*Maslaha*) can be achieved under the guidance of *Shari'ah*.

Theory of social justice in conventional system

The term of social justice, first introduced by J. S. Mill is based on two concepts, one is merit and desert and the other is related to need and equality. Generally, social justice is also known as distributive justice. Hayek said, "There can be no distributive justice where no one distributes"[1] (Friedrich Hayek, cited in Burke 2010, p. 297). Novak argues in this way: "Social justice is a virtue, an attribute of individuals, or it is a fraud" (cited in Burke 2010, p. 297). The role of individuals, a group of people and customs are very much important in maintaining justice (Burke 2010).

In the current literature, theories about justice are divided under two subcategories:

(i) Procedural theories of justice
(ii) Distributive/Economic theories of justice

Distributive justice advocates the just allocation of goods and services among the members of society and establishing more administrative, political and social institutions. This leads to a stronger role of the political institutions and emphasizes more the regulation of the market as well as the economy and is consequently able to establish social justice. There are different theories that have emerged in the literature related to the abovementioned discussion, among them Rawl's theory of justice as fairness and the differences between people, Dworkin's resource-based approach to social justice and Sen's capability approach to social justice got the most attention among academic circles.

Rawls (1971, 1999) supported the general welfare with each individual's welfare and connected with the cooperative venture for mutual advantage which as a result supports the political intervention. His notion of fairness suggests that benefits and burdens are equally distributed among the participants. In his opinion all the participants are free, equal, reasonable and rational. However, Rawls purposed a hypothetical situation which he called the original position, where every participant is free and has equal rights to select the primary goods, i.e., basic rights and liberties. Vargovic (2012) explained how justice will be selected in the world of Rawls,

> Rawls argues parties in the original position would choose the following two principles of justice by using maximin strategy: (1) the principle of equal liberty for all and (2) the principle of equality of opportunity and the difference principle, according to which social and economic inequalities should benefit the least-advantage in the society
>
> (Vargovic, 2012, p. 15)

Hampton (1998) criticizes Rawls and commented that Rawls allows some inequalities whereas people should be treated equally despite differences in culture, religion, habits, talents, abilities and so on. In the words of Hampton, "Rawls has failed to acknowledge the proper role that effort, merit and responsibility should have in the distribution of resources" (Hampton 1998, p. 143 cited in Vargovic 2012, p. 16).

Dworkin (2000, 2006, 2011) explains equality of resources and equality of welfare. In his opinion the state is responsible for providing the resources and individuals are responsible for their own well-being. In Hampton's (1998) view that Dworkin did not advocate absolute equality. However, this is the responsibility of the state and society to help people whatever the circumstances, for example disabled members of the society need extra help and care. However, it creates another problem: what resources should be allocated to the disabled members of the society? However, Rawls and Dworkin support the idea that society is responsible for social justice and for the achievement of social equality. The capability approach developed by Sen (Nobel Price holder), and Nussbaum's human functioning approach, discussed indirectly social justice in terms of interpersonal well-being, both approaches consequently require the role of society in terms of the redistribution of required resources and opportunities. Vargovic (2012, p. 18) comments on the capability approach and stated:

> The capability approach is focused on the ends because it is believed that people significantly differ in their ability to convert means into valuable opportunities (capabilities) or outcomes (functionings). However, the point is to place people in conditions in which they can pursue their ultimate ends.
>
> (Vargovic, 2012, p. 18)

However, according to Minogue (2005) social justice is an abstract term which is different under different systems such as socialism, communism, the system of a welfare state and also a mixture of an idea and a political project. Hayek (2001) opines that social justice is a meaningless concept. As Morison (2005) stated that according to Hayek remunerations based on performance or needs set by the government are known as social justice as a result an individual or group of individuals enjoying themselves at the cost of others, however, under a system of the free market, distribution of income is a byproduct of the impersonal process of the free market whereas individuals involved in the economic exchange have biases towards others.

According to Leanne Ho (2011),[2] it is the joint responsibility of the society and the individuals to establish social justice and also to maintain an optimal balance between the two ends. She further added that joint responsibility is

> to address systemic/structural poverty, inequality and unfairness (emphasizes responsibility of the system or government to provide), fair redistribution of resources, equal access to opportunities and rights, fair

system of law and due process, ability to take up opportunities and exercise rights, protection of vulnerable and disadvantaged people, Individual responsibility

(Ho, 2011, p. 4)

and

getting what you deserve according to: status (emphasizes an individual's social position as a determinant of the share of resources an individual deserves), moral responsibility (emphasizes the behavior of those who are poor, excluded or disadvantaged), workforce participation (emphasizes workforce participation as the only legitimate way for an individual to contribute to society and be socially included), individual capability (emphasizes the personal characteristics that enable people to take advantage of opportunities.

(Ho, 2011, p. 4)

Function of market, government and society in conventional system

Classical liberates are of the opinion that the role of the government should be minimum and there should be freedom for individuals and the market and limited powers for the government. However, experts on the other hand, have different opinions and support the government's role in establishing the welfare state. They believe that the byproducts of the market are undesirable, i.e., inequality, unequal distribution of income, exploitation of the poor, value free functioning and etc. Keeping that in mind, experts have asked the question of whether the invisible hand of the market is sufficient to establish social justice or is it necessary for the government to intervene and achieve this objective (Vargovic 2012).

In the current literature one can find a discussion of the role of the market, the role of the government and the interrelationship in between these two institutions for the achievement of the goal of social justice. Is it possible for the free market to resolve the issue of social justice without greater government? This is always being asked by the academicians and policymakers. Simultaneously, they are also trying to solve the issue of whether of not the market complements society or not.

It is evident that the free market produces inequalities, greediness, selfishness and it has also been taken under consideration that the market does not distribute benefits in a justified way. However, on the other hand, it is also assumed that the market mechanism will be able to produce an efficient production and consumption system and simultaneously efficient utilization of dispersed individual knowledge (Vargovic 2012). Policymakers are always trying to solve the issue of social justice which is related to government intervention and undesirable market outcomes.[3] The main issue is how the conflict between the functions of the free market and the intervention of government could be resolved, and simultaneously, how the political authorities can solve the issue of efficiency and equity.

Briggs (1961) stated that the basic purpose of the welfare state is to modify market forces, to provide a minimum level of income to individuals and families, to maintain a minimum standard of security and to guarantee the minimum the highest level of living standards to all citizens. Goodin (1988) argued that the responsibility of the welfare state is to reduce the poverty level, redistribute the available resources among the members of the society in a justified way and also promote a level of social responsibility. In his opinion the responsibility of the state and society was to help, to care and to look after the vulnerable members of the society. He further argued that it is the responsibility of the government and society to provide the public goods due to the failure of the market and efforts should be made to reduce the dependency of the deprived members of the society. In his opinion, the market economy would not be able to provide social justice in an optimal manner because it produces disparities, dependency, corruption and exploitation. Hasnas (2003) agreed that state has the responsibility to provide the public with goods but other segments of society should also feel equal responsibility besides the state. In Vargovic's (2012) view,

> the most promoting argument for promoting distributive justice is that reasonable people perceive that certain market outcomes are simply unjust and that it is the duty of the state to cover them through redistributive policies and regulation in order to create a more just society.
>
> (p. 22)

However, Hampton (1998) perceived that the actions of the welfare state are not justified because it is not possible to satisfy all the members of society; so a small group may be unsatisfied. In Hayek's view it is the state which abuses its power in order to implement its predetermined political agenda and ideas, whereas Nozick's (1999) argued that government interventions violate the rights of the members of the society. Kymlicka (2001) stated that morally the state should play a minimum role and it is the responsibility of state to protect the rights of the individuals, i.e., natural and prepolitical, more intervention of the state violates the individual rights.

Hayek (1978) argued that extensive intervention by the government does not match the idea of equality, distributive justice does not represent social justice and a predetermined political agenda would not be able to create an environment of social justice. In his opinion, greater government does not lead to the equal treatment of individuals. He said,

> formal equality before the law is incompatible with any governmental activity which deliberately aims at a material or substantive equality of different people—therefore, in order to produce the same outcome for

different people, they would have to be treated differently because to give different people the same objective benefits does not mean to give them the same subjective opportunity

(Hayek 1978, p. 106 cited in Vargovic 2012, p. 26)

He further added that demand for social justice is based on the narrow understanding the functioning of the market system which leads to the extensive government interventions and redistributions (Vargovic 2012). In Hayek's view, social justice is meaningless in the market system because it is not predictable, human reasons are limited, the nature of knowledge is dispersed, the nature of society is complex and also based on the luck of the players of the market. And it is purely based on a game of skill and luck which is known as *catallaxy*, i.e. to exchange or to admit in the community. In Hayek's view, market society produces a high degree of harmonization of the expectations of different people and most efficient utilizations of the knowledge and skills of different members of society (Vargovic 2012, p. 35). The market outcome does not depend on a predetermined agenda, idea or project. However, in his opinion, government power ultimately leads to an abuse of powers and creates biases and an unjust environment. He said the market is for all and not for a selected groups or individuals and increases the efficiency and productivity of the economy. As a result, it reduces the dependency of the individual on the society and state. Cragg (1983) supports the Hayek's idea and said that there is no predetermined agenda in the market system and it is not possible to redistribute the resources without any intervention. However Plant (2005) argued that if any member of society is unable to achieve success within the framework of the market then he should be entitled to receive help from the state and society if not then it will be considered as injustice. On contrary Shearmur (2003) supports the market society and claims that morally the market society is more desirable and assistance can only be provided in the case of natural disasters or people suffering under severe hardship. He further added that we should find out why people would choose a system which is morally unacceptable and unjust. Vargovic (2012) concluded as:

In conclusion, returning to the starting question, does social justice matter in the end? The answer is fairly straightforward—'Yes it does' because the notion of justice has been highly valued in every society at all times in history. However, the notion of social justice understood only as distributive justice, although attractive as an ideal, has no such value and it is purely rhetorical in complex contemporary societies.

(p. 29)

According to Kymlicka (2001) once property rights are recognized then a free market in factors of production is morally required (cited by Vargovic 2012, p. 40)

However the counter arguments of Olsaretti (2004) are: she describes the market as being value free and not functioning on the basis of moral merit, it is not governed by any regulations and does not follow any of the independently formulated principles. She further elaborated that the free market should function within the framework of two arguments, i.e., compensation and contribution argument. In her opinion, a politically just society is one where individuals are independent and free to make their choices.

Sautter (2001) is in favor of the government's corrective measures. He supports a strong legal and just system which is able to monitor the functions of the market in a proper way. The state must reduce inequalities through its corrective measures which are produced by the free market. He further elaborated that it is difficult to draw a fine line between the long-term success of the market economy and its negative and damaging impact on the society. Narveson (1998) stated that the current prevailing inequalities are due to different expertise, skill and knowledge attained by the different members of the society and the duties imposed by the government for reducing inequalities promote individual dependency on others.

Hayek's elaborated: "Providing assistance to the weakest members in a society is a matter of public charity which is compatible with a free market system as long as it is provided outside the market and without restricting its freedom" (Hayek 1998 cited in Vargovic 2012, p. 45). Vargovic (2012, p. 45) summarizes Hayek's argument related to state intervention as:

> [I]t is in the interest of all, it may be perceived as a general moral duty to assist those who cannot help themselves and earn enough for a decent life (for any reason), it is important for social and political stability.
>
> (Vargovic, 2012, p. 45)

In Hayek's (1998) point of view, in the free market system society enables one to find new ways to utilize scarce resources and satisfies more individuals because there is no predetermined agenda. However, if there is intervention from the state, it may be that in the short-run it will reduce the gap between the haves and have-nots but as a result it will reduce the amount of opportunities in the society. In a nutshell, the free market system allows its members to use their knowledge in an efficient and productive way and enables them to contribute to the welfare of the economy without any predetermined objective.

From the above discussion we can conclude the following results:

(i) If a society requires social justice then the role of the state is very important and for the achievement of specific goals and objectives, the state should impose some restrictions on society.
(ii) If individuals demand freedom, then the free market system is morally necessary and acceptable.

As Tatian (n.d.) considered the true spirit of social justice, she concluded that morals, social security and personal well-being are strictly linked with each other. Any system which is based on the abovementioned three ingredients creates that environment of social justice which provides a dignified status to the members of the society.

Complementarity of society, market and government in the Islamic framework

Islamic system is purely based on a universal set of morals. Tatian (n.d.) explained that we have three types of morals:

(i) Morals of duty
(ii) Morals of free beliefs
(iii) Morals of responsibility

She said that every moral has two dimensions.[4] Islam recommends and respect nos. "i" and "iii" whereas "ii" is not appreciated. The system of Islam is based on honesty, fairness, benevolence to others, truthfulness, kindness, brotherhood and justice. Islam has provided its own morals which are not free from its beliefs. It is not possible for anyone to understand social justice (which is the subset of universal set) in the system of Islam without understanding the Islamic concept of the universe, life and mankind. It gives us a comprehensive theory for the understanding of individual issues. Every segment of life is interconnected with one another which is the subset of the universal and comprehensive theory and leads to the welfare of the mankind. Qutub (1980) argued that no solution exists in isolation from all other issues. Islam has its own universal philosophy which is guided by the Holy Book of the *Qur'an* and the traditions (*sunnah*) of the Prophet (*SAW*). These are the basic sources which guide how Muslims should spend their lives, how the laws are supposed to be formulated, what the modes of worship are and how Muslims are supposed to behave in their economic and social life. These sources also guide the relationship between the creator and creation, between man and universe, between individual and society, between communities and between one nations. Islam develops a balance in between all these relations. These relationships have not any type of opposition, resistance, hostility, antagonism, conflict, exploitation or disagreement. No one can exploit another due to his natural advantage or after acquiring a worldly power. *Maqsad* of *shari'ah* is to serve humanity and increase the welfare of mankind in both of his lives, i.e. present life and life hereafter.

Islam develops the concept of social justice in a unique manner where all the agents of the society and economy complement one another. Every social and economic agent in this scenario supports one another in promoting and enhancing social justice. The teachings of Islam lead to that path which is an integrated one, where life in this world and the hereafter are connected with one faith, where worship and work are going on the same path and have the same objective, the objective of all of the above is to please Allah. The norms of love, mercy, help, cooperation, brotherhood, equity and maintaining a reasonable equality among human beings. In the system of Islam only that person considers as superior who has fear of Allah in his heart and that is a preferred one in the eyes of Allah.. Everyone has the freedom to use his abilities to achieve his goals and this is not forbidden. Islam appreciates the differences in abilities in different members of society.[5] Because a perfect equality is not a natural one. Every individual has his own potential and by using that potential he can efficiently contribute to the economy and receive a reward according to his abilities. Islam recognizes and admits the merits of good doers.

In this system one can find a universal set of values which comprises the economic, social, religious and psychological values, the justice in the society is based on all the above mentioned values whereas economic values are a subset of its universal set of values. That society is known as a just society where true values play a significant role and money itself is not considered to be the only source of value like in conventional economies. Islam treats the body and soul as one unit and the whole human being is considering to be one body, all individuals are interdependent, every individual has his rights (*haqquq*) on other individual, this is the duty of every individual to take care of others, this leads to a just and productive society. Social justice in an Islamic environment is a comprehensive concept and not merely dependent on economic materials.

According to Qutub (1980) there are three foundations of social justice in the Islamic framework:

(i) Absolute freedom of conscience
(ii) The complete equality of all men
(iii) The permanent mutual responsibility of society

Islam gives priority to the freedom of human beings and human equality but these are under some limits and constraints, Islam places some restrictions on the behavior of its followers, however, few behaviors are not allowed whereas most are permissible. However, Islam also puts social and mutual responsibilities on members of society or on the community as a - whole,[6] i.e., responsibility between man and his soul, between a man on his family, between the individual and society, between one community and another and one nation to another nation. Islam defines the morals of the society and identifies the limits of the individuals and community. It is not possible for individuals and society to cross the limits which are imposed by the *Shariah* (Islamic Jurisprudence).

However this is the obligatory duty of the state to look after the affairs and needs of all its citizens.[7] Furthermore, this is the duty of the Muslims to look after other Muslim brothers and if any Muslim has worldly material in surplus then he is advised to give to the other Muslim brothers.[8] Even every citizen of the Islamic state has the right to the treasury of the state.[9] Similarly this is the duty of the community to provide the destitute segment of the society.[10]

Every individual has his rights on others especially neighbor has more rights on his neighbors, so much so if one sleeps hungry while another has food then he is not considered to be a Muslim.[11] Likewise it is the duty of the community to look after the poor members of the community and provide them the basic needs. It is consensus among the Muslim scholars that the basic ingredient of social justice in the Islamic environment is social interdependence. Ibn Hazm, a great Muslim jurist. He says:

> It is the duty of the rich that they should meet the needs of the poor and the destitute of their village or town. And if the treasury is not sufficient to meet their needs, then the state has the right to take their surplus wealth, if necessary by force, to meet the needs of the poor in the community. He further says that all the companions of the Holy Prophet are agreed upon this that if there is anyone hungry or naked or without shelter, it is incumbent upon the state to supply his needs from the surplus wealth of the rich (in case its own treasury is insufficient).
>
> (cited by Chaudhry, n.d.)

Table 3.1 explains justice in the conventional as well within the Islamic framework.

In following we are trying to present three illustrations of social interdependence at the micro as well as macro level within an Islamic framework.

Illustration 1: at a macro level: the system of Zakat and Charity

Social interdependence is the responsibility of the individuals or community towards society. It requires to cover the basic needs of the needy segment of the society.[12] Generally these functions are performed through charity/philanthropy. This is the religious duty of Muslims to give a proportion of their income to the needy who are economically and socially deprived.[13] This obligatory duty is known as *Zakat*.[14] *Zakat* is the obligatory duty on Muslims known as *sahib-i-nisab*, transfer payments to the poor segment of society. If the volume of *Zakat* is not sufficient then this is the responsibility of the rich people to transfer more funds to the needy segment of the society or the state should collect more funds from rich people and fill the gap. This is the duty of the government to collect the *Zakat* and transfer it to the deprived segment of society. It also creates an environment of social interaction among the givers and the beneficiaries. It is the source of sharing the resources among the different segments of the society which ultimately

Table 3.1 Definitions of justice

Scholastic Term	Modern Term	Definition in conventional framework	Definition in Islamic framework
Justice	Justice	To give what is owed	Not harm anyone and follow the rules of *Shariah*
Commutative Justice	Commutative Justice	What is owed between two persons in exchange	Morally and economically no suppression among the members of society
Distributive Justice	None	Obligations between a community and its members, divided into general and particular justice	Distribution of the economic, social, psychological, religious and human capital on a merit basis
General Justice or Legal Justice	Social Justice	What the members of a community owe to that community	Interpersonal dependency and moral environment with its basic traits
Particular Justice	Distributive Justice	What a community owes to its members	Market, government and society complement each other and fill that gap which is not filled by others

Source: Burke (2010)
Note: the 4th column was added by the authors.

increases the strength of the Muslim *ummah*. Through the transfer of funds from higher income group to lower income group, Islam creates a strong community of believers (Hassan 2007).

It is discussed by Azid and Qureshi (2015) that in Islamic society, charity plays a very important role and it increases the universal set of capital which comprises psychological capital, social capital, religious capital and human capital. Which is not possible within the framework of the free market. However, this incremental change in the universal set of capital enhancing the social as well as distributive justice. In this scenario government, market and voluntary sector (society) work simultaneously and also support each other. The Islamic economy in real terms is the moral economy with its traits of brotherhood, kindness, fairness, justice and a high degree of generosity. Consequently, the market does not produce inequalities and disparities in the moral economy, similarly government officials do not abuse their powers, whereas society is always ready to give to the deprived segment of the society. All of these three institutions complement each other and create an environment of harmony. In the Islamic sense free market does not mean that market is value free. *Sahriah* has imposed some ethical constraints on the functioning of government, market as well on the society. This is an example of the distributive or social justice at a macro level. Because in this case the whole economy benefits and enjoys the social justice.

However, if someone has earned income by unjust means then according to the ruling of *Shariah* his income should be taken by the government, if he pays the *Zakat*, this will not purify his income, and this will not lead to social justice. On the contrary if he earned his income by just means then he has to pay the *Zakat* according to the *nisab*.

Illustration 2 venture philanthropy

It is a major question how the philanthropy will be channelized in the Islamic system and also without wastage of resources, how it can be used properly for the welfare of the individuals, local community and Muslim *ummah*. In the current scenario, Islamic financial institutions can play a very pivotal role and also through venture philanthropy they can maintain the social justice in the Islamic society/community. As it is observed that Islamic financial institutions (IFIs) are developing *shariah* compliant products, and their major objective is also to serve the community beyond their commercial activities. In that way society, government and the market can play a very positive role for the development of the social structure of the society and will be able to help the needy segments of the community. Islamic financial institutions invest the amount of philanthropy in the *Shariah* compliant instruments, i.e. venture philanthropy. And the profit of venture philanthropy may be used for the training of the members of the lower income group, for the provision of education and health facilities, for the other services to the society and also to develop human capital. Consequently, a nexus will be built up with the set of philanthropy and IFIs for *Shariah* compliant venture philanthropy. This step leads towards the marketization of the whole cycle. IFIs will provide training to the beneficiaries and produce the market-oriented products and services. And then this will start a circular flow towards the group of philanthropists. As a result, the size of the philanthropy group will also snow ball because of the generation of new resources in this world system. Through this process the beneficiaries would understand the importance of sharing and the value of almsgiving in all the aspects of life (religious, psychological, social and economic). In this process we are unable to see any crux of Hayek's theory or any root of Polany's double movement. Table 3.2 explains the circular causation flow of philanthropy.

Illustration 3 at a micro level: distributive justice through firm

Within the Islamic framework, firms work on the *Musharakah* or *Mudharabah* basis. If firms earn profits then it is distributed among the *Mudharib*

Table 3.2 Circular causation flow of philanthropy

	Universal Set of Philanthropy: Originated from the Philanthropist Group				Islamic Financial Institutions (IFIs)	
Stages of Philanthropy	*Type of Capital*	*Impact*	*Change*		*Shariah Compliant*	*Training* / *Function of IFIs*
Stage 1	Religious	Reward in the life hereafter	Generation of resources		Venture Philanthropy, e.g. cash *waqf* (as trustee), part-nership, etc.	Improving the social environment reinvestment
Stage 2	Psychological	Happiness				Provision of education and health facilities
Stage 3	Social	Satisfaction				
Stage 4	Human	Utility				Disbursement of philanthropy
Σ	Moral Economy	*Flah*	Incremental Change in the resources		Generation of new profit	Production of a new set of market-oriented products and services
Final Output	Increasing the size of Philanthropist Group and again enters stage 1					

Source: Azid and Qureshi (2015)

(worker) and *Rab ul Ma'al* (supplier of funds). In this scenario, the firm satisfies the requirement of distributive justice. The returns are based on the number of shares. However, if a firm earns a reasonable profit then workers will also benefit. So workers and shareholders are both working together to achieve the objective of the firm. Both parties produce goods and services. Like the conventional system, labor is not considered to be the cost of the firm and is not included in the cost. This structure does not create friction among the shareholders and the workers of the firm. Owing to the environment of brotherhood the workers are receiving deserts as well as being compensating by the management. Firms should pay workers according to their work and the wages should be paid before their sweat is dried.[15] Firms within the Islamic framework follow exactly the distributive justice which is synonymous with social justice. If a firm doesn't distribute among the workers or shareholders as they deserve then it means that the firm does not follow distributive justice. If firms are not able to distribute according to distributive justice then conflict and differences will tend to increase which will disturb the harmony of the economy as well society. If the government provides a pleasant environment, punishing criminals, enforcing laws of contracts in a proper way, it is considered to be the input of the firm then the government has the right to get a share from the firms by way of taxes and duties (Azid and Rawashdeh 2018).

Conclusions

Social justice is the product of government intervention and policies of the government to maintain the equity and justice among the members of society. However, in a conventional setting, the free market does not support social justice, so government policies are required to build social and ethical foundations for the market to grow on a long-term basis and to help society to create a universal capital group. It has been argued by experts that social justice and development are positively correlated and enhance the degree of a moral and just environment within a country. Generally, it is the consensus among the social scientists that development leads to social justice, the approach to the deprived segment of the society and provides them with the basic needs in a dignified way. However, in a conventional setting the market, government and society do not complement each other.

However, within the Islamic framework, the state, market and society develop as a triangle base for the substantial degree of social justice. Venture philanthropy within the Islamic environment generates a universal set of capital which results in increases to the degree of social justice.

We can conclude that the Islamic world is completely different from the conventional one because the instruments and tools of Islamic *Shariah* have their unique and different concepts which are not understandable in a conventional setting.

Notes

1 Social justice, distributive justice and economic justice are synonymous and related to the re-distribution of income. Whereas commutative justice is what is due in exchange among the persons and distributive justice is what is due in between community and its members. "While social justice relates an individual to his community, distributive justice relates the community to its members" (Burke 2010, p. 301).

2 Leanne Ho defines different approaches of social justice in the following manner:

   i   Utilitarianism (J.S. Mill): In practice, this view reflected an unequal distribution on the basis of status as it was often the disadvantaged whose rights were sacrificed for the good of the privileged classes of society (p. 6).
   ii Rawls: This view of social justice relates to justice in a systemic form, applied to society as a whole rather than individuals. It emphasizes unequal distribution on the basis of an individual's needs or requirements with a particular focus on the needs of the disadvantaged, and equality of opportunity (pp. 6–7).
   iii Nozcik: This view of social justice emphasizes distribution according to the existing system of individual property ownership and does not support any kind of redistribution (p. 7).
   iv Miller (p. 7) This view of social justice emphasizes unequal distribution according to what an individual deserves based on their moral responsibility or behavior (p. 7).
   v   Sen: This idea of social justice emphasizes developing individual capabilities (p. 8).

3 Among other things, social justice advocates endorse the exercise of government power to redistribute wealth/income and to regulate behavior to produce a more just outcome across the whole of society (Rose 2013 www.libertylawsite.org/tag/egalitarianism/).

4 **Morales of duty**: 1) morals of duty to a society (or a community, or collective), characterized by attitudes of collective consciousness, when public interest has importance over and above the personal; 2) morals of duty to God in which a moral life is lived in correspondence to the divine instructions of God, guaranteeing finding salvation. **Morales of free belief:** 1) the morals of individuals based on individualist consciousness, when personal interests are higher than public interests; 2) the morals of "the imposter", when the key principle is based on the idea of "the means justifies the ends. **Morales of responsibility:** 1) the morals of responsibility to "yours", when people correlate their interests to the interests of their class, their country, their nation, etc.; 2) the morals of responsibility to all mankind (global ethics).

5 And Allah hath favored some of you above others in provision) 16:71).

6 The Messenger of Allah said: No one's faith amongst you is reliable until he likes for his brother (in Islam) what he likes for himself (Bukhari).

7 The Messenger of Allah said: The government is the guardian of anyone who has no guardian (Abu Dawood; Tirmizi).

8 Abu Saeed Khudhri reports that the Holy Prophet said; "Anyone who possesses goods more than his needs, should give the surplus goods to the weak (and poor); and whosoever possesses food more than his needs should give the surplus food to the needy and the destitute." He further added that the Holy

Prophet went on referring to different kinds of goods in similar manner until we thought that none of us had any right over his surplus wealth.") Ibn Hazam)

9 Caliph Umar once said: Each and every Muslim has a right in the property of Bait-ul-Mal whether he exercises it or not (Kitab al Amwal).

10 Ali is reported to have said that "God has made it obligatory on the rich to meet the economic needs of the poor up to the extent of their absolute necessities. If they are hungry or naked or involved in other financial difficulties, it will be merely because the rich are not doing their duty. Therefore God will question them about it on the Day of Judgment and will give them due punishment." (Ibn Hazam)

11 The Prophet of Islam is reported to have said: If anyone spent a night in a town and he remained hungry till morning, the promise of God's protection for that town came to an end (Musnad Ahmad).

12 Believe in Allah and His messenger, and spend of that whereof He hath made you trustees ... (57:7).

13 And in whose wealth there is a right acknowledged. For the beggar and the destitute (70:24)

14 The alms are only for the poor and the needy, and those who collect them, and those whose hearts are to be reconciled and to free the captives and the debtors, and for the cause of Allah, and (for) the wayfarers; a duty imposed by Allah. Allah is Knower, Wise (9:60) .

15 Give full measure and full weight, in0 justice ... (11:85).

References

Azid, T. & Qureshi, M. A. (2015). Philanthropy, Markets, and Islamic Financial Institutions. Paper is presented in the International Conference on Islamic Financial Institutions will be held in International Islamic University, Islamabad, Pakistan, Organized by the Islamic Development Bank and IRTI.

Azid, T. & Rawashdeh, O. H. (2018). The Notion of "Moral Firm" and Distributive Justice in an Islamic Framework, *Intellcutal Discourse* (forthcoming).

Briggs, A. (1961). The Welfare State in Historical Perspective, *Archives Europeennes de Sociologie, II*

Burke, J. (2010). Distributive Justice and Subsidiarity: The Firm and the State in the Social Order. *Journal of Markets & Morality*, 13(2), 297–317.

Chaudhry, M. S. (n.d.) Social Justice. Chapter 16 in *Fundamentals of Islamic Economic System*. Retrieved from www.muslimtents.com/shaufi/b16/b16_16.htm, accessed on March 10, 2016.

Cragg, A. W. (1983). Hayek, Justice and Market. *Canadian Journal of Philosophy*, 13 (4), 575–584

Dworkin, R. (2000). *Sovereign Virtue: The Theory and Practice of Equality*. Cambridge, MA: Harvard University Press.

Dworkin, R. (2006). *Justice in Robes*. Cambridge, MA: Harvard University Press.

Dworkin, R. (2011). *Justice for Hedgehogs*. Cambridge, MA: Harvard University Press.

Goodin, R. (1988). *Reasons for Welfare: The Political Theory of the Welfare State*. Princeton, NJ: Princeton University Press.

Hampton, J. (1998). *Political Philosophy*. Boulder, CO: Westview Press.

Hasnas, J. (2003). Reflections on the Minimal State. *Politics, Philosophy*, 2(1), 115–128.

Hassan, R. (2007). Giving and Gaining: Philanthropy and Social Justice in Muslim Societies. *Lahore Journal of Policy Studies*, 1(1), 25–34.

Hayek, F. A. (1978). The Atavism of Social Justice. In F. A. von Hayek (Ed.) *New Studies in Philosophy,Politics, Economics and the History of Ideas* (chap. 5, pp. 57–68). London: Routledge & Kegan Paul.

Hayek, F. A. (1998). *Law, Legislations and Liberty.* London: Routledge.

Hayek, F. A. (2001). *The Road to Serfdom.* Westminster: The Institute of Economic Affairs.

Ho, L. (2011). What Is Social Justice? Occasional paper # 1, Sydney: National Pro Bono Resource Centre.

Kymlicka, W. (2001). *Cotemporary Political Philosophy.* Oxford: Oxford University Press.

Minogue, K. (2005). Social Justice in Theory and Practice. In B. David & K. Paul (Eds.), *Social Justice from Hume to Walzer* (pp. 255–267).

Morison, S. T. (2005). A Hayekian Theory of Social Justice. *NYU Journal Law and Liberty*, 1, 225–247.

Narveson, J. (1998). Libertarianism vs Maxism: Reflection on G.A. Cohen's Self Ownership, Freedom, and Equality. *The Journal of Ethics*, 2(1), 1–26.

Nozick, R. (1999). *Anarchy, State and Utopia.* Oxford, Cambridge: Blackwell Publishers, Ltd.

Olsaretti, S. (2004). *Liberty, Desert and the Market: A Philosophical Study.* Cambridge: Cambridge University Press.

Plant, R. (2005). Social Justice in Theory and Practice. In D. Boucher & P. Kelly (Eds.), *Perspective on Socail Justice from Hume to Walzer* (pp. 269–283), Abingdon: Routledge.

Qutub, S. (1980). *The Nature of Social Justice in Islam.* New York, NY: Octagon Books.

Rawls, J. (1971). *A Theory of Justice.* Cambridge, MA: Harvard University Press.

Rawls, J. (1999). *Law of Peoples.* Cambridge, MA: Harvard University Press.

Rose, D. C. (2013). Social Justice Theory: A Solution in Search of a Problem: In Response to What Social Justice. Retrieved from www.lawliberty.org/liberty-forum/social-justice-theory-a-solution-in-search-of-a-problem/ accessed on 15 December, 2018.

Sautter, H. (2001). *Introduction in Social Justice in a Market Economy,* H. Sautter & R. Schinke (Eds.). Frankfurt, Germany: Peter Lang.

Shearmur, J. (2003). *Hayek and After: Hayekian Liberalism as a Research Programme.* London: Routledge.

Tatian, S. (n.d.). The Morals of Responsibility, Social Justice and Social Security of the Person, Social Work and Society. *International Online Journal.* Accessed on March 10, 2016.

Vargovic, E. (2012). Social Justice and the Moral Justification of a Market Society. Master of Art thesis submitted to Department of Political Science, Central.

4 Contractual freedom, market and social justice

The "invisible hand" of God-man's agency relationship (*khilafah and real*)

Valentino Cattelan

1. Introduction Islamic economics, God-man's agency relationship (khilafah) and real contractual/human freedom

While contemporary capitalism is experiencing remarkable changes both with regard to the rise of the so-called "sharing economy," with its innovative models of collaborative agency, networking and venture business (on the subject, Gold, 2004; more recently, Chase, 2015; Kramer, 2015; Stephany, 2015) and an emerging favor towards principles of sustainable development, with criteria of profitability that are tamed in the light of community welfare and ethical values (see, for instance, Sen, 2009; Stiglitz, 2015; Velasquez, 2011), Islamic economics, as is well-known, inherently provides an alternative paradigm for the contemporary market economy that is grounded for Muslim believers on God's Guidance as revealed by the *shari'ah*.

The construction of this alternative paradigm (on some open issues in this regard, Cattelan, 2013c) has certainly benefitted from a variety of important academic contributions (as reference texts, for instance, see Chapra, 1992; Naqvi, 1981; Siddiqui, 1981), emphasizing the equality of the individuals in their relations with the Creator in the *tawhid* (the profession of unity of Allah) framework of Islamic justice. This *tawhidi* background, which is at the same time ontological (in God's creation) and deontological (with regard to God's justice, *'adl*) directly implies criteria of social welfare for the promotion of a *shari'ah*-based economy, where the believer is responsible for performing the "right" (*haqq*) as the result of God's revealed "decree" (*hukm*) (on this point see in the text, § 2.3). Accordingly, as reported by Asutay (2013, p. 57), Al-Makarim (1974, p. 25) defines Islamic economics as "the science that deals with wealth and its relation to man from the point of view of the realization of justice in all forms of economic activities," while Khan (1984, p. 55) identifies its fundamental objective in the "study of *falah* ['salvation', 'prosperity', 'welfare'] achieved by organising the resources of earth on the basis of cooperation and participation" (on these criteria, see here both § 2.3 and § 3).

This chapter intends to contribute to the investigation of Islamic economics as a distinct paradigm for the market economy by interpreting the conceptualization of contractual freedom in Islam as the direct outcome of God-man's agency relationship (*khilafah*), i.e. the status of God's vice-regent on Earth for the human being that "outlines [his] responsibilities [as Muslim believer] and provides the reasons of [his] existence" (Asutay, 2007, p. 8).

> *Khilafah* is the empowerment of humans by their Creator as agent-trustee to extend His love and compassion to one another, materially through the resources provided to them by the Creator and non-materially through the manifestation of unconditional love for their own kind as well as for the rest of creation.
>
> (Askari *et al.*, 2015, p. 30)

As remarked by Ahmad (1979, p. 12), from this God-man's agency relationship (*khilafah*) derives "the unique Islamic concept of individual's trusteeship, moral, political and economic, and the principles of social organization" and it is exactly within this unique framework that the present chapter aims at outlining a *shari'ah*-based understanding of the role of contractual freedom in market economy.

In this way, the study intends to look at one of the most challenging points such as how to construct a distinct Islamic theory and practice for the market economy by embedding the criteria of *social* justice which inherently belongs to the Right Path of *shari'ah*, while recognizing the *freedom* of God's agent/vice-regent on Earth (*khalifah*) in pursuing his *own* economic interest through daily commercial transactions.

The issue is somehow different (and more demanding, from a social science perspective) than evaluating the existence (or not) of a doctrine of contractual freedom in Islamic law. As the normative foundation of contemporary Islamic economics and finance, classical *fiqh* (i.e. the "understanding" of God's *shari'ah*) certainly shows a great variance with regard to the admissibility of contracts that were not codified by the tradition, with the Hanafis, Malikis and Shafi'is limiting the principle of permissibility (*ibaha*), which was on the contrary subscribed by the Hanbalis.[1] In fact, while the position of the latter found support in numerous passages of the *Qur'an* and the *Sunna*,[2] the former ascribed to these passages the simple value of moral imperatives, in the light of more restrictive textual references.[3]

But, inasmuch as the existence of a critical elaboration and debate in Islamic law about something *comparable* to the concept of contractual freedom in the Western tradition—as a fundamental aspect of the conventional model of the market economy—cannot be denied, the specific problem in this study is to investigate *how* Islamic economics (through its *own shari'ah*-based foundation of the agent-trustee relationship, *khilafah*) does *reformulate* the aforementioned principle in the daily life of Muslim believers.

Accordingly, much hermeneutical concern is needed when dealing with contractual freedom as an aspect of Muslim *human* freedom as comprehensively grounded on Islamic values, through an interpretative perspective able to contextualize the legal prescriptions transmitted by the tradition of *fiqh* within the socioeconomics of a market grounded on Islamic social justice. In other terms, if these prescriptions have certainly to be implemented in an Islamic market economy functioning according to the criteria of commutative justice (at a microeconomic level), the understanding of broader rationales of distributive justice (at a macroeconomic level) underpinning Islamic economics requires to preliminarily investigate the historical, philosophical and sociological background of the Western notion of the "free market," in order to recognize *how* the Islamic paradigm of contractual freedom is an *alternative* to that which is embedded in conventional capitalism.

This chapter aims at providing an interpretative contribution towards this direction by comparing (according to a multi- and interdisciplinary social science approach) the Western and Islamic conception of contractual/human freedom, from the idea of the "invisible hand" by Adam Smith to the specific ontology and deontology of Islam as a direct result of God's Will. To this objective, the text will first investigate the conceptual distance between the "blind justice" of an *abstract* principle of contractual freedom (as maintained in conventional economics) and the *real* freedom of God's agent (*khalifah*) as embedding in the divine *'adl* through the performance of the trustee-agency relationship (*khilafah*) (§ 2).

Following this comparative study, the normative dimension of Islamic *fiqh* will be later contextualized within a *reality* of community development where the trustee-agent relationship of *khilafah* leads market actors towards strategies of wealth production and financial inclusion based on mutual aid, profit- and risk-sharing and substitutes the centrality of the economic *exchange* (with a corresponding parameter of *efficiency* to measure the success of the "invisible hand") with the centrality of the social *person* as God's agent (and a criterion of *legitimacy* of his action to be judged in the light of the Guidance—*shari'ah*—of the revealed Word). Accordingly, after briefly referring to the historical experience of the Islamic economy in the past of Muslim communities, from the time of the Prophet to the Ottoman Empire, the text will examine valuable tools for the implementation of *real* contractual freedom in contemporary market economy, from retail banking and microfinance to project finance and the rediscovery of *waqf* (§ 3).

To conclude, the chapter will add some final considerations about the current gap between the social justice embedded in the *real* human freedom of *khilafah* and the practice of Islamic finance at a global stage, by locating the action of the human being as "being of the (revealed) Word" in between the *market* (as a place of social interaction) and the *state* (as beholder of political power and responsible for financial regulation). In this way, the *real* freedom of the trustee-agent relationship, i.e. the freedom embracing the full benefits of the "invisible hand" of *khilafah*, will be linked to factors of political economy that cannot be marginalized in the functioning of an alternative *human*-oriented capitalism able to reflect the paradigm of Islamic economics (§ 4).

2. The "invisible hand" of the market economy: comparing the Western and Islamic conception of contractual/human freedom

Adam Smith's "invisible hand" and the autonomie de la volonté

As remarked above, when dealing with the conceptualization of social justice in contemporary market economy, the understanding of human freedom becomes of paramount importance: it is of such a paramount relevance that the "story" of this concept can be traced back directly to the very foundation of economics as a discipline by Adam Smith's *Wealth of Nations* (1776).[4]

More precisely, the "story" of the role of human freedom in the market is connected to the interpretation of the well-known metaphor used by Adam Smith (1723–1790) to describe unintended social benefits from individual actions, that is to say the "invisible hand" governing human economy.

Appearing for the first time in his *History of Astronomy* (written before 1758), as something to which the ignorant refer to to explain what they do not understand about natural phenomena, Smith speaks of *an* invisible hand (never of *the* invisible hand) with respect to income distribution in of *The Theory of Moral Sentiments* (1759) and with regard to issues of production in *The Wealth of Nations* (1776).

The first passage, of 1759, deals with an invisible hand leading a selfish landlord to distribute his harvest to the workers (Part IV, Ch. 1); the second extract (1776) with the force by which man's natural tendency towards self-interest results, beyond his own personal intentions, in society prosperity:

> [E]very individual necessarily labors to render the annual revenue of the society as great as he can. He generally neither intends to promote the public interest, nor knows how much he is promoting it ... [H]e intends only his own gain, and he is in this, as in many other cases, led by an invisible hand to promote an end which was no part of his intention. Nor is it always the worse for society that it was no part of his intention. By pursuing his own interest he frequently promotes that of the society more effectually than when he really intends to promote it.
>
> (*The Wealth of Nations*, Book IV, Ch. 2, § 9)

Ironically, what future generations would consider the most iconic quotation of Smith's idea of the free market does not employ the metaphor:

> It is not from the benevolence of the butcher, the brewer, or the baker, that we expect our dinner, but from their regard to their own interest. We address ourselves, not to their humanity but to their self-love, and never talk to them of our own necessities but of their advantages.
>
> (*The Wealth of Nations*, Book I, Ch. 2, § 2)

Our contemporary understanding of Adam Smith's "invisible hand" is affected by the diverse interpretations that economists have given of his idea.

For instance, Velasquez (2011) equates the "hand" to the utilitarian conception of an unregulated market able to foster common benefits through competition. Beside him, by explaining the "hand" as the possibility of a "social coordination without a co-ordinator," sociologist Aldridge compares Smith's idea to Darwin's "natural selection" (*On the Origin of Species*, 1859), with evolution seen as adjustment of organisms to their environment, out of their intention, as economic self-interest fosters wealth creation beyond individual motives (2005, p. 10 *et seq.*). The self-love of economic actors as engine for socially desirable development lies also behind the notion of *laissez-faire* and neoclassical economic theories (Slater & Tonkiss, 2000, pp. 54–55), as well as behind any legal doctrine concerning contractual freedom as cornerstone of a libertarian conceptualization of the marketplace (Dagan & Heller, 2013).

In this way, Adam Smith's "invisible hand" is tightly shaken with the "autonomous hand" of an individual acting through his own self-regulating rationality, whose philosophical foundations can be dated back to the French Enlightenment of 19th century (Ranouil, 1980), when Western legal doctrine assumed the *autonomie de la volonté* (i.e. the "autonomy" or "self-determination" of the human will: see in this regard also Gutmann, 2013) as cornerstone of contractual theory.

Although, as highlighted by Atiyah some decades ago (1979), Western legislation has moved away from a self-feeding conception of the freedom of contracts, determining its "fall" towards a more in-depth social approach to the market, a libertarian assumption still characterizes the Western conceptualization of the marketplace, holding the single individual able

(i) to assess his interest to enter a contract, as well as whether to contract or not with a certain counterparty;
(ii) to define the best regulation of his economic interests in the interaction with this counterparty (thus creating, modifying or removing certain legal relations);
(iii) to choose, among existing contractual types, the best "form" to rule these relations, or even to structure new contractual types (by creating new forms, or combining existing contracts), be this solution the most efficient to undertake.

Accordingly, from a historical perspective, contractual freedom has been fostered or tamed at different degrees in the Western legal tradition,

  (i) by limiting more or less extensively the access to the contract by "weak" subjects (e.g. the minor in age; the mad person; the inexperienced or vulnerable subject; the consumer; the investor in the financial market ...);

 (ii) by exalting the freedom of contract as a slogan for *laissez-faire* capitalism or, reversely, by opting for the protection of the weak party in the interaction with the strong one;

(iii) promoting parties' self-regulation, either through their choice of the best contract or the invention of new contracts, as expression of the powerful "invisible hand" of the market.

The "invisible hand" of Divine Providence? Smith and Islamic economic thought

As previously stated, our contemporary interpretation of Adam Smith's "invisible hand" has to be located within a historical evolution of an idea that has been contextualized within the legal philosophy of the Enlightenment, and later adapted to new social approaches.

Significantly, in his recent book on debt economy (2011), David Graeber provides a historical understanding of Smith's idea in connection with Isaac Newton (1642–1727) and his new foundation of physical science, as the outcome of Divine Providence.

> Newton had represented God as a cosmic watchmaker who had created the physical machinery of the universe in such a way that it would operate for the ultimate benefit of humans and then let it run on its own. Smith was trying to make a similar, Newtonian argument. God—or Divine Providence, as he put it—had arranged matters in such a way that our pursuit of self-interest would nonetheless, given an unfettered market, be guided "as if by an invisible hand" to promote the general welfare. Smith's famous invisible hand was, as he says in his *Theory of Moral Sentiments* [IV.I.10], the agent of Divine Providence. It was literally the hand of God.
>
> (Graeber, 2011, p. 44; and p. 396, note 3)

Graeber's argumentation is based on some textual evidence of Smith's *Theory of Moral Sentiments*, while there is no explicit description of the "invisible hand" in *The Wealth of Nations* as a theological reference to God's capacity as a divine planner.

But what is most interesting is that Graeber also postulates a possible connection between Smith and medieval Islam by noting how Muslim legal scholars embraced the Prophet's saying that in a free-market situation "prices depend on the will of God."[5]

> Most legal scholars interpreted Mohammed's decision to mean that any government interference in market mechanisms should be considered similarly sacrilegious, since markets were designed by God to regulate themselves. If all this bears a striking resemblance to Adam Smith's "invisible hand" (which was also the hand of Divine Providence), it might not be a complete coincidence.
>
> (*ibidem*, 2011, p. 279)

In his book Graeber explicitly refers both to al-Ghazali (AD 1058–1111) and Tusi (AD 1201–1274), underlining the existence of some similarities in their arguments to those used in Smith's reasoning. For instance,

> Smith's most famous example of division of labor, the pin factory, where it takes eighteen separate operations to produce one pin, already appears in Ghazali's *Ihya*, in which he describes a needle factory, where it takes twenty-five different operations to produce a needle.
>
> (*ibidem*, 2011, p. 279)

But, as Graeber immediately specifies, "differences, however, are just as significant as the similarities." In actual fact,

> like Smith, Tusi begins his treatise on economics with a discussion of the division of labor; but where for Smith, the division of labor is actually an outgrowth of our "natural propensity to truck and barter" in pursuit of *individual advantage*, for Tusi, it was an extension of *mutual aid*.
>
> (*ibidem*, 2011, p. 279; italics not in the original text)

It is indeed this fundamental shift

- from the idea of an "invisible hand" leading to the *division* of goods through the *competition* among economic actors (Western economic thought)
- to a Divine Providence fostering a *sharing* of economic resources through the *cooperation* among human beings in the market as a locus of personal interaction (on this conceptual shift see Cattelan, 2013a, pp. 6–7)

that the Islamic conception of contractual freedom can find a proper understanding.

From the "abstract" contractual freedom to the "reality" of God's justice for His agent (khalifah**) in Islam**

The understanding of the Islamic conception of contractual freedom requires a preliminary outline of the specific ontology and cosmology of Islam, looking at the unity (*tawhid*) of the universe as the direct result of God's creation (Netton, 1989).

In the Islamic conception of justice (Smirnov, 1996), not only is the "real" (*haqq*) deeply moralized as materialization of God's Will (*hukm*), but also the "right" (*haqq*, again) reflects in its conceptual structure the unity (*tawhid*) of the creation (Netton, 1989, p. 22 *et seq.*; Geertz, 1983, pp. 177–178).

Within this *tawhidi* framework, where God's Will constructs everything real (Q. II:117: "To Him is due the primal origin of the heavens and earth. When He decrees a matter, He says only 'Be', and it is"),[6] human beings become responsible for their deeds by "acquiring" (*kasb*) God's creation[7]: more precisely, as His vice-regents on Earth, Muslim believers perform an agent-trustee relationship (*khilafah*) on the basis of which they will be judged by the Creator. Furthermore, the status of God's agent (*khalifah*) implies that, by participating in the unique creation by God, any human being *shares* with the others a common destiny of salvation, whose benefits have been generously provided by the Creator: in other terms, their opposition for the conquest of (individual) wealth and justice is substituted by a (divine) "invisible hand" (see above, § 2.2) that guarantees social justice for all through the performance of *khilafah*. Accordingly, an opposition between the "right" and the "obligation," which leads in Western economic thought to a *division* of property rights for which human beings have to *compete*, does not exist anymore:

> the Shari'ah does not seek to eliminate the distinction between rights and obligations or to emphasize their duality and division [...]. In the Qur'an, right and duty merge into justice so much so that they become, in principle, an extension of one another. [...] *hukm* (ruling) subsumes both rights and obligations. The relationship between ruling and justice is also of means and ends: a ruling is the means towards justice, while the fulfilment and realization of *haqq* in its dual capacities of right and obligation is predicated upon justice. Islam thus seeks to establish justice by enforcing Shari'ah rulings which, in turn, is expected simultaneously to mean the proper fulfilment of rights and duties.
> (Kamali, 1993, p. 357)

Subsequently,

• the *abstract* auto-regulation of human freedom (as postulated by the *autonomie de la volonté* of legal Enlightenment: Ranouil, 1980), where it

is the self-interest of the independent actor to foster (out of his intention) the general welfare of the community (hence the intervention of
Smith's "invisible hand")

• is replaced in Islamic economic thought by the *reality* of God's creation,
to which human beings participate as God's agents by *sharing* the
resources that Allah has generously offered to them and by *cooperating*
in the market as a place of *mutual aid* (see above, Tusi).

This fundamental conceptual shift in the understanding of human freedom
as foundation of the market has been recently highlighted in a meaningful
way by well-known legal scholar Wael B. Hallaq (2009), comparing the
Western dichotomy between the "real" economy and the abstract "rule" of
contractual freedom with the Islamic identity between the "real" and the
search for justice through a human freedom located within the *shari'ah*.

The Western conception of the free market, in fact, postulates an abstract
and general conception of contractual freedom as equally applicable to all,
for individuals seen as indistinguishable members of a generic species,
"standing in perfect parity before a blind lady of justice" (Hallaq, 2009,
p. 166). In reverse, the logic of Islamic justice, mirroring the perpetual
actualization of God's supremacy in man's agency (where the right, *haqq*,
realizes, in the proper sense of "making actual", God's decree, *hukm*, in the
creation), proceeds by deeming each individual and circumstance as unique
and *ijtihad* necessarily occurrence-specific. In this sense, inasmuch as the
West separates the general rule of contractual freedom from the real economic conditions of market actors, Islamic economy connects the "real" to
the "particular" "right" (*haqq*) of the parties as established by God's decree
(*hukm*).

Hence, the abstract reference to the "invisible hand" of contractual freedom, as a hidden mechanism regulating the efficiency of the market, is
deprived of any consistency in the logic of Islamic economy, as Islam has
never accepted the notion of blind justice, for it allowed the rich and the
powerful to stand on a par with the poor and the weak. On the contrary,

> [i]n the *Shari'a*, the latter ... [has] to be protected, and their disadvan-
> tage ... turned into an advantage in the *Shari'a* courts of law ... [as] an
> *ijtihadic* process, a continuously renewed exercise of interpretation. [In
> classical Islam, law] was an effort at mustering principles as located in
> specific life-situations, requiring the legists to do what was right at
> a particular moment of human existence. Even in its most detailed and
> comprehensive accounts, the law was mostly a guide that directed the
> judge and all legal personnel on the ground to resolve a situation in
> due consideration of the unique facts involved therein ... Islamic law
> was not fully revealed unto society until the principles meshed with
> social reality and until the interaction of countless social, moral,

material and other types of human relations involved in a particular case was made to come full circle.

(Hallaq, 2009, pp. 166–167)

It is exactly by "contextualizing" the principle of contractual freedom within the *reality* deriving from the countless aspects of human life that Islamic economy connects the *haqq* of God's creation to the social dimension of the market by locating human freedom within the right Path of *shari'ah* and the performance of *khilafah*.

Moving from a descriptive to a normative approach, § 3 of the chapter will draw from this Islamic understanding of market freedom relevant inputs for the promotion of social justice in an Islamic economy. In particular, in order to "commensurate" human freedom to the real economic conditions of market actors, the work will suggest that Islamic economic tools should be contextualized as much as possible within a community dimension, for the market to represent a *locus* of mutual aid and cooperation, a common enterprise of profit- and risk-sharing among all its participants. To this aim, references to some historical examples of the community dimension of Islamic market economy, from the time of the Prophet to the Ottoman Empire, will also be made.

3. The social justice of *khilafah* in an Islamic economy: the market as a shared enterprise of mutual cooperation

The social dimension of Islamic economy: market and community development

As remarked in the previous paragraph, Islamic justice postulates the participation in the market in the light of principles of *sharing* and *cooperation*, where the human being, as God's agent (*khalifah*), does not refer to an abstract notion of "contractual freedom" (equally applicable to all as indistinguishable members of a generic species, equal before the "blind lady" of justice, as in the Western tradition), but recognizes social differences and is ready to turn the disadvantage of the poor into an advantage in the light of *shari'ah*. As Hallaq notes, this implies an *ijtihad*, "an effort at mustering principles as located in specific life-situations [... and] meshed with social reality ... [through] the interaction of countless social, moral, material and other types of human relations" (Hallaq, 2009, p. 166).

Therefore, the Islamic economy substitutes the centrality of the economic *exchange* (with a corresponding parameter of *efficiency* to measure the success of the "invisible hand") with the centrality of the social *person* as God's agent in participating in the market (with a criterion of *legitimacy* of the action to be judged in the light of the Guidance—*shari'ah*—of the revealed Word). The recognition of the centrality of the person transforms the market into a place of social interactions (and not merely of economic exchange) which immediately looks at the comprehensive development of the *community* as its core objective.

Accordingly, it is by looking at the community (and not more at the self-interest and self-love of the single individual) that

> Islam [has] never accepted the notion of blind justice, for it allowed the rich and the powerful to stand on a par with the poor and the weak. In the Shari'ah, the latter ... [has] to be protected, and their disadvantage ... turned into an advantage.
>
> (Hallaq, 2009, p. 166)

Hence, Islamic economic thought cannot be fully understood (and practiced) unless the Islamic idea of contractual freedom is entwined with a market founded on mutual trust and cooperation (the "mutual aid" to which Tusi refers in his works), where consumers, merchants and bankers participate in a common economic venture. In a nutshell, *human freedom* makes sense in an *Islamic market economy* only when directed towards *social justice* in the light of the Guidance given by the revealed Word and through the performance of *khilafah*.

It is precisely with reference to this notion of social justice that community development is actually fostered in an Islamic economy according to criteria of *socioeconomic inclusion*, looking at the market as a common enterprise of profit- and risk-sharing.

These core criteria of socioeconomic inclusion at the roots of the conceptual paradigm of Islamic economics can be found both in the historical development of the idea of free market in Muslim communities, from the time of the Prophet to the Ottoman Empire (§ 3.2) and provides valuable tools to *reformulate* the market from a place of *exchanges* to a place of *human interactions* in the contemporary economy (§ 3.3).

Islamic social market in history: from the Prophet to the Ottoman Empire

As is well-known, from the very beginning, Islam has had a positive attitude towards commerce and trade, as well as towards the market as a place of social interaction: "Mohammed himself had begun his adult life as a merchant, and no Islamic thinker ever treated the honest pursuit of profit as itself intrinsically immoral or inimical to faith" (Graeber, 2011, p. 275).

In fact, historical research has confirmed the broad development of commercial partnerships in medieval Islam (see especially Udovitch, 1970), as well as of a complex system of credit instruments, from the *sakk*, "check" (pl. *sukuk*—from which the name of the financial instruments sold in the contemporary Islamic capital market) and *ruq'a* ("credit note") to the *suftaja* ("letter of credit," "bill of exchange") and *hawala* ("assignment of debt") (Ray, 1997; Udovitch, 1967).

These historical data are extremely relevant for our discussion for two reasons.

On the one side, they actually contradict a common point of criticism by mainstream economics against the contemporary Islamic financial system (the idea that the prohibitions of "interest," *riba*, "uncertainty," *gharar* and "gambling," *maysir*, are excessively restrictive), as credit and commercial institutions actually flourished in medieval Islam by following the teaching of the Qur'an and the exemplary life of the Prophet. On the other side, by removing interest as a form of unlawful gain (Q. II:125: "... Allah hath permitted trade and forbidden *riba*"), the mercantile society that flourished in medieval Islam found its core element in criteria of *cooperation* and *sharing* (see above), looking at economic actors as participants in a common enterprise of welfare, in the light of the principles of the sacred *shari'ah* as embedded in the proactive role of the human being as God's agent (*khalifah*).

A striking example of the shift of paradigm from conventional to Islamic economics with regard to the meaning of contractual freedom within the frame of *khilafah* can be also found in the constitution of charitable foundations/endowments (*awqaf*, pl. of *waqf*) at the time of the Ottoman Empire. As an institution belonging to the Islamic legal tradition, public a*wqaf* have always been functional to the promotion of local development, creating the structural conditions for the persistence of wealth pooling within a certain community, thus indirectly promoting a process of economic and financial inclusion. Furthermore, as highlighted by Çizakça, evidence found in the Ottoman archives

> has confirmed that endowments ... applied a process of capital pooling among themselves. [...] [T]he borrowers were not entrepreneurs but consumers and ... the capital supplied by the cash *awqaf* was not accumulated at the hands of a few enterprising individuals but was diffused throughout the society. To conclude, research has revealed that cash *awqaf* which originally appeared as a promising and unique Ottoman institution of capital accumulation, actually functioned as an institution of capital distribution.
>
> (1998, pp. 59–60)

As we are going to see in the next paragraph, the socioeconomics of *sharing* and *cooperation* which is embedded in the God-man's agency relationship (*khilafah*) should rediscover these means of economic development and inclusion in the pursuit of poverty alleviation (in this regard see also Habib, 2004; Shirazi, 2014). Furthermore, to this objective, specific attention should be given not to the application *per se* of "Islamic law" in the structuring of *shari'ah*-compliant products, but to the performance of God's Will (§ 2) in the marketplace also in a broader socioeconomic perspective, in order to "convert" the abstract contractual freedom into *real* social justice.

The socioeconomics of khilafah: strategies of economic and financial inclusion

Not only does this shared commitment towards socioeconomic inclusion in an Islamic economy embrace *Zakat* as a significant instrument of poverty alleviation (as one of the Pillars of Islam), but it also promotes a conceptual *re*formulation of the market, according to strategies that should foster the development of Islamic banking and finance from a socioeconomic stance.[8] Above all, it should not be the mere insertion of these instruments into the mainstream capitalistic model (that is to say, the simple "readaptation" of conventional financial contracts from "Western" to "Islamic" finance) to be considered a viable path for a *shari'ah*-based market: rather, it is a community-based conception of the market (i.e. the attention towards its social dimension as the center of interpersonal inter-actions linked—but not limited—to commercial exchanges) to indicate appropriate models for a social economy rooted in the Guidance of the revealed Word.

To this objective, the promotion of a community development through the market, according to the criteria of social and financial inclusion, should embrace, for instance,

- instruments of retail banking,
- microfinance,
- project finance,
- as well as the adoption of social impact *sukuk*,
- and the rediscovery of the *waqf* (as a community means for resources management, as at the time of the Ottoman Empire: see above),

in order to foster the "real" market freedom of Islam as outcome of God's creation, merging His Will (*hukm*) with the right (*haqq*) conceived in the light of distributive justice, thus *realizing* the benefits of *khilafah*.

As argued in the first part of the chapter (§ 2), when the "invisible hand" of Western capitalism is replaced in Islamic economy with the Guidance of the revealed Word through the performance of *shari'ah* by God's agent (*khalifah*), the abstract and general concept of "human freedom" is substi-tuted within the *reality* of welfare of community development, moving from a logic of division and competition to a logic of *cooperation* which trans-forms the market into a *shared* venture (Cattelan, 2013a).

Accordingly, the fundamental rationales of Islamic property rights (from the primacy of the real economy to the requirements of equilibrium in the transaction and the parameters of risk-sharing and equity: Cattelan, 2013b) transform the function of financial intermediation from the "trade of money" (as in conventional capitalism) into the mobilization of funds for the promotion of a community-based development.

In this light, it is not the application *per se* of "Islamic law" in the struc-turing of *shari'ah*-compliant products to "convert" the abstract contractual freedom into an Islamic economy aimed at social justice, but rather, as previously remarked, the implementation of strategies of *economic and financial inclusion*, able to channel the (global) financial market towards (local) responsible investments.

Within the underlying paradigm of community development, for instance, a new flourishing for *waqf* institutions should be welcomed to promote the eradication of poverty by "contextualizing" social impact *sukuk* investments into local justice, thus fulfilling the rationale of contractual freedom according to an Islamic perspective (Cattelan, 2015). The efficiency of local management of Islamic charitable endowments should also comprise representatives of local communities (similarly to the governance of cooperatives), in order to uphold the legitimacy of economic choices according to the real needs of civil society. Furthermore, in the effort "at mustering principles as located in specific life-situations" (Hallaq, 2009, p. 166), also the role of scholars sitting in the *shari'ah* boards of Islamic financial institutions should be evaluated in the light of a "monitoring" function aimed at verifying the real economic development of the local community, where the institution operates to promote social justice according to Islamic values.

> Hence, corresponding mechanisms and procedures addressed to involve locally based *shari'ah* scholars in the shaping of business plans, social investment strategies and wealth creation, as required by the local community, should be fostered; at the same time, the responsibility of *shari'ah* scholars should be framed in the light of their satisfactory (or unsatisfactory) accomplishment to fulfil the function of contextualizing economic justice.
>
> (Cattelan, 2015)

Apart from the rediscovery of *waqf* as a modern institution to channel global investments to local opportunities for development, the shift from the abstract to the "real" contractual freedom of Islamic justice (as materialization of God's Will in the creation of man's agency, *khilafah*), can be pursued through fostering the access to retail banking by instruments of microcredit and microfinance (similarly to the well-known model of the "bank for the poor" of Grameen Bank, by Nobel laureate Prof. Muhammad Yunus—readapted through the elimination of *riba*). This would be also an important opportunity for local empowerment and support to the private sector that will be primarily beneficial to small and medium enterprises.

The access to banking services through microfinance and the provision of tailored-products for low-income savers could be another important step in the mobilization of funds for social impact purposes, in order to promote the full realization of a function of financial intermediation beyond the mere "trade of money" of debt-capitalism (as cornerstone of the contemporary economic system). This could also contribute to policies of local empowerment, social inclusion and support to the medium and small enterprise system, thus matching criteria of economic growth with wealth redistribution.

Last but certainly not least, the fundamental parameters of the primacy of the real economy and the conception of the market as a shared business venture perfectly match project finance strategies of development, directing the flow of international capitals towards forms of private and public partnerships, able to absorb workforce and reduce social tension. The specific socioeconomic role of project finance investments, from the perspective of Islamic economy, has been recently highlighted also as a means of reconstruction in the aftermath of Arab uprisings, with the President of the Islamic Development Bank (IDB), Dr. Ahmad Mohamed Ali, declaring in September 2011 that

> the recent developments in some Arab countries make it imperative for the IDB Group to assist in the country-owed formulation and implementation of an employment-focused reform and development agenda. In this regard, the IDB Group has formulated a multi-tiered program to assist the affected Arab countries in achieving better alignments between economic growth and employment generation objectives ...
> (El Haouti, 2012, pp. 28–29)

Of course, if the level of promotion of human freedom is closely related to employment opportunities, from which the channeling of financial resources can be later invested in the real economy through further consumption and production, the "community-based approach" of social justice that fosters Islamic economy, as argued in this chapter, calls for a final evaluation of the current distance between the theory and the practice of Islamic finance objectives, also in the light of open issues of political economy in contemporary Muslim countries and the level of "human freedom" of God's agent (*khalifah*) as related to civic empowerment.

4. Conclusions. The "invisible hand" of *khilafah*: real contractual freedom, social justice and open issues of political economy

Dealing with the description of Muslim ethics in classical theology, Steffen A. J. Stelzer remarks how Islamic religion shapes

> the human being as ... a being of the word. [...] Humans can therefore not be adequately understood in their ethical dimension as already constituted beings "before the Law" who are then asked to find out by which means they will reply. Or rather, they can be understood in this way only because the law as particular manifestation of the divine Word constitutes them *by way of word*.
> (2008, p. 169; italics in the original text)

Looking at the construction of a *shari'ah*-based paradigm for Islamic economics in the light of the God-man's agency relationship (*khilafah*), this chapter has investigated the notion of social justice in an Islamic economic system in the light of the contractual/human freedom as cornerstone of a functioning market (§ 1).

To this aim, the work has preliminarily connected the Western conception of contractual freedom to the metaphor of the "invisible hand" by Adam Smith and to the legal doctrine of the *autonomie de la volonté* (where the final outcome of the efficiency of the market appears beyond the self-interest of the single actors, *competing* among themselves for the *division* of economic resources). Later on, the chapter has highlighted how in Islamic economy, in reverse, *real* contractual freedom exists only *within* the unity (*tawhid*) of God's creation, where men are constituted *by way of word* and participate in the market by *sharing* resources in a venture of *cooperation* aimed at community development. In this light, the text has shown how if particular similarities can be found between Smith's "invisible hand" (originally, the Divine Providence, according to Graeber) and the Islamic conception of the Guidance by the revealed Word (as in al-Ghazali and Tusi), most significant differences are related to the socioeconomics of the market conceived either as a place of competition or, conversely, mutual aid, when fostered by God-man's agency relationship (*khilafah*) (§ 2).

In fact, if the individual freedom is framed in Western thought as an "abstract" and "general" principle disconnected from real economic conditions and overcome by a logic of competition, it is the rationale of "mutual aid" that shapes the "reality" of the market as God's creation for His agent (*khalifah*) in an Islamic economic system, thus leading to the historical development of an advanced trade community in medieval Islam and institutions of financial inclusion (*awqaf*) in the Ottoman Empire, as well as, today, towards policy strategies that should favor economic and financial instruments aimed at community development, as mentioned at § 3 (namely retail banking, microfinance, project finance, social impact *sukuk* and the employ of *waqf* as a tool for collective property management).

But if the promotion of social justice through the materialization of the divine Word in the market postulates to "commensurate" human freedom to real economic conditions, through a community dimension addressed to mutual aid, profit- and risk-sharing, how much has the shift from the (conventional) "invisible hand" to the agent-trustee relationship (*khilafah*) of God's Guidance been actually realized in the practice of the Islamic financial market?

Since the development of Islamic finance has been primarily concentrated on the *efficiency* of the market by replicating conventional standards (as simply readapted to Islamic legal rules), the fundamental *legitimacy* of human action (as assessed in the light of God's Guidance) has been marginalised, thus maintaining a disconnection between an abstract (and in some ways artificial) human freedom and the real distributive justice in the market as embedded in the principle of *khilafah*.

Furthermore, the effectiveness of the "community development" as cornerstone of a legitimate Islamic economy has been rarely measured in the last decades also in the light of the active participation of the civil society as protagonist of the market (a condition that has played a central role in the rise of the Arab Springs, where persistent situations of unemployment denied *a priori* any economic freedom: see § 3.3). In the light of this, the adoption of an (Islamic) paradigm of community—rather than (Western) market-oriented development—will not be achieved unless the human freedom directed to entrepreneurship activities is also supported by effective civic empowerment. A necessity that is still burdened by open issues in the political economy of many Muslim countries, where structural weaknesses in the governance of the market are related to the persistent lack of real policies of wealth redistribution.

The arguments of this chapter, from the descriptive comparison of the conceptualization of human freedom in the Western and Islamic economies (§ 2) to the normative suggestion of viable tools for community development (§ 3), have underlined how the future of the Islamic financial market will depend on the sound and appropriate implementation of the *Word* in the action of the human being as ethical being *by way of the word*. But, at the same time, it will be the responsibility of the national governments of Muslim countries to promote an *alternative* capitalism through a person-oriented development of the market as a way of human empowerment through the *real* freedom of a distributive justice grounded on the principle of *khilafah*.

In summary, only the combination between appropriate *state* policymaking in the regulation of the financial market and free *market* economy tools, according to parameter of *real* social justice in the light of *khilafah*, will prospectively guarantee the development of Islamic economy as a sound alternative to conventional capitalism. In other terms, the shift from Smith's "invisible hand" to the "invisible hand" of *khilafah* (with the God-man's agency relationship leading to a *human*-oriented market based on criteria of *cooperation* and *sharing*) will depend on concurrent factors of civic empowerment and political economy, whose full promotion will represent one of the fundamental challenges for the democratic future of the Muslim world.

Acknowledgements

I would like to express here my deep gratitude to Prof. Mehmet Saraç for his precious comments on the original version of the manuscript, and in particular for his suggestion to refer directly to the core concept of agency (*khilafah*) to better conceptualize the notion of human freedom in the Islamic economy. This idea, already implicit in the original text, has been better outlined in this revised version and has definitely improved the quality of the manuscript. I am also grateful to Prof. Toseef Azid and Dr. Lüfti Sunar for their patient editorial work, and valuable recommendations.

Notes

1   The early jurists were concerned that all contracts were free from suspicion of usury and uncertainty, characteristics which served to nullify any transaction.

As a result of this, they decided that individuals should contract according to the rules of nominate contracts, and thus, not generally free to establish or create any new and possibly illegal stipulations. Nevertheless, the Hanbali jurists constituted an exception, for they permitted freedom of contract under the doctrine of *ibaha*: non-restriction was, for the Hanbalis, the general rule.

(El-Hassan, 1985, p. 54)

2 Passages such as "O ye who believe! Fulfil (all) obligations" (Q. V:1); "O ye you believe! Eat not up your property among yourselves in vanities: but let there be amongst you traffic and trade by mutual good-will" (Q. IV:29); and the Sunna: "Muslim are bound by their stipulations" (Abu Dawud; Tirmidhi; Nasa'i; Ibn Hanbal; Hakim) were seen by the Hanbalis as evidence of the general admissibility of *any* agreement not explicitly forbidden
3 Opposing to the doctrine of *ibaha*, Hanafis, Malikis and Shafi'is generally argued for a limitation of contractual freedom by referring to Q. II:190 ("But do not transgress limits; for Allah loveth not transgressors"), supplemented by the *Sunna*:

How can men stipulate conditions which are not in the Book of Allah? All stipulations which are not in the Book of Allah are invalid, be they a hundred in number. Allah's judgement alone is true and His stipulations alone are binding.

(El-Hassan, 1985, p. 57)

4 Shortened title of *An Inquiry into the Nature and Causes of the Wealth of Nations*.
5

For Mohammed this natural regulation of the market corresponds to a cosmic regulation. Prices rise and fall as night follows day, as low tides follow high, and price imposition is not only an injustice to the merchant, but a disordering of the natural order of things.

(Essid, 1995, p. 153)

6 See also Q. III:47 and 59; VI:73; XVI:40; XXXVI:82; XL:68.
7 The intertwined God-man's agency is explained by Muslim philosopher al-Ghazali in the following terms:

And if human beings are agents, how is it that God most High is agent? Or if God Most High is an agent, how is a human being an agent? There is no way of understanding "acting" as between two agents. In response, I would say: indeed, there can be no understanding when there is but one meaning for "agent". But if it had two meanings, then the term comprehended could be attributed to each of them without contradiction [...]. The sense in which God Most High is agent is that He is the originator of existing things ..., while the sense in which a human being is an agent is that he is the locus [*mahall*] in which power is created after will has been created after knowledge has been created, so that power depends on will, and action is linked to power, as a conditioned to its condition.

(Al-Ghazali, 2001, p. 276)

8 On the present distance between the theory and the practice of the Islamic economic model some considerations will be advanced at the end of this chapter

References

Ahmad, K. (1979). *Economic Development in an Islamic Framework*. Leicester: The Islamic Foundation.
Aldridge, A. (2005). *The Market*. Cambridge: Polity.

Al-Ghazali, A. H. M. (2001). *Faith in Divine Unity and Trust in Divine Providence (The Revival of the Religious Sciences*, Book XXXV), tr. by D.B. Burrell. Louisville, KY: Fons Vitae.

Al-Makarim, Z. A. (1974). *Ilm al-'Adl al-Iqtisadi* [The Science of Just Economy]. Cairo: Dar al Turath.

Askari, H., Iqbal, Z., & Mirakhor, A. (2015). *Introduction to Islamic Economics. Theory and Application.* Chichester, UK: John Wiley & Sons.

Asutay, M. (2007). A Political Economy Approach to Islamic Economics: Systemic Understanding for an Alternative Economic System. *Kyoto Journal of Islamic Area Studies*, 1(2), 3–18.

Asutay, M. (2013). Islamic Moral Economy as the Foundation of Islamic Finance. In V. Cattelan (Ed.), *Islamic Finance in Europe: Towards a Plural Financial System* (pp. 55–68). Cheltenham, UK & Northampton, MA: Edward Elgar.

Atiyah, P. S. (1979). *The Rise and Fall of Freedom of Contract.* Oxford: Oxford University Press.

Cattelan, V. (2013a). Babel, Islamic Finance and Europe: Preliminary Notes on Property Rights Pluralism. In V. Cattelan (Ed.), *Islamic Finance in Europe: Towards a Plural Financial System* (pp. 1–12). Cheltenham, UK & Northampton, MA: Edward Elgar.

Cattelan, V. (2013b). A Glimpse through the Veil of Maya: Islamic Finance and Its Truth on Property Rights. In V. Cattelan (Ed.), *Islamic Finance in Europe: Towards a Plural Financial System* (pp. 32–51). Cheltenham, UK & Northampton, MA: Edward Elgar.

Cattelan, V. (2013c). *Shari'ah* Economics as Autonomous Paradigm: Theoretical Approach and Operative Outcomes. *Journal of Islamic Perspective on Science, Technology and Society*, 1(1), 3–11.

Cattelan, V. (2015). Performing God's Will in Market Economy: Islamic Contract Law, *Fiqh* and the Law of Islamic Finance. In *Harnessing Waqf into a Bankable Social Financing and Investment Asset Class* (pp. 90–100). Proceedings of the SC-OCIS Roundtable 2014, 22–23 March 2014, Kuala Lumpur, Malaysia.

Chapra, M. U. (1992). *Islam and the Economic Challenge.* Leicester: The Islamic Foundation.

Chase, R. (2015). *Peers Inc.: How People and Platform Are Inventing the Collaborative Economy and Re-Inventing Capitalism.* New York, NY: PublicAffairs.

Çizakça, M. (1998). *Awqaf* in History and Its Implications for Modern Islamic Economies. *Islamic Economic Studies*, 6(1), 43–70.

Dagan, H., & Heller, M. (2013). Freedom of Contracts. *Columbia Law and Economics Working Papers* No. 458 (draft; available at www.ssrn.com).

Darwin, C. R. (1859). *On the Origin of Species by Means of Natural Selection, or the Preservation of Favoured Races in the Struggle for Life.* London: John Murray.

El Haouti, A. (2012). The Role of Islamic Infrastructure Funds in the Aftermath of the Arab Spring. 25 January, *Islamic Finance News*.

El-Hassan, A. W. A. (1985). Freedom of Contract, the Doctrine of Frustration, and Sanctity of Contracts in Sudan Law and Islamic Law. *Arab Law Quarterly*, 1(1), 51–59.

Essid, Y. (1995). *A Critique of the Origins of Islamic Economic Thought.* Leiden: Brill.

Geertz, C. (1983). Local Knowledge: Fact and Law in Comparative Perspective. In C. Geertz (Ed.), *Local Knowledge. Further Essays in Interpretive Anthropology* (pp. 167–234). New York, NY: Basic Books.

Gold, L. (2004). *The Sharing Economy: Solidarity Networks Transforming Globalization.* Farnham, UK & Burlington, VT: Ashgate.

Graeber, D. (2011). *Debt: The First 5,000 Years*. Brooklyn, NY: Melville House Publishing.

Gutmann, T. (2013). Theories of Contract and the Concept of Autonomy. *Preprints and Working Papers of the Centre for Advanced Study of Bioethics* 2013/55, Münster.

Habib, A. (2004). *Role of* Zakat *and* Awqaf *in Poverty Alleviation*. Occasional Paper No. 8. Jeddah: Islamic Research & Training Institute, Islamic Development Bank Group.

Hallaq, W. B. (2009). *An Introduction to Islamic Law*. Cambridge: Cambridge University Press.

Kamali, M. H. (1993). Fundamental Rights of the Individual: An Analysis of *Haqq* (right) in Islamic Law. *The American Journal of Islamic Social Sciences*, 10(3), 340–366.

Khan, A. (1984). Islamic Economics, Nature and Need. *Journal for Research in Islamic Economics*, 1(2), 55–61.

Kramer, B. J. (2015). *Shareology: How Sharing Is Powering the Human Economy*. New York, NY: Morgan James.

Naqvi, S. N. H. (1981). *Ethics and Economics: An Islamic Synthesis*. Leicester: The Islamic Foundation.

Netton, I. R. (1989). *Allah Transcendent: Studies in the Structure and Semiotics of Islamic Philosophy, Theology and Cosmology*. London: Routledge.

Ranouil, V. (1980). *L'autonomie de la Volonté. Naissance and Évolution d'un Concept*. Travaux et Recherches de l'Université de Droit, d'Économie et des Sciences Sociales de Paris. Paris: Presses Universitaires de France.

Ray, N. D. (1997). The Medieval Islamic System of Credit and Historical Considerations. *Arab Law Quarterly*, 12(1), 43–90.

Sen, A. (2009). *The Idea of Justice*. Harvard, MA: Harvard University Press & London: Allen Lane.

Shirazi, N. S. (2014). Integrating *Zakat* and *Waqf* into the Poverty Reduction Strategy of the IDB Member Countries. *Islamic Economic Studies*, 22(1), 79–108.

Siddiqui, M. N. (1981). *Muslim Economic Thinking: A Survey of Contemporary Literature*. Leicester: The Islamic Foundation.

Slater, D., & Tonkiss, F. (2000). *Market Society: Markets and Modern Social Theory*. Cambridge: Polity.

Smirnov, A. (1996). Understanding Justice in an Islamic Context: Some Points of Contrast with Western Theories. *Philosophy East and West*, 46(3), 337–350.

Smith, A. (1759). *The Theory of Moral Sentiments*. London: A. Millar; Edinburgh: A. Kincaid & J. Bell.

Smith, A. (1776). *An Inquiry into the Nature and Causes of the Wealth of Nations* (reproduced 2007). Petersfield, UK: Harriman House.

Stelzer, S. A. J. (2008). Ethics. In T. Winter (Ed.), *The Cambridge Companion to Classical Islamic Theology* (pp. 161–179). Cambridge: Cambridge University Press.

Stephany, A. (2015). *The Business of Sharing: Making It in the New Sharing Economy*. Basingstoke: Palgrave MacMillan.

Stiglitz, J. E. (2015). *The Great Divide: Unequal Societies and What We Can Do about Them*. New York, NY: W.W. Norton & Company.

Udovitch, A. L. (1967). Credit as a Means of Investment in Medieval Islamic Trade. *Journal of the American Oriental Society*, 87(3), 260–264.

Udovitch, A. L. (1970). *Partnership and Profit in Medieval Islam*. Princeton, NJ: Princeton University Press.

Velasquez, M. G. (2011). *Business Ethics: Concepts and Cases* (7th ed.). London: Pearson.

5 How can Islamic banks achieve social justice?

A discourse

Khoutem Ben Jedidia

Islamic economics is governed by Islamic law (*Sharia*) based on the *Qur'an, Sunna* and jurisprudence (*Ijmaa*). It is based on a paradigm whose primary objective is socio-economic justice (Chapra, 1996). In fact, Islamic economics' attempts to carry out justice and social welfare by individuals and organizations in a society whose members cooperate to reach *falah* (happiness).

Since Islamic finance is unsuitable for usury, debt rescheduling, speculative transfers, gambling or waste and other purely monetary activities, it seems to be an effective avenue for justice and social well-being. It can be associated with other initiatives of Islamic redistributive mechanisms such as *Zakat, Sadaqat* and *Waqf* all of which aim to enhance social justice.

Conventionally, the economic behavior is independent of any particular ethical position or normative judgment (Friedman, 1953). However, Islamic banking does not solely focus on profit maximization but also on establishing distributive justice (Usmani, 2002). So, social justice is one of the main features of the *Sharia*-compliant banking system. Nevertheless, social justice has many aspects (distributive, relational and retributive justice) which imply the consideration of different elements in banking transactions.[1] The social and environmental responsibilities of Islamic banks advise them to finance wealth and income growth with socioeconomic goals (ethical and corporate social responsibility investment). The question is how Islamic private banks can reconcile their own profit seeking and achieving the social objectives which might be against their own interest.

In a recent paper, Ali (2015) emphasizes that "an articulate theory and corresponding policies to put the ideas of Islamic social justice into practice need renewed attention" (p. xiv). So, the aim of this chapter is to specify the principles and mechanisms of social justice in Islamic banking finance and to discuss whether Islamic banks have achieved these objectives of social justice in practice and if they have favored one aspect over another.

The remaining of this chapter is organized as follows: the second section presents a review of the literature. The third section examines the Islamic banking principles that pave the way to social justice. The fourth section, however, discusses the mechanisms through which Islamic bank financing can practically achieve social justice. The fifth section tries to ascertain the extent to which Islamic banking has contributed to social justice. Finally, section six offers some conclusions and policy recommendations.

Literature review

The Islamic banks seek to comply with *Maqassid al Sharia*. Abu Hamed al-Ghazali argues that

> the objectives of the *shari'ah* are to promote the well-being of mankind, which lies in safeguarding their faith (*din*), human self (*nafs*), their intellect (*aql*), their posterity (*nasl*) and their wealth. Whatever ensures the safeguard of these five serves public interest and is desirable.
>
> (1937, p. 139)

The Islamic financial system aims at preserving certain social objectives such as distributive justice, poverty alleviation and social equity (Venardos, 2005). The Islamic banks have a religious duty to achieve social welfare (Farook, 2008). Islamic bank activity is then inextricably linked to social justice as it is considered as one of its vanguards. The twofold functions of Islamic banks are profit-oriented and social-oriented (Hasan, 2012). As explained by Farook (2008), this does not mean that Islamic banks become merely charitable or uncompetitive institutions but they are required to assume an important role in order to regain the community's trust.

Several studies highlight the social justice role of Islamic banks by emphasizing different elements contributing to build social justice.

Islamic banking contributes to build the social justice by ensuring financial stability. In fact, as an anticrisis system, Islamic banking can avoid instability and stimulate growth fairly. Small Islamic banks tend to be financially stronger than small conventional banks (Čihák & Hesse, 2010). Hasan and Dridi (2010) showed that Islamic banks remained stable during the period of the *subprime crisis* as their credit and asset growth performed better than that of conventional banks. Besides, Maghrebi and Mirakhor (2015) state that the asset-backed equity-financing characterized by shared return can guarantee financial stability. Yet, in the conventional systems, the financial liberalization causes financial instability and crisis. Cecchetti and Kharroubi (2015) assert that financial booms are not growth-enhancing since the financial sector competes with the rest of the economy for resources and drains them from the real economy.

Furthermore, Islamic banking financing which tries to reduce inequality contributes to build social justice. Social justice and particularly the elimination of extreme poverty are among priority areas of Islamic financing strategies (Khan & Khan, 2010). Islamic financial institutions can help achieve the balance between allocative efficiency and distributional equity (Hassan & Chachi, 2005). Thakur (1996) states that in our contemporary context, social justice primarily refers to distributive justice. However, in a conventional economy, a minimum level of financial development is a necessary precondition to reduce income inequality. In other words, the initial stage of financial development would hurt the poor more and exacerbate income inequality. Nevertheless, the second or even third development stage would decrease inequality (Greenwood & Jovanovic, 1990).

Obviously, the social standing of Islamic banks is embodied through the attention to the human aspect of their activities. Overall, in Islamic economics, the attention given to the human side of development is unique (Chapra, 2010). The problem is not only the maximization of material wealth but who would benefit from this wealth. The ethical investment is a relevant concern for Islamic banks. Ahmed (2011) considers that the Islamic financial system is expected to "entail risk-sharing features and serve all categories of the population thereby bringing about equity, stability and growth" (p. 1). Besides, Islamic banks bring ethical values and corporate social responsibility to banking activities (Dusuki & Abdullah, 2007).

Moreover, Islamic banking can address the issue of "financial inclusion" or "access to finance" through risk-sharing contracts (Mohieldin, et al. 2012) and consequently they serve the purpose of social justice. As argued by Burgess and Pande (2005), the lack of access to finance is considered as a key reason for the poor to remain poor. Islamic banking offers greater opportunity for the poor to have access to credit (Iqbal, 2002). This enables them to invest in their own employment generating income (Hassan & Alamgir, 2002). Yet, in the situation of a lack of credit availability because banks are less willing to provide loans to the poor, who would address the informal lending sector at high interest rates? They consequently find themselves in a vicious cycle of credit and poverty (Hassan & Alamgir, 2002). According to El Melki and Ben Arab (2009), the Islamic banking financing should benefit all parties involved in market transactions and promote social harmony. This means that they should care for the less fortunate in society in order to maintain equilibrium and social justice (El Melki & Ben Arab, 2009). Empirically, many studies like those of Demirguc-Kunt et al. (2013) and Ben Naceur et al. (2015) have ascertained the role of Islamic finance in financial inclusion.

The novelty of this study lies in the fact that it investigates the relationship between Islamic banking principles and social justice; to discuss how Islamic banking contributes to the three objectives of social justice: (1) a fair and equitable distribution of wealth; (2) the provision of basic necessities of life to the needy; (3) the protection of the weak against economic hardships.[2] Ultimately, this research evaluated objectively whether the Islamic banking system has played a genuine role in establishing social justice.

Islamic banking principles and social justice

The underlying principles of Islamic banking make it distinct from conventional one. In fact, Islamic banks are invited to respect many principles and avoid any involvement with all contracts that contain any or all prohibitions such as: interdiction of *Riba*, interdiction of *Gharar* and *Maysir* and interdiction of illicit sector. In addition, they have to respect the principles of Profits and Losses Sharing (PLS) and Assets Backing. These principles involve social justice. In this section, we tried to address different aspects of social justice advocated by these principles which characterize Islamic banking activity.

First of all, Islam's doctrinal and general principles do covey the values of equity, cooperation and social justice. The concept of social justice itself is derived from divine foundations (divine knowledge) (Ali, 2015). In fact, the principle of *Tawhid* (unity) supposes equality before God and the principle of *adl* means equality between individuals, and both of them sustain social justice in its distributive, relational and retributive dimensions.

Riba prohibition

The Islamic finance major principle is the prohibition of *Riba* (interest and usury). In fact, money itself has no intrinsic value. It can only be a means of transactions. Thus, money is a "potential capital" that requires its association with the entrepreneur service in order to transform this potentiality into a reality (Iqbal & Mirakhor, 2006).

This principle of interest rate prohibition stands for social justice. For instance, the money holder has no reward without taking risk and the remuneration is related to the involvement of the financial capital to create wealth. This means that unless the capital is exposed to business risk, it be assigned no reward (Ahmed, 1995). Nevertheless, if the fund holder requires a fixed remuneration, he is likely to take advantage of the borrower as he benefits from a return without achieving any task or sharing any risk. So, interest charging is considered as to be an unjust and exploitative instrument of financing (Khan & Mould, 2008). Interest-free transactions avoid economic exploitation and guarantee relational social justice.

Furthermore, the abolition of interest rate discourages wealth concentration[3] leading to an achievement of more social justice. The interest charge increases inequality between the poor and the rich and the tension between self-interest and fairness to others. This leads to distributional justice.

In sum, forbidding the *Riba* seeks to ensure both relational and distributional justice.

Gharar and Maysir prohibition

The Sharia formally forbids contracts and transactions that are based on, or involve, *Maysir* and/or *Gharar*. *Gharar* is related to uncertainty. *Maysir* is associated with games of chance (i.e. gambling). It occurs when one loses a part or all of one's wealth. *Maysir* is an example of *Gharar*.

Since *Gharar* exposes the economic agent the situations of uncertainty where he could suffer from unexpected losses, it, therefore, results in economic injustice. *Sharia* advises believers to write any promise or contract that they make (2:282) to guarantee transparent transactions and fairness and avoid social injustice.

In addition, games based on *Kimar* and *Maysir* lead to a single winner while other participants are losers. The gain is based on luck and not on work or effort. It is related to wasteful activities and not justified according to the Islamic religion.

So, this principle of forbidding *Gharar* and *Maysir* enhances relational and distributional justice as it enhances equality between economic agents.

Illicit sectors prohibition

According to *Sharia* principles, it is illicit to earn money by investing in activities dealing with alcohol, pork, drugs and pornography. Islamic banks screen for such activities to ensure their compliance with *Halal* (permissible) sectors and international standards (Belabes, 2010). Forbidding such sectors leads to avoid financing harmful and sinful goods which may result in a high social and economic cost. Consequently, by avoiding illicit sectors, Islamic banking contributes to social justice.

Profits and losses sharing principle

Under the rules of *Sharia*, no one can claim any compensation without incurring risk. This rule is called *al-ghounm bi al-ghourm* and the paradigm of Profits and Losses Sharing (PLS) emerged from such a rule. PLS assumes that financial transaction parties have to share risks as well as returns together. This leads to a key principle of equitable sharing. The coparticipation in risk and return which carries out a more equitable distribution of resources can promote economic justice and social fairness. Indeed, the fixed return is replaced by a proportionate share which ensures an equitable return of capital related to project results and macroeconomic conditions. Therefore, the principle of profit and losses sharing encourages equal income distribution for the benefits of social justice.

Asset backing principle

All financial transactions should systematically be linked to real assets. Money is, accordingly, in the service of the real economy. Therefore, the strong relationships between real and financial spheres avoid the problem of their development "discordance." This association generates more value-added wealth since more funds would be oriented towards a more productive system. In this context, Islamic bank's financing avoids growth-inhibiting financial crisis that occurs in the case of excessive growth of credit as suggested by Rousseau and Wachtel (2011) in the conventional system. Furthermore, Dabla-Norris et al. (2015) argued that before the *subprime* crisis, the resources were diverted towards the financial sector, away from more productive sectors in advanced economies. Besides, following this principle of asset backing, Islamic banks do not create money *ex nihilo* which causes excessive inflation and speculative bubbles. So, social justice is granted by avoiding inflation that impoverishes creditors and profits debtors.

Deductively, the principle of asset backing principle prevents Islamic banking activity from growth-inhibiting financial crisis and injustice distribution of revenues.

Nevertheless, social justice is not solely based on Islamic basic principles; it also needs an adequate implementation (Hasan, 2007). The author explains that the problem is not with concept and dicta of social justice, but it rather lies in the "process and approach of its implementation." As suggested to Abu Zaharah's theory of *Maqasid al Sharia,* the justice should be defined in relation, or according to, the context of its application. This is what we tried to develop in the following paragraphs.

Islamic banking mechanisms toward social justice

We have already discussed how Islamic banking can serve the three objectives of social justice, what ought to be ensured and how it can be guaranteed.

Wealth equitable distribution

Islamic banking can address the wealth equitable distribution issue from two perspectives: the first is achieved through proving risk-sharing financing (*Musharakah* and *Mudharabah*), and the other through the mobilization of savings of investment accounts.

On the asset side, Islamic banking financing is distinguished from the conventional one by *Musharakah* and *Mudharabah. Musharakah* is equity participation (active participation) of an Islamic bank in the capital of a firm. *Mudharabah* is a passive participation where the Islamic bank is an investor that provides the capital full amount while the client is responsible for business management. Profits are shared in agreed portion, but potential losses are endured by the Islamic bank only except for in the case of manager negligence.

The PLS financing (*Musharakah* and *Mudharabah*) allows a more efficient and equitable distribution of wealth and income (Hassan & Kayed, 2009). In fact, the allocation of funds is based on viability and expected profitability/productivity of a project rather than on creditworthiness of the entrepreneur in conventional banking.

At the liability side, the equitable distribution of resources is carried out among depositors of investment account and Islamic bank. Profit-sharing investment accounts (PSIA) are not insured accounts, or capital certain. The *ex-ante* rate of return on investment (interest rate premium in conventional banks) is replaced by an uncertain *ex-post* rate of return.

Consequently, the participative intermediation based on investment deposits on the liability side and *Musharakah* and *Mudharabah* on the asset side is the best tool to perform social justice through risk sharing leading to an equitable distribution of wealth. In fact, this model of risk sharing is different from the risk strategies in the conventional finance: (1) no risk like in *riba*; (2) excessive risk like speculation and gambling; and (3) transfer risk as in the case of borrowers who bear all the risk of their investment while the lender enjoys a fixed interest income (Hassan & Kayed, 2009). Kuran (2002) considers risk transfer to be unjust and inequitable given that borrowers should pay back both the borrowed capital and the interest thereof out of their personal wealth. Askari and Krichene (2010) claimed that the development of disparity in revenue and wealth in USA over the previous four decades is attributed to the conventional finance system. Even the non-PLS Islamic banking products i.e. sale contract (*murabaha, salam, istisnaa*) based on risk transfer, they do not lead to the same outcome as the conventional finance. In others words, Unlike conventional banking where, the risk shifting in these sale contracts is a win-loses strategy, it is rather a win-win strategy in the Islamic context (Seif, 2009).

Contribution to the supply of basic necessities of life

The ability of Islamic banks to enhance economic development leads to better welfare and consequently improves the economic situation of the poor.

The principle of distribution in an Islamic economy is first need and followed by sufficiency (the basic necessities of life like food, clothing and shelter) for every citizen regardless of his nationality and religion. Islamic banks can, therefore, provide the basic needs to the poor and fulfill basic human needs, enabling them to contribute to social justice. Indeed, Islamic banks perform a social intermediation (Ben Jedidia, 2012). On the one hand, this type of banking is distinguished from the conventional one by the "*Zakat*"[4] accounts in which the amounts due to the obligation of *Zakat* is paid on behalf of the Muslim Bank shareholders, the bank's immediate holding company and the bank's ultimate holding company.[5] The Islamic banks are responsible for managing the use of these funds. For example, the Emirates Islamic Bank stated in its report of 2015, that the "*Zakat* is disbursed to *Sharia* channels through a committee formed by the management" (p. 56).[6] This *Zakat* financing helps to satisfy the poor and involve them in the sphere of production. However, one can suggest that the role of Islamic banks is not to collect and distribute *Zakat*. We think that since Islamic banks raise the *Zakat* funds, they can support foundations for social activities[7] or they create their own foundations.

Further, the Islamic banking system makes funds available to the poor through microcredits on the basis of a *Qard Hassan* (interest-free loan). *Qard Hassan* is a social lending for people in difficulty, for young innovative and emerging entrepreneurs. Such financing may enable the poor to become more productive and reduce unemployment.

This social financial intermediation helps solve poverty problems and fulfill the basic needs. In return, this can reduce social disparities among economic agents.

Equality of access to finance and protection of the weak against economic hardships

The Islamic banking can be considered as a pillar of financial inclusion.[8] It can enable a wider array of individuals (including low-income people and rural residents) and enterprises to access the financial services. So, Islamic banks try to overcome financial exclusion by providing financing to small businesses and workers (Asutay, 2008). This contributes to justice in term of access to finance (equal access to markets, investment and technology) which promotes equality in society. If access to credit improved thanks to easing the financing constraints for smaller and younger firms, entrepreneurship would increase and poverty would be consequently reduced (Ben Naceur et al., 2015). The study of Global Financial Development Report of the World Bank (2014) emphasizes that Islamic banking is associated with a lower incidence of religious self-exclusion and a lower share of firms citing access to Islamic banking finance as a significant obstacle.

Furthermore, the "associative finance" encourages entrepreneurship and protects the weak against economic hardships through *Mudharabah* and notably *Musharakah*. *Musharakah* means that Islamic banks support firms and consolidate the implementation and development of its projects.

To sum up, it seems that the intervention of Islamic banks can ensure the three aspects of social justice: an equitable distribution of wealth; the provision of the basic needs to the poor; and the protection of the weak against economic hardships. It is interesting to discuss whether in practice Islamic banks have achieved these objectives of social justice and/or if they have favored one aspect over another.

Islamic banking role in social justice appraisal

Since Islamic banks represented about four-fifths of the total Islamic finance assets in 2013 (IFSB, 2014), they could enjoy an important role in establishing social justice. As argued by Ali (2015), it is important to evaluate the socioeconomic progress under the guidance the Islamic religion.

We have shown that following Islamic principles, Islamic banks are able to establish social justice goals but they need to adopt practical actions to achieve the potential of Islamic banking in fulfilling social justice.

From a social viewpoint, there is a gap between Islamic banks' promised social role and their practical performance in this field. Overall, Islamic banking has *de facto* failed to meet the social and ethical goals claimed by *Sharia* (Ahmed, 2011). The practice of Islamic banking misrepresents Islam and does not contribute to solving social problems (Mansour et al., 2015). Asutay (2008) argued that following their profits, Islamic financial institutions which have become too "commercialized" have lost their social origins as the profit maximization objective negates the importance of the banks' societal responsibility. The author concluded that Islamic financial institutions have deviated from the social welfare objectives and failed to internalize social justice in their operational function.

It seems that after almost 40 years of experience, Islamic banks are far from fulfilling their excepted social justice objective in its three aspects as stated in the fourth section. This can be argued by many factors such as:

- The limited share of *Musharakah* and *Murabahah* in Islamic banking financing hinders the objective of an equitable distribution of income because the risk and return sharing is not the dominant criterion of resources allocation. The Islamic financial instruments are mostly based on bond-like specificities notably the *Murabaha*. For example, investments in *Mudharabah* and *Musharakah* made by Islamic banks in Bangladesh represent only 1.9% of total banking investments (Quarterly Report Preparation Committee, 2015). The monitoring of PLS arrangements, full of complexities, leads to the rise of asymmetric information problems (Daher et al., 2015).[9] So, the dominance of the conventional finance quasi-products does not allow Islamic banking to alleviate social injustice and inequity. Islamic financial products, similar to the conventional ones, lead to the same social effect.
- The practice of the Islamic banking industry shows that this industry does not benefit a large spectrum of people (Mansour et al., 2015). Recent empirical studies interested in Islamic banks and financial inclusion have found mixed results. For example, Ben Naceur et al. (2015) investigated the relationship between the development of Islamic banking and financial inclusion.[10] They concluded that there is a weak evidence of a positive impact of the Islamic banking related to some inclusion types. Indeed, their results show that Islamic banking in OIC countries is weakly associated with greater use of bank credit by both households and firms (for investment purposes) while there is no significant association with ownership of accounts by households. In addition, the empirical study of Demirguc-Kunt et al. (2013) highlights that the

size of the Islamic finance industry is not related to the differences in financial inclusion between Muslim and non-Muslim. In addition, instead of investing funds in Muslim countries, there is a tendency to invest them abroad depriving Muslim populations from benefiting from their services. Thus, the equality of access to finance does not seem to be fully achieved by Islamic banks.

- Social lending (*Qard Hassan*) is limited since it represents only 1% of the financing offered by Islamic banks. This fact hampers the expected social-building capacity of Islamic banking. This also does not comply with the expected role of the supply of basic necessities of life by Islamic banks.

We can conclude that while Islamic banks have largely complied with the principles of Islamic finance, they do not seem to make enough effort to implement the mechanisms for the practical establishment of social justice. There is rather a focus on the profitability and survival of Islamic banks. Thereby, Islamic banks have tried to achieve a bit of every aspect of social justice.

Conclusion and recommendations

Achieving a social balance is a requirement of Islamic economics characterized by ethical and moral values. In particular, Islamic banks dominate the Islamic monetary and financial landscape. Since the Islamic banking sector experienced an annual growth at a rate of about 17% in the period 2009–2013 (Hussain et al., 2015), it can play a key role in channeling economies towards social justice at distributive, relational and retributive levels and doing so, it can participate in social development.

Islamic banking principles convey the relational and distribution justice and require mechanisms to put the justice values into practice. In fact, the prohibition of *Riba, Gharar* and *Maysir*, illicit sectors can ensure both relational and distributional justice. Besides, the principle of profits and losses sharing encourages equal income distribution. The principle of asset backing is able to prevent Islamic banking activity from growth-inhibiting financial crisis and unfair revenues distribution. However, the compliance of Islamic banking to these principles does not guarantee the achievement of social justice. Rather, Islamic banks should undertake practical actions that help accomplish this objective.

We have shown that the PLS financing (*Musharakah* and *Mudharabah*), the *Qard Hassan* and the choice of viable projects enable Islamic banks to achieve an equitable distribution of wealth and supply the basic necessities of life. Besides, Islamic banking could support efforts to improve access to financial services and the protection of the weak against economic hardships. Consequently, Islamic Banks can contribute to establish social justice (social solidarity and social balance) within the financial sphere and then to spread them through the whole economy.

Nevertheless, we have concluded that there is a wide gap between what Islamic banks are expected to achieve in their social role and their practical performance in this field. So, several challenges still lie ahead of the Islamic banking to really fulfill its potential social justice role.

Islamic banks are then invited to:

- Pay more attention to the issue of social justice by revising their strategies through the integration of the social aspect of their activities. Kamla and Rammal (2013) recommend a positive change in Islamic banks' actual social roles.[11] In fact, Islamic banks seem to be more concerned with legal and mechanistic aspects of adherence to Islamic law rather than with promoting Islamic ethical values (Nienhaus, 2011). Asutay (2008) requires "new models of institutional developments beyond commercial Islamic financial institutions" to reorienting social banking. Chapra (2012) argues that Islamic banks have to promote the claimed *Maqasid al-Shari'ah* which is far from being true in today's practice. Thus, Islamic banks should stick to the social and economic ends of their financial transactions.
- Enable more customers to access financing in order to enhance their financial inclusion and increase their productive capacity. Ben Naceur et al. (2015) have already proposed some changes to the Islamic banks operating model such as the creation of separate Small Medium Enterprise business units that can improve the financial inclusion.
- Increase their PLS investment and promote the risk sharing culture which allows an equitable distribution of wealth and income. As PLS financing does not exceed 5% of Islamic banking financing, Islamic banks are not really able to contribute to an equitable distribution of wealth and an equal access to finance. Due to moral hazard behavior and excessive risk taking, Hamza (2016) recommends the development of a new generation of investment deposits for better saving mobilization.
- Build a "social justice committee," *via* the *Sharia committee*, to investigate the banking transactions ends compliance not only to financial principles but also to justice. In fact, it is critical to have a social committee within Islamic banks to adopt social strategies. However, this committee might result in extra costs, which in return affects the efficiency of Islamic banks. Given the additional governance problems that may arise from the implementation of this new committee, it is advisable to combine both the social committee and the *Sharia* committee.
- Resort to specialists, human capital, and qualified talents to improve the training of bank personnel in social justice-compliant instruments. In fact, as outlined by Jabr (2003), the ability of Islamic banks to expand the outreach of their services is limited since they face a dearth of

qualified talent and are compelled to recruit staff trained in conventional banking.

Nevertheless, at the macroeconomic level, the social justice role of Islamic banks would require an important condition: the public authorities have to acquire a social justice strategy to support Islamic banks in their efforts notably with the competition of conventional banks. In this trend, the authorities are required to conceive of a social justice agenda, which will avoid Islamic banks being attached only to their survival and their profitability. Furthermore, there is a need to create an enhancing environment for economic and social development by improving the financial infrastructure, the efficiency of the legal and supervisory system and the financial education. These reforms might enhance the effectiveness of Islamic banking for establishing social justice. Ultimately, Islamic banks need to expand further in order to make a noticeable impact on social justice in the economy.

Notes

1 The three important criteria of Islamic ethics are *adl* (justice), *amanah* (trust), and *ihsan* (benevolence) (Beekun and Badawi 2005).
2 These aspects of social justice are presented by Hassan and Kayed (2009, p.49). Unlike the paper of Hassan and Kayed (2009) which discusses the risk management and social justice in Islam, our study considers the role of the whole bank activity in achieving the social justice objectives.
3 The Holy Coran is against exploitation, it warns: "Wealth should not only circulate between the rich amongst you" (59:7).
4 Zakat is a religious tax of wealth. It is a pillar of Islam. It is paid on the wealthy capital that reached the taxable threshold (nissâb) and was hoarded for a year.
5 For example, the report of Emirates Islamic bank (2015) note in the Article (72-G): "The shareholders shall independently provide Zakat (Alms) for their money (paid up capital) and the Company shall calculate for them the due Zakat per share and notify them thereof every year. As for the money held by the Company as reserves, retained earnings and others, on which Zakat is due, the Company shall pay their Zakat as decided by the Fatwa and Shari'ah Supervisory Board and transfer such Zakat to the Zakat Fund stipulated in Article (75) of Chapter 10 of the Articles of Association." The Zakat on shareholders' equity (except paid up capital) is discharged from the retained earnings.
6 The *Zakat* payable by Emirates Islamic Bank is AED 33,483 million in 2015 and AED 16,826 Million in 2014.
7 For example, Bank Mandiri, an Islamic Indonesian bank supports the Titian Foundation Scholarship.
8 Financial inclusion is the share of the population who use financial services. It means a broad access to financial services.
9 Islamic banks favor like-debt and short-run financing such as Murabahah lending rather than providing more PLS financing (Musharakah and Mudharabah) because they are less risky. Furthermore, PLS intermediation is more costly for the bank aiming at reducing risks and improving the information collection. The equity-based instruments pose operational problems and they suffer from the lack of institutional and regulatory framework that guarantees more enforcement and

transparency especially those involving profit and loss sharing financing scheme (see Ben Jedidia and Ben Ayed (2012) for more discussion).

10 They notice that various indicators of financial inclusion tend to be lower in Muslim countries members of the Organization for Islamic Cooperation (OIC). In fact, the use of financial services has not growing as quickly as the physical access to these financial services.

11 Kamla and Rammal (2013) try to explain the reasons for disclosures and silences in Islamic banks annual reports and web sites vis-à-vis to social justice for a sample of 19 banks. They note that while Islamic banks disclosures highlight their religious character through claims (adhere to *sharia*'s teachings); they lack specific or detailed information regarding schemes or initiatives to poverty eradication and social justice enhancement.

References

Ahmed, A. (1995). The Evolution of Islamic Banking. In Institute of Islamic Banking and Insurance (Ed.), *Encyclopedia of Islamic Banking* (pp. 21–23). London: Institute of Islamic Banking and Insurance.

Ahmed, H. (2011). Defining Ethics in Islamic Finance: Looking Beyond Legality. Paper presented at the 8th International Conference on Islamic Economics and Finance of *Sustainable Growth and Inclusive Economic Development from an Islamic Perspective*, December 19–21, Doha, Qatar. Retrieved from www.conference.qfis.edu.qa/app/media/290.

Al-Ghazali, A. (1937). *Al-Mustasfa*. 1109. Cairo: al-Maktabah al-Tijariyyah al-Kubra.

Ali, S. S. (2015). Islamic Economics and Social Justice Essays on Theory and Policy. In H. A. El-Karanshawy et al. (Eds.), *Islamic Economic: Theory, Policy and Social Justice* (pp. xi–xiv). Doha, Qatar: Bloomsbury Qatar Foundation.

Askari, H., & Krichene, N. (2010). Malaysia-Gateway to Islamic Finance. The Muslim Observer, November 4, 2010. Retrieved from http://muslimmedianetwork .com/mmn/?p=7221?pfstyle=wp.

Asutay, M. (2008). Islamic Banking and Finance: Social Failure. New Horizon. Retrieved from www.islamic-banking.com/IIBI_magazine.aspx.

Beekun, R. I., & Badawi, J. A. (2005). Balancing Ethical Responsibility among Multiple Organizational Stakeholders: The Islamic Perspective. *Journal of Business Ethics*, 60(2), 131–145. Doi:10.1007/s10551-004-8204-5.

Belabes, A. (2010). Épistémologie des Principes de la Finance Islamique. *Cahiers De La Finance Islamique*, 2, 5–11.

Ben Jedidia, K. (2012). L'intermédiation financière participative des banques islamiques. *Etudes en Economie Islamique*, 6(1), 17–31.

Ben Jedidia, K., & Ben Ayed, N. (2012). Islamic Participative Financial Intermediation and Economic Growth. *Journal of Islamic Economics, Banking and Finance*, 8(3), 44–59.

Ben Naceur, S., Barajas, A., & Massara, A. (2015). Can Islamic Banking Increase Financial Inclusion? IMF, WP/15/31. Retrieved from www.imf.org/external/pubs/ft/wp/2015/wp1531.pdf.

Burgess, R., & Pande, R. (2005). Do Rural Banks Matter? Evidence from the Indian Social Banking Experiment. *The American Economic Review*, 95(3), 780–795.

Cecchetti, S., & Kharroubi, E. (2015). Why Does Financial Sector Growth Crowd Out Real Economic Growth? *BIS Working Paper* No. 490, February 2015. Retrieved from www.bis.org/publ/work490.pdf.

Chapra, U. (1996). Monetary Management in an Islamic Economy. *Islamic Economic Studies*, 4(1), 1–35.

Chapra, U. (2010). Speech, Panel Discussion, *The Impact of Islamic Finance on Economic Development: A Roundtable Discussion*, Islamic Finance Project, Harvard Law School, October 12.

Chapra, U. (2012). The Future of Islamic Economics, Speech at the Workshop on *The Future of Islamic Economics*, November 12–13, Jeddah.

Čihák, M., & Hesse, H. (2010). Islamic Banks and Financial Stability: An Empirical Analysis. *Journal of Financial Services Research*, 38(2), 95–113.

Dabla-Norris, E., Guo, S., Haksar, V., Kim, M., Kochhar, K., Wiseman, K., & Zdzienicka, A. (2015). The New Normal: A Sector-Level Perspective on Growth and Productivity Trends in Advanced Economies. *IMF Staff Discussion* Note International Monetary Fund, Washington, DC. Retrieved from www.imf.org/external/pubs/ft/sdn/2015/sdn1503.pdf.

Daher, H., Masih, M., & Ibrahim, M. (2015). The Unique Risk Exposures of Islamic Banks' Capital Buffers: A Dynamic Panel Data Analysis. *Journal of International Financial Markets, Institutions and Money*, 36(3), 36–52.

Demirguc-Kunt, A., Klapper, L., & Randall, D. (2013). Islamic Finance and Financial Inclusion: Measuring Use of and Demand for Formal Financial Services among Muslim Adults. *Policy Research Working Paper Series* 6642, World Bank. Retrieved from http://elibrary.worldbank.org/doi/pdf/10.1596/1813-9450-6642.

Dusuki, A. W., & Abdullah, N. I. (2007). Why Do Malaysia Customers Patronize Islamic Banks? *International Journal of Bank Marketing*, 25(3), 142–160. Doi:10.1108/02652320710739850.

El Melki, A., & Ben Arab, M. (2009). Ethical Investment and the Social Responsibilities of the Islamic Banks. *International Business Research*, 2(2), 123–130.

Emirates Islamic Bank Report. (2015). On Behalf of the Shari'a Supervisory Board-Emirates Islamic. Retrieved from www.emiratesislamic.ae/eng/assets/files/annualreports/EI_AnnualReport_2015_Eng.pdf.

Farook, S. (2008). Social Responsibility for Islamic Financial Institutions: Laying Down a Framework. *Journal of Islamic Economics, Banking and Finance*, 4(1), 61–82.

Friedman, M. (1953). The Methodology of Positive Economics. In M. Friedman (Ed.), *Essays in Positive Economics* (pp. 3–43). Chicago, IL: University of Chicago Press.

Global Financial Development Report. (2014). *Financial Inclusion*. Washington, DC: World Bank. Retrieved from https://openknowledge.worldbank.org/bitstream/handle/10986/16238/9780821399859.pdf?sequence=4.

Greenwood, J., & Jovanovic, B. (1990). Financial Development, Growth, and the Distribution of Income. *Journal of Political Economy*, 98(5), 1076–1107.

Hamza, H. (2016). Does Investment Deposit Return in Islamic Banks Reflect PLS Principle? *Borsa Istanbul Review*, 16(1), 32–42. Doi: 10.1016/j.bir.2015.12.001.

Hasan, M., & Dridi, J. (2010). The Effects of the Global Crisis on Islamic and Conventional Banks: A Comparative Study. IMF working Paper 10/201, International Monetary Fund, Washington, DC, p. 47. Retrieved from www.imf.org/external/pubs/ft/wp/2010/wp10201.pdf.

Hasan, S. (2007). Islamic Concept of Social Justice: Its Possible Contribution Harmony and Peaceful Coexistence in a Globalized World. *Macquarie Law Journal*, 7, 167–183.

Hasan, Z. (2012). Corporate Governance in Islamic Financial Institutions: An Ethical Perspective. *Prime Journals of Business Administration and Management*, 2(1), 405–411.

Hassan, A., & Chachi, A. (2005). The Role of Islamic Financial Institutions in Sustainable Development. In M. Iqbal, & A. Ausaf (Eds.), *Islamic Finance and Economic Development* (pp. 59–93). New York, NY: Palgrave Macmillan.

Hassan, M. K., & Alamgir, D. A. H. (2002). Micro Financial Services and Poverty Alleviation in Bangladesh: A Comparative Analysis of Secular and Islamic NGOs. In M. Iqbal (Ed.), *Islamic Economics Institutions and the Elimination of Poverty* (pp. 113–168). Leicester, UK: The Islamic Foundation.

Hassan, M. K., & Kayed, R. S. (2009). The Global Financial Crisis, Risk Management and Social Justice in Islamic Finance. *ISRA International Journal of Islamic Finance*, 1(1), 33–58.

Hussain, M., Shahmoradi, A., & Turk, R. (2015). An Overview of Islamic Finance, IMF Working Paper African, European, and Middle East and Central Asia Departments, June 2015. Retrieved from www.imf.org/external/pubs/ft/wp/2015/wp15120.pdf.

Iqbal, M. (2002). Introduction. In M. Iqbal (Ed.), *Islamic Economics Institutions and the Elimination of Poverty* (pp. 1–24). Leicester, UK: The Islamic Foundation.

Iqbal, Z., & Mirakhor, A. (2006). *An Introduction to Islamic Finance—Theory and Practice*. Hoboken, NJ: John Wiley & Sons.

Islamic Financial Services Board (IFSB). (2014). *Islamic Financial Services Industry Stability Report*. Kuala Lumpur: IFSB. Retrieved from http://ifsb.org/docs/IFSB%20-%20IFSI%20Stability%20Report%20TEXT%20FINAL%20(OUTPUT).pdf.

Jabr, H. (2003). Islamic Banking in Palestine: Challenges and Prospects. *An – Najah Univ. J. Res. (H.Sc)*, 17(1), 261–275.

Kamla, R., & Rammal, H. G. (2013). Social Reporting by Islamic Banks: Does Social Justice Matter? *Accounting, Auditing & Accountability Journal*, 26(6), 911–945. Doi: 10.1108/AAAJ-03-2013-1268.

Khan, A., & Mould, H. (2008). *Islam and Debt*. Birmingham, United Kingdom: Islamic Relief.

Khan, M. F., & Khan, M. M. (2010). Islamic Financial System Needs Market Reforms. *Journal of Islamic Economics, Banking and Finance*, 6(3), 9–36.

Kuran, T. (2002). Islamic Discipline of Economics Emerged in Late Colonial India. *Islamic Economics Bulletin*, 12(6), 1–4.

Maghrebi, N., & Mirakhor, A. (2015). Risk Sharing and Shared Prosperity in Islamic Finance. *Islamic Economic Studies*, 23(2), 85–115. Doi:10.12816/0015021.

Mansour, W., Ben Jedidia, K., & Majdoub, J. (2015). How Ethical Is Islamic Banking in the Light of the Objectives of Islamic Law? *Journal of Religious Ethics*, 43(1), 833–859. Doi:10.1111/jore.12086.

Mohieldin, M., Rostom, A., Fu, X., & Iqbal, Z. (2012). The Role of Islamic Finance in Enhancing Financial Inclusion in Organization of Islamic Cooperation (OIC) Countries. *Islamic Economic Studies*, 20(2), 55–120.

Nienhaus, V. (2011). Islamic Finance Ethics and Shari'ah Law in the Aftermath of the Crisis: Concept and Practice of Shari'ah Compliant Finance. *Ethical Perspectives*, 18(4), 591–623. Doi:10.2143/EP.18.4.2141849.

Quarterly Report Preparation Committee. (2015). Development of Islamic Banking in Bangladesh, Developments of Islamic Banking Industry in Bangladesh during April-June 2015. Retrieved from www.bb.org.bd/pub/quaterly/islamic_banking/apr_jun_2015.pdf.

Rousseau, P., & Wachtel, P. (2011). What Is Happening to the Impact of Financial Deepening on Economic Growth? *Economic Inquiry*, 49(1), 276–288. Doi:10.1111/j.1465-7295.2009.00197.x.

Seif, I. T. (2009). The Current Financial and Economic Crisis within the Markets: An Overview. Paper Presented at the Harvard-LSE Workshop on *Risk Management Islamic Economics and Islamic Ethico-Legal Perspectives on Current Financial Crisis*, London School of Economics, February 26.

Thakur, S. C. (1996). *Religion and Social Justice*. New York, NY: St Martin's Press.

Usmani, M. T. (2002). *An Introduction to Islamic Finance. Arab and Islamic Law Series*. Amsterdam: Kluwer Law International.

Venardos, A. (2005). *Islamic Banking and Finance in South-East Asia: Its Development and Future*. Singapore: World Scientific Publishing.

6 Social aids and willingness to work

Developing a social aid framework within the context of Islam

Omer Faruk Tekdogan and Mehmet Tarik Eraslan

Social policies and the fight against poverty has gained importance especially in developed and developing countries (Góra & Schmidt, 1998). Although family-based cooperation and traditional methods still retain their importance, they are far from sufficient for the struggling poor in the modern era. Thus, countries have designed and applied policies (Góra & Schmidt, 1998), primarily economic and social, in order to achieve their targets in this field. Social assistance policies are a part of this large social policy genre, which carries importance in terms of the battle against poverty. The fight against poverty necessitates an integrative approach in terms of policy building, which means that these policies cannot be designed independently from other policy areas. The indirect effects of these social aids are as important as their direct effects (Surender et al., 2010).

As Ditch (1999) expresses that there are generally two key objectives for social assistance, that is, to prevent extreme hardship among those with no other resources and to prevent social marginalization and exclusion. He also emphasizes that financial support should be available to people who do not get alternative support and it should also be sufficient to maintain a minimum standard of living, and supported people should be encouraged to work rather than dependent on state support.

Góra and Schmidt (1998) asserts that the purpose of social assistance should primarily be supporting individuals and families with low income. The eligibility to receive it should be determined by a means test, which is fashionable in most countries today. It is also emphasized that there is no institutional link between unemployment insurance and social assistance, as many social benefit applicants could be both unemployed and not eligible for unemployment benefits.

Social assistance or social aids are financial help for people in need that is paid through government tax incomes. Social assistance programs are generally one sided, only towards people in need and do not necessitate any payback. The need for assistance in the poor and vulnerable people makes it mandatory for the government to step in and organize the financial transactions. Otherwise, if people in need are left to the mercy of charities and NGOs, only some will obtain this aid. Not only will the government make payments and adjust help through taxes but also will take on an important role in organizing charities working in the field.

Social assistance policies and programs which keep people in poverty doesn't make things better for them as in the long term these individuals stay poor. The main objective should be to take those people up to a higher wealth level. We need to make sure that people who are capable of working are motivated to be employed and make policies which help not to make them state dependent on benefits. If the opposite happens, not only will people keep on getting social aid and living poorly, but they will also transfer this poverty to the next generations (Kenworthy, 1998).

To prevent extreme hardship, most OECD countries implement transfer programs and apply a low-income criterion as a primary condition. With this financial support, an acceptable standard of living for low-income families is ensured. Especially during recession periods, more people apply for unemployment benefits, because long-term unemployment rises (OECD, 2014).

Types of social assistance programs

Different groups of social insurance programs differ in structure, part of them rely on premiums and do not cover all citizens. In some countries even if they cover all the people, they generally do not go beyond health care and pensions. Social assistance is a step further, taking in and protecting all citizens who are in need and who have no protection whatsoever. While helping and protecting the citizen with social assistance, the state does not ask for a payback or put the individual in debt.

Kinds of Social Assistance:[1]

• Social services and welfare support: this assistance is given to highly vulnerable groups such as the mentally or physically disabled, children without families, drug addicts etc.
• Assistance based on income tests: this kind of assistance is given to all individuals who are below a certain income level. Even if the individual has some kind of low-level income, this type of assistance focuses on the determined threshold and is given to all those below it.
• Cash or in-kind transfers: examples of this kind of assistance are food stamps and family allowances. This type of aid is towards regular or extraordinary needs. It may be giving out stamps which enables them to be used just for food or in some cases housing benefits which supply the basic housing needs of a citizen.
• Temporary subsidies: lifeline support, food assistance in times of crises etc. are good examples of this kind of assistance.

We need to specifically mention unemployment benefits which are typically received during an initial phase of unemployment, such as unemployment insurance in most countries. Instead unemployment insurance, some countries apply a means-test to applicants. Previous employment or insurance contributions and active job search are generally required for eligibility (OECD, 2014).

Lessons learned from past experiences

After decades of program implementation, developed countries have initiated new social assistance programs in order to reconnect people to the labor market while obtaining social assistance. These programs, in line with the economic and social policies, aim to decrease the dependencies towards social assistance and direct them towards the labor market[2] (Riphahn, 2001). In that way, the number of people who are enrolled for these financial assistance tools would be decreased.

Some studies support the claim about the adverse relationship between generous social assistance benefits and employment. Lemieux and Milligan (2008) examined the incentive effects of transfer programs and found that, in addition to the negative effect of social benefits on employment, those transfers can affect behavioral influences, such as changing family structure or living arrangements. Therefore, some part of the unemployment rates of some countries can be explained by such generous benefits which have work disincentives.

Baumberg (2014) searched the perceptions of British people towards spending on benefits. People struggling with the cost of living were more likely to support the benefits system, whereas, people in working households did not favor benefit claimants, whose claims are unfair and undeserving, as they said. This was supported by the search results as, in 2013, 54% of the British public agreed that "most unemployed people could find a job if they really wanted one" and 57% thought that "unemployment benefits are too high" and discourage people from finding paid work. Moreover, 77% argued that "large numbers of people" falsely claim benefits.

Basically, this is the problem of the individual's choice between income and leisure. As we remember from microeconomics textbooks, this is the utility function of consumption and leisure. We assume leisure gives satisfaction directly and income, as a source of purchasing power, gives satisfaction indirectly. Every individual has different utility functions with their own preference levels of consumption and leisure. As we add social benefits to this function, leisure becomes preferable at low wage rates. Therefore, a new balance would be needed between the wage rates and social benefits. Schneider and Uhlendorff (2005) supportively argue that the ratio between wages and social benefits positively affects the probability of a transition to employment for households with a higher wage income than their social benefits. They suggest workfare programs as an alternative to reduction of the social assistance levels.

It should also be taken into account that, without creating a connection between social aid and employment, this will harm the motivation of those people in the labor market who work very hard each day in an unfavorable situation. This discomfort towards poor people (beneficiaries) in the nation will cause a rise in tensions between different classes and hurt social peace in the community. Besides, if poor people are put back into the labor force, this will increase productivity in the nation hence stimulating economic development.

On the other hand, for poor people who are not able to work, it is obligatory for these individuals to benefit from regular social assistance programs and increase their standard of living. Another important fact in decreasing poverty permanently is to erase poverty for children in need. In order to achieve this very important target, children in poverty should be assisted especially in the areas of education and health. If social assistance programs have tools for the young and teenagers of poor families which would promote their health services and education needs, this will help in a very substitutional way in decreasing and erasing poverty risks. As the level of education rises in an individual and as he/she gets healthier in physical and mental ways, this change on its own brings an increase in earnings to the person (Barrientos & Santıbáñez, 2009). Thus, poverty for these individuals is no longer a trap to be afraid of. These kinds of policies which invest in human capital are also an equal opportunity chance for the young at the beginning of their lives.

Therefore, separating employment, education and health policies from social assistance programs and not giving these policies the relevant importance and just focusing on financial help may be a simpler approach but it does not serve well for the honor of people and it does not do much for the communities' peace and the development of the country. Countries should approach social assistance taking these matters into account and bring an integrative formula to the table. It may seem a simpler choice to confine policies towards financial aids and accept the fact that these people will stay poor; the hard way would be to challenge poverty and support financial aid with other tools that serve well for human capital.

Social assistance programs that encourage the poor who are able to work to join the labor market doesn't necessitate cutting their financial aids. If these people continue to be poor while working, they should be able to benefit from social assistance programs. The main pillar of the system should be to keep people in social aids until their needs are done even if they have a job.[3]

Social assistance and motivation to work

Poverty is an important sign that shows a part of society that cannot integrate itself to the community and labor market. As mentioned, the most important cause of poverty is the problems with labor market integration and the income gap between individuals. Social policies aim at these week points and try to develop certain tools in order to fix the related problems. Very different financing models are being used also, above taxes and voluntary funds.

An important example to the problem raised above is put forward by Arslan (2014) where she examines the motivation of social assistance beneficiaries towards working with interviews of different families. The study shows that 23% of social aid beneficiaries openly state that they would seek the existing assistance even if a regular paid job in the formal labor market is available.

Table 6.1 also shows the amount of spending made towards unemployment policies. Public social expenditures for unemployment as a share of total spending is 3.6% on OECD average. Many European countries are near to, or above, this average. Immervoll et al. (2015) argue that rates of social aid benefit receipt are greater for individuals who have received social aid before than individuals who have not. They list some reasons for state dependence in unemployment for working-age individuals:

- Being without a job makes a worker's skills and experience ("human capital") less valuable and they may lose their labor market value, and in turn, increase the likelihood of future unemployment.
- If employers decide to hire potential employees on the basis of their past unemployment, state dependence may arise.
- Unemployed people may lower their wage expectation with the passage of time and accept poorer quality jobs that are more likely to be liquidated. For this reason, they will be unemployed again.

So, that policies towards giving financial support to individuals and not following up is not working. On the contrary, it is understood that the step that comes after social aids are very important for the social development of the individual. These further steps actually are the main drivers that create a person who is self-sufficient. The most important focus of this latter step is the integration of the individual into the labor market.

When developed countries are examined, one can see that the focus of social assistance has turned to active labor market policies (Geldof, 1999). The reason behind this turn is as abovementioned; solely financial aids themselves do not carry a motivation towards joining the labor market. In most cases they can cause the opposite. The change in production methods brought an important change to the labor market. This fluctuation affected different ages of civilians causing a gap in the functioning of the labor market. Some jobs were there but the unemployed did not have the qualifications to do them and on the other side there was a supply of unskilled labor which was more than needed. This excess supply of labor lacking the necessary skills would not be motivated to find a job if given nothing more than financial assistance. The need is to activate the individual while he or

Table 6.1 Public social expenditure in OECD countries: levels and composition, 2007

	Total	Cash	Income tested	Old age	Survivors	Incapacity related	Health	Family	Active labor market prog.	Unemployment	Housing	Other social policy areas
	in % of GDP			In % of total spending								
Australia	16.4	7.3	5.6	28.7	1.2	13.4	34.8	15.2	1.8	2.4	1.8	0.6
United Kingdom	20.4	9.9	5.0	27.9	1.0	12.3	33.8	16.2	1.5	1.0	5.4	1.0
Ireland	16.7	8.9	4.3	18.5	4.8	10.7	35.1	17.3	3.6	6.0	1.8	2.4
France	29.7	17.1	4.1	37.2	6.0	6.0	29.2	10.1	3.0	4.7	2.7	1.0
Iceland	15.3	5.6	4.0	15.2	0.0	14.6	37.7	23.2	0.0	1.3	4.0	4.0
Canada	16.8	8.7	3.6	21.8	2.4	5.3	41.2	6.5	1.8	3.5	2.4	15.3
Netherlands	21.1	10.1	3.6	25.1	0.9	14.2	33.2	9.0	5.2	5.2	1.9	5.2
New Zealand	18.6	9.6	3.3	22.8	0.5	14.7	38.0	16.3	1.6	1.1	4.3	0.5
Germany	25.1	14.5	3.3	33.9	8.4	8.4	30.7	7.2	2.8	5.6	2.4	0.8
Portugal	22.7	15.0	2.7	40.4	7.0	9.2	29.4	5.3	2.2	5.3	0.0	1.3
Spain	21.3	12.8	2.6	30.4	8.9	11.2	28.5	6.1	3.7	8.4	0.9	1.4
Greece	21.6	14.1	2.2	46.8	9.3	4.2	27.3	5.1	0.9	2.3	2.3	1.9
Slovenia	19.5	12.8	1.9	42.3	7.7	10.8	28.9	5.2	1.0	1.5	0.0	2.6
Austria	26.3	17.4	1.9	40.8	7.3	8.8	25.6	9.9	2.7	3.4	0.4	1.1
Switzerland	18.5	10.7	1.7	33.9	2.2	16.1	30.1	7.0	3.2	3.2	0.5	3.8
Denmark	26.5	12.6	1.6	27.7	0.0	16.3	25.4	13.3	4.9	7.2	2.7	2.7
Hungary	23.0	14.6	1.5	36.4	6.1	11.7	22.5	14.7	1.3	3.0	3.9	0.4

(Continued)

Table 6.1 (Cont.)

	Total	Cash	Income tested	Old age	Survivors	Incapacity related	Health	Family	Active labor market prog.	Unemp- loyment	Housing	Other social policy areas
	in % of GDP			In % of total spending								
Norway	20.5	10.0	1.4	29.8	1.5	20.5	27.3	13.7	2.9	1.0	0.5	2.9
Finland	24.7	14.2	1.4	34.1	3.3	14.6	24.0	11.4	3.7	6.1	0.8	2.0
Belgium	26.0	16.0	1.4	27.3	7.3	8.8	26.9	10.0	4.6	11.9	0.4	2.7
Italy	24.7	16.7	1.2	47.6	9.8	6.9	26.8	5.7	1.6	1.6	0.0	0.0
United States	16.3	7.9	1.2	32.5	4.3	8.0	45.4	4.3	0.6	1.8		3.1
Sweden	27.3	12.8	1.1	32.8	1.8	18.6	23.7	12.4	4.0	2.6	1.8	2.2
Slovak Republic	15.7	9.4	1.0	34.2	5.1	9.5	32.9	11.4	1.3	2.5	0.0	3.2
Poland	19.7	14.2	0.9	43.9	10.1	12.1	22.7	5.6	2.5	1.5	0.5	1.0
Israel	15.5	9.0	0.9	28.6	4.5	18.8	26.0	13.6	1.3	1.9	0.0	5.2
Mexico	6.9	2.2	0.8	16.2	2.9	1.5	38.2	14.7	0.0			11.8
Korea	7.7	2.8	0.8	21.4	3.3	7.4	45.8	7.0	1.7	3.3	14.7	10.2
Czech Republic	18.1	11.4	0.7	36.5	3.9	12.7	30.9	10.5	1.1	3.3	0.6	0.6
Luxembourg	20.3	12.2	0.6	23.8	8.4	13.4	29.7	15.3	2.5	4.5	0.5	2.0
Japan	18.7	10.5	0.6	46.8	6.9	4.3	33.5	4.3	1.1	1.6		1.6
Chile	9.4	5.7	0.4	46.2	6.5	6.5	30.1	8.6	2.2	0.0	0.0	0.0
Turkey	10.5	6.3	0.3	48.1	11.5	1.0	39.4	0.0	0.0	0.0		0.0
Estonia	12.7	8.2	0.1	40.2	0.8	14.2	29.9	12.6	0.8	0.8	0.0	0.8
OECD–Total	**19.2**	**10.9**	**3.7**	**32.4**	**5.1**	**10.6**	**29.3**	**10.1**	**2.3**	**3.6**	**3.0**	**3.5**

Source: Immervoll et al. (2015).

she is receiving these funds. Otherwise people become addicted to social assistance after a certain time and lose their motivation to find a job (Lemieux & Milligan, 2008).

In the developed world we can say that there are many social policy programs aimed at disadvantaged individuals. The amount of social assistance payments is not a major percentage but it has been steadily rising in the last couple of decades. The important reason behind this development is the failure of the disadvantaged and the poor to integrate into the labor market. Thus, one can come to the conclusion that individuals are losing their motivation to find a job and stand on their own income. The social assistance programs are sometimes so generous that when a person compares the amount of effort he/she has to put forward for a full-time job, settling for the financial aid and not working becomes more attractive Rawlings (2004). This problem has been on the agenda of developed countries and technical staffs have been trying to formulate alternative policies that can force the poor with working capabilities to search for a job.

Social assistance programs linked to the individuals' labor market search are a result of this issue. Additional motivation has to be found for some individuals who are below certain income levels. This approach and the programs that followed do not necessitate a cut of social assistance for the poor who have working capabilities. Further, it aims to make these individuals search the labor market for adequate jobs or give them the necessary training to find one while receiving these benefits. Governments have made programs that has put the private sector in this frame by creating incentives that make it very attractive for these companies to hire below income level citizens searching for jobs. As mentioned above, the major aim is more than giving these people financial help but to integrate them into the community with a job that will create self-esteem.

These programs towards integrating the poor to the labor market have different structures from country to country. Some countries focus on motivating the individual by supplying necessary training programs and focusing on increasing the quality of these programs. If the individual is to put forward the necessary effort, additional incentives are also given. Some countries on the other hand have closely tied job searching effort of the individual with the amount of social assistance that he or she will receive. In these countries, the beneficiary is expected to do whatever is necessary to find a suitable job in order for the social assistance to continue (Bolvig et al., 2003). If the person is reluctant to search the labor market or obtain the necessary training supplied by the government, then gradually he or she will face losing parts of their social aids.

Beneficiaries who have the capability to work generally are motivated by these programs which force them to search for an adequate job or lose their benefits. But, if the market is not monitored properly by the government, it may result in citizens accepting jobs that are financially very insufficient that come along with bad working conditions. Companies know that some of these individuals have no choice in finding a better job in the short term so they can take advantage of the social assistance beneficiaries as cheap labor. Issues like these make it obligatory for the government to monitor the beneficiaries until they obtain the skills to choose between alternative jobs.

Distribution of public social expenditures

Referring to Table 3.1, health assistance and assistance to elder people have the highest shares on public social expenditures in OECD countries. In some countries, we can see that health expenditures exceed the amount of social expenditures made for the aged. The reasons behind this fact are that, in these countries the amount of aged population is relatively low and health expenditures and insurances are supplied by the state rather than the involvement of the private sector. Average unemployment expenditures in OECD countries are 3.6% of the total public spending and developed European countries are above this average.

Table 6.1 alone is not sufficient to make evaluations, as it only comprises social assistance expenditures of the state. As seen on Table 6.1, the social spending level of Turkey at 10.5% is very low when compared to OECD countries. This does not necessarily mean that Turkey is insufficient in this area; one must take into account that (*Zakat, sadaqa, awqaf*, etc.) play an important role in Muslim countries as an additional support mechanism to the state's social spending.

As seen in the Figure 6.1, Muslim countries have the highest-level social expenditure only among low-income countries. In high-level countries, only Bahrain is listed and it is among the last countries in the social expenditure. In middle-income countries, we see Tunisia, Iran and Morocco among the highest rankings and Turkey, Indonesia, Malaysia, Pakistan, etc. among the lowest. Especially in low- and middle-income Muslim countries, social structure and close family ties enable the state to take a lesser role in this area. On the other hand, we don't have sufficient data for the voluntary assistance supplied by individuals and charity organizations, this scarcity constrains our ability to compare Muslim and non-Muslim countries in total social assistance spending. In this respect, it is very important for the state to institutionalize organizations which work in the area of social assistance for building up a more efficient and effective system.

As we observed from Table 6.1, the average social spending of OECD countries as a percentage to GDP was 19.2%. Roughly one third of this expenditure was in health, so we can say that in average 15.6% is the amount of spending when health is excluded. In Figure 6.2, we can see social protection and health care spending of OIC countries separated in income levels. As seen from these figures, none of the OIC countries is near the OECD average in social policy spending, excluding or including health care expenditures. The closest countries to the OECD average are Egypt, Turkey and Iran at 13.21%, 13.11% and 12.53% respectively. The main

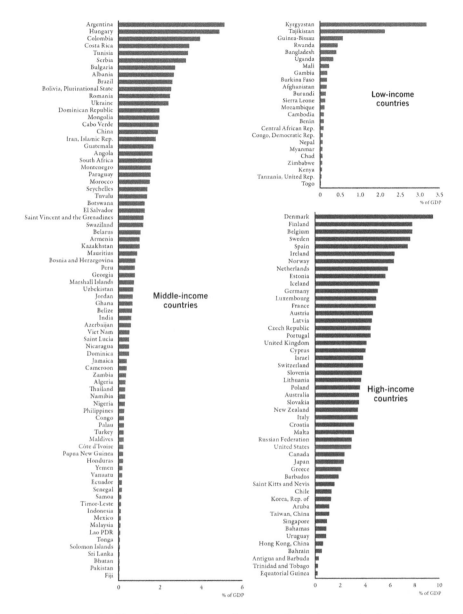

Figure 6.1 Nonhealth public social protection expenditure for people of working age, by national income (percentage of GDP), 2010/11

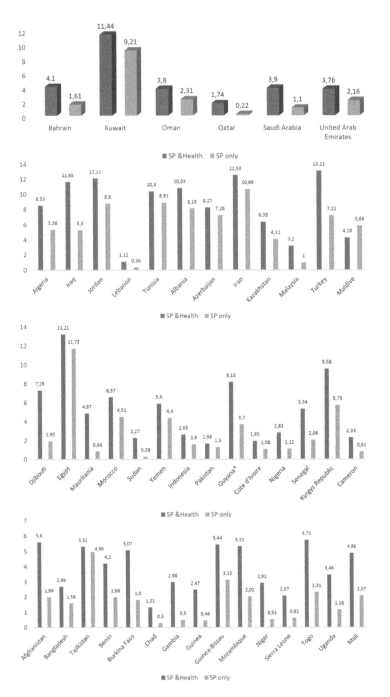

Figure 6.2 Total public social protection and health care expenditure (% of GDP) in high-income, upper middle-income, lower middle-income and low-income (respectively) Organisation of Islamic Cooperation (OIC) countries

causes behind this difference between Western countries and Muslim countries other than income levels is the fact that Muslim countries have a social and family structure which supplies a safety net and voluntary organizations, whom also take on a very important role, whereas Western countries choose to institutionalize social assistance system led by the various states.

An Islamic prospect of social aid

Islam orders some obligatory actions or recommends some voluntary actions, such as *zakah, sadaqa, waqf*, in order to sustain social justice and social solidarity within the society. Islamic history shows us that the institutionalization of these tools facilitated social justice among societies, not only with government itself but also with contributions of nongovernmental organizations. These actions aims to save poor or needy people from poverty and then make them wealthy and ready to help other people. All Muslims should show devoutness and an effort to earn their subsistence without being dependent on the help of others. Islam does not approve of the action of a person who is healthy or rich or strong and willing to take a share from poor people. Accordingly, some *hadiths* reported from Sunan Abu-Dawud quoted here:

> Narrated Ubaydullah ibn Adl ibn al-Khiyar: two men informed me that they went to the Prophet (*pbuh*) when he was at the Farewell Pilgrimage while he was distributing the *sadaqa* and asked him for some of it. He looked us up and down, and seeing that we were robust, he said: If you wish, I shall give you something, but there is nothing spare in it for a rich man or for one who is strong and able to earn a living.
>
> Narrated Abdullah ibn Amr ibn al-'As: the Prophet (*pbuh*) said: *Sadaqa* may not be given to a rich man or to one who has strength and is sound in limbs.
>
> Narrated Ata ibn Yasar: the Prophet (*pbuh*) said: *Sadaqa* may not be given to rich man, with the exception of five classes: one who fights in Allah's path, or who collects it, or a debtor, or a man who buys it with his money, or a man who has a poor neighbour who has been given *sadaqa* and gives a present to the rich man.
> (Sunan Abu-Dawud, Kitab Al-Zakat, Hadith No: 1629–1631)

Sunan ibn Majah reports another *hadith* from Anas bin Malik. He narrated that:

> A man from among the Ansar came to the Prophet (*pbuh*) and begged from him. He said, "Do you have anything in your house?" He said: "Yes, a blanket, part of which we cover ourselves with and part we spread beneath us, and a bowl from which we drink water." He said:

"Give them to me." So he brought them to him, and the Messenger of Allah (*pbuh*) took them in his hand and said, "Who will buy these two things?" A man said: "I will by them for one Dirham." He said: "Who will offer more than a Dirham?" two or three times. A man said: "I will buy them for two Dirham." So he gave them to him and took the two Dirham, which he gave to the Ansari and said: "Buy food with one of them and give it to your family, and buy an axe with the other and bring it to me." So he did that, and the Messenger of Allah (*pbuh*) took it and fixed a handle to it, and said: "Go and gather firewood, and I do not want to see you for fifteen days." So he went and gathered firewood and sold it, then he came back, and he had earned ten Dirham. The Prophet (*pbuh*) said: "Buy food with some of it and clothes with some." Then he said: "This is better for you than coming with begging (appearing) as a spot on your face on the Day of Resurrection. Begging is only appropriate for one who is extremely poor or who is in severe debt, or one who must pay painful blood money."

(Sunan Ibn Majah, Vol. 3, Book 12, Hadith 2198)

We can infer from the last *hadith* that, a healthy person should not only depend on his own labor, but he should also make use of his belongings. This might seem like an extreme example as we live in an era in which many people supply their labor and avoid entrepreneurship. But, this example shows us how Islam encourages entrepreneurship. Here we listen to the Gleams from Said Nursi, his inference about unemployment and entrepreneurship:

There is nothing idle in existence; the unemployed man works on account of nonexistence. The most miserable, wretched, and distressed person, is the unemployed. For idleness is nonexistence within existence, death within life. Whereas exertion is the life of existence, and the waking state of life!

(The Words, Gleams, p. 764)

Today, many people declare that they are poor and needy and look for help. It became a serious matter for *zakah* and *sadaqa* givers and for charity institutions to distinguish the real poor from healthy and workable aid dependents. We call them dependent because they are addicted to laziness and free money, which in turn affects social order and economic welfare negatively.

From the *maqasid al-Shari'ah* perspective, Jan et al. (2015) defines three goals to be reached for the development of the society, where work or *a'mal* is counted as the second important goal. In Islam, it is a duty of every able-bodied Muslim to earn *halal rizq* or lawful earning through work and a duty of the community to build the earth and develop its resources for the benefit of humanity. Therefore, Islam encourages all capable people to work both for their self-improvement and for the community but also to gain the pleasure of Allah to achieve *falah* in hereafter. Third important goal is social welfare security system, which should function in four areas according to Kamali (as cited in Jan et al., 2015). It should begin with family which is the inner circle, and then it should go through outer circles, respectively the community at large, followed by cooperation among smaller groups and association and lastly supported through the legal payments of alms and voluntary charities. In Islam, all essential needs of citizens, such as food, clothing, shelter, health and education, should be fulfilled. This collective obligation of the society is a guarantee for social and economic justice among the citizens.

Origins of zakah, sadaqa *and* waqf

Zakah is a compulsory obligation for Muslims, whereas *sadakah* is a voluntary action. For non-Muslims, there are other compulsory payments, if they live in a Muslim country. All these payments have effects on the economy and social life. We know who should pay *zakah* and who has the right on it from the Holy Qur'an and from the Prophet's (*pbuh*) hadiths.

The government used to collect and distribute *zakah* within the era of the Prophet (*pbuh*) and Khulafa-e-Rashideen. In this period and in the early Umayyad period, *zakah* officials used to assess the *zakatable* assets of potential *zakah* payers and collect the amount due. Referring to Ahmed (2004), in that period, distribution of *zakah* was local, meaning that *zakah* proceeds were disbursed in the same region where they were collected. He refers to some reports which claim that this tradition was continued during the time of Umar bin Abdul Aziz (99-101H). Ahmed (2004) also shows us some evidence from the time of Umar bin Al-Khattab (13-22H) and Umar bin Abdul Aziz, which prove that poverty was eliminated in some regions during that time, so that *zakah* collections could not be distributed in those regions due to lack of poor. Therefore, these undistributed collections used to be gathered in Bayt-al Mal, which was established properly and institutionalized during the period of Umar bin Al-Khattab.

As *zakah* is imposed on idle wealth of the *zakah* payers, those *zakah* payers are supposed to mobilize their idle wealth to productive areas, if they do not want to pay *zakah*. This is a kind of punishment on idle wealth owners by taking a part of it and giving to the poor, so that it can compulsorily be productive at poors' hands.

Waqf (pl. *awqaf*) is a voluntary charity and it is also used to refer to a charitable institution, which is the institutionalized form of this voluntary action. It developed in the Muslim world long before it did in the West and facilitated the development of Muslim societies. There are also philanthropic actions which financed many public services and facilities including the construction or establishment of mosques, institutes of education, libraries, hospitals, soup kitchens, public fountains and bridges has been financed by the *waqf* system (Ismail et al., 2013).

The Islamic fundamental of *waqf* comes from the concept of *sadaqa jariya*, which can be translated as ongoing charity. The Prophet (*pbuh*) promotes giving *sadaqa* which has continuing benefits, as narrated by Abu Huraira: *Allah's Messenger (pbuh)* said:

> When the son of Adam dies no further reward is recorded for his actions, with three exceptions: charity whose benefit is continuous, knowledge from which benefit continues to be reaped, or the supplication of a righteous son (for him).
>
> (Imam An Nawawi, n.d.)

Kahf (n.d.) argues that the first *waqf* action of the Prophet (*pbuh*) was the purchase of the land and construction of the mosque of Madinah. His companions followed him on this purpose and many *awqaf* were created. One example for this is the *waqf* of Umar bin Al-Khattab, as reported from Ibn Umar:

> Umar acquired a piece of land at Khaibar. He came to Allah's Apostle (may peace be upon him) and sought his advice in regard to it. He said: Allah's Messenger, I have acquired land in Khaibar. I have never acquired property more valuable for me than this, so what do you command me to do with it? Thereupon he (Allah's Apostle) said: If you like, you may keep the corpus intact and give its produce as Sadaqa. So Umar gave it as Sadaqa declaring that property must not be sold or inherited or given away as gift. And Umar devoted it to the poor, to the nearest kin, and to the emancipation of slaves, aired in the way of Allah and guests. There is no sin for one, who administers it if he eats something from it in a reasonable manner, or if he feeds his friends and does not hoard goods (for himself). He (the narrator) said: I narrated this hadith to Muhammad, but as I reached the (words) "without hoarding (for himself) out of it." he (Muhammad said: "without storing the property with a view to becoming rich." Ibn Aun said: He who reads this book (pertaining to waqf) informed me that in it (the words are) "without storing the property with a view to becoming rich."
>
> (Sahih Muslim, Book 013, Hadith 4006)

Ahmed (2004) classifies *awqaf* in three groups according to their objectives. In the first group, the objective of the *waqf* is the society at large, that is called as philantrophic (*khayri*) or public (*amm*). In the second group, the objective is related to the family and descendants of the *waqf*'s creator or another specific person. This kind of *waqf* is called as family (*ahli*) or private (*khass*). The last group has combined objectives to partly serve both the family and descendants and partly the society.

As outlined by Ahmed (2004), many scholars including the Shafiites, the Hanbalites and Abu Yusuf and Muhammad of the Hanafites support the ownership of *waqf* assets or properties belong to Allah. The founder of the *waqf* sets the objectives for which the *waqf* property can be used and sets the rules for which the *waqf* should be managed. *Awqaf* are generally perpetual, however no clue exists imposing a restriction for a temporary *waqf* (Ahmed, 2004).

Productive utilization of zakah, sadaqa *and* waqf *sources*

Kahf (n.d.) summarizes the *fiqhi* position of distribution of *zakah, sadaqa* and *waqf* sources that targets poverty elimination. Primarily, a person or a family may be given as much as needed for their physical, physiologic and social needs. A healthy and workable person would be given what he needs enabling him to be a productive earner. Other than being financial aid as a seed capital for start-up business, this may be in form of training, rehabilitation or craft's tools. *Zakah* proceeds also can be used to establish productive projects and making *zakah* recipients a share owner and maybe a manager of that project.

Senadjki and Sulaiman (2015) studied the roles of Islamic values in alleviating poverty and encouraging people to have a better life. To alleviate poverty, they divided responsibilities into three parts and assigned them to three parties, such as everyone's self-responsibility, community's responsibility and the state's responsibility. We already said that, in principle, every Muslim should be productive and rely on their selves for their income. *Zakah, sadaqa* and *waqf* and maybe other forms of social aids and charity constitute the community's responsibility. As the obligation of an Islamic state, the minimum livelihood of people who cannot afford their subsistence like the poor, widows, disabled people and others should be guaranteed. They conducted a one-way ANOVA test to assess the effect of self-responsibility and behavior on the welfare of households. Results listed below are confirming our arguments:

- Those who prayed to Allah and made an effort had a higher mean income than who only prayed Allah and those who neither prayed nor made an effort.
- Those who believed poorness is their destiny therefore spent no effort and had less mean income than those who refused that idea.
- Those who believed that resources were not sufficient therefore they cannot find a job or work had less mean income than those who refused this idea.
- Those who seek for *zakah* had less mean income than those who never or seldom seek *zakah*.
- Those who never seek *sadaqa* had higher mean income than those who sometimes seek it.
- People who generally borrow an interest-free loan had higher income than the others who seldom or never did it.
- The poor who seek assistance in the form of *zakah, sadaqa* and an interest-free loan in investments and savings had higher income than those who spent them all.

Kahf (n.d.) claims that cash and investment *awqaf* were invented by Muslims, which is dated to the end of the first *hijri* century. Once cash granted to *waqf*, operation of cash *waqf* can be in the form of cash given as lending to borrowers or in the form of cash invested and its return assigned to *waqf* beneficiaries (Ahmed, 2004).

Other than Hanafites, many scholars accept the endowment of cash and movable property since they do not seek the perpetuity feature for validity of a *waqf*. Cash *awqaf* established during the period of the Ottoman Empire were generally based upon Imam Zufar's fatwa. According to the records of Istanbul religious courts, cash *awqaf* was first established in the time of Fatih Sultan Muhammad. The rapid spread of cash *awqaf* across the country was fostered by some factors, such as *waqf* property getting damaged as time went by and their repair and maintenance was costly, whereas endowed cash did not require such costs. In addition to that, economic disruption at that time increased the need for cash and this need was saturated by cash *awqaf* (Kurt, 2011).

In the 19th century, some criticisms were raised by various intellectuals of that time, mainly arguing that these institutions were harmful for Muslim societies, as they hinder social and economic development (*terakki*), prevent individual ownership and entrepreneurship and promote idleness, laziness, poverty and fatalism. Elmalılı Hamdi Yazir, a Muslim scholar of that time, did not share those criticisms. He claimed that these could be true if only people were taught to earn their living by resting on others help and *sadaqa*. Islam indoctrinates human beings the opposite way, it suggests that people help/aid, not to seek help/aid. He also supports that a *waqf* which constantly spends to teach the poor how to earn wealth as being more beneficial than a *waqf* which sometimes spends to feed the poor (Cilingir, 2015).

Conclusion and some policy implications

In light of the discussed Islamic perspective of social aids, we can infer some policies which can lead us to the efficient and righteous utilization of sources available for the poor and needy. First of all, individuals have to be encouraged to work in order to get over their laziness. Laziness is a significant factor contributing to poverty, so we need to define its causes. The Flashes (2009) gives us a clue:

> Excess of wastefulness leads to lack of contentment. And lack of contentment destroys enthusiasm for work; it causes laziness, opens the door to complaining about life, and makes the dissatisfied person complain continuously. Also, it destroys sincerity, and opens the door to hypocrisy. And it destroys self-respect, and points the way to begging.
>
> (as cited in Umar et al., 2015)

In Nursi's views, too much spending may lead to, through illegal means of finding money, higher consumption and lower production. Lending more money for consumption causes less money to be left in the treasury that would otherwise be used for productivity in the economy. This would result in higher prices and an increased number of poor people. The main cause for poverty is the misuse of economic resources and too much consumption. (Umar et al., 2015)

Secondly, Islamic countries have an advantage as they have *zakah* and *waqf* foundations, which have been developed and institutionalized throughout history with great contributions to social welfare. Family-based and community-based cooperation and traditional methods are significant means for fighting against poverty in these countries. Therefore, Islamic countries do not need to mimic western countries and try to implement more state-oriented social aid policies. What has to be done is to make government responsible for monitoring and regulating *zakah* and *waqf* activities in their country, to ensure social aids are going to the right place just in time. The most crucial point is the coordination of these parties. This requires the formation of a database, in which all social aids from the government and charities are recorded in detail. Combined with other policy implications, this would be a huge first step for productive utilization of both government's social assistance and *zakah* and *waqf* resources. This would increase effectiveness of social aid programs, save money and facilitate the elimination of poverty.

As a next step, the government should collaborate with charitable foundations, to connect people to the labor market and give them permanent jobs with sufficient salaries. If these employed people stay poor while working and are not able to meet their basic needs, they should be getting social aids as long as their status remains the same. Other than financial support, poor people should have access to health and education services, in order to have equal opportunity like others and to be qualified for all kinds of work. If we want to connect people to the labor market, we should focus on giving training programs and decreasing financial aids, so that these people can stand on their own feet.

Social policy measures focusing on education and training, social services and community work are better for longer term goals, such as encouraging and facilitating individual growth, development and social integration. On the contrary, if the aim is to minimize disincentives to work and to promote individual responsibility in the short term, then the focus should be on conditions of eligibility and the adjustment of social assistance rates with earnings levels (Ditch, 1999).

Notes

1 Many different kinds of social assistance implementations have been classified by Barrientos A., Rebecca, H., & Scott, J. (2008). *Social Assistance in Developing Countries Database*. Brooks World Poverty Institute.
2 These policies include a wide range of different programs including; labor market trainings, subsidized employment, public employment services, youth programs and programs for the disabled.

3 A good example for this implementation is in England, where citizens continue to receive social assistance if the job they have generates income below a certain threshold (www.gov.uk/income-support).

References

Ahmed, H. (2004). *Role of Zakah and Awqaf in Poverty Alleviation (Occasional Paper)*, IRTI Occasional Paper 201. The Islamic Research and Teaching Institute (IRTI).

Arslan, N. (2014). Sosyal Yardımlar ve İstihdam İlişkisinin İncelenmesi: Sivas İlinde Bir Alan Araştırması. *Cumhuriyet University EUL Journal of Social Sciences*, V(I), 16–31.

Barrientos, A., Holmes, R., & Scott, J. (2008). *Social Assistance in Developing Countries Database (Version 4.0 August 2008)*. Manchester: Brooks World Poverty Institute. Retrieved from www.chronicpoverty.org/uploads/publication_files/Social_Assistance_Database_Version4_August2008.pdf.

Barrientos, A., & Santıbáñez, C. (2009). New Forms of Social Assistance and the Evolution of Social Protection in Latin America. *Journal of Latin American Studies*, 41(1), 1–26.

Baumberg, B. (2014). Benefits and the Cost of Living. *British Social Attitudes*, 31, NatCen Social Research.

Bolvig, I., Jensen, P., & Rosholm, M. (2003). *The Employment Effects of Active Social Policy*, IZA DP No. 736.

Cilingir, H. (2015). Elmalılı Muhammed Hamdi Yazır on Waqf Issues in the Last Period of Ottoman Empire. *İnsan ve Toplum (Humanity & Society)*, 5(9), 33–52. Doi:10.12658/human.society.5.9.M0111.

Ditch, J. (1999). The Structure and Dynamics of Social Assistance in the European Union. In *Linking Welfare and Work* (pp. 59–70). Luxembourg: European Foundation for the Improvement of Living and Working Conditions.

Geldof, G. (1999). New Activation Policies: Promises and Risks. In *Linking Welfare and Work* (pp. 13–26) Luxembourg: European Foundation for the Improvement of Living and Working Conditions.

Góra, M., & Schmidt, C. M. (1998). Long-Term Unemployment, Unemployment Benefits and Social Assistance: The Polish Experience. *Empirical Economics*, 23(1/2), 23–85. Retrieved from https://ssrn.com/abstract=122948.

Imam An Nawawi. (n.d.). *Riyadh as-Salihin (The Gardens of the Righteous) (Abridged)*. Dar Al-Manarah Vol. 2, Chapter 151, p. 653, No. 486. Retrieved from www.salaattime.com/hadith-three-exceptions/.

Immervoll, H., Jenkins, S. P., & Königs, S. (2015). *Are Recipients of Social Assistance "Benefit Dependent"? Concepts, Measurement and Results for Selected Countries*. OECD Social, Employment and Migration Working Papers, No. 162. OECD Publishing. Retrieved from http://dx.doi.org/10.1787/5jxrcmgpc6mn-en.

Ismail, A. G., Zaenal, M. H., & Shafiai, H. (2013). *Philanthrophy in Islam: A Promise to Welfare Economics System*, IRTI Working Paper 1435-03.

Jan, S., Ullah, K., & Asutay, M. (2015). Knowledge, Work, and Social Welfare as Islamic Socio-Economic Development Goals. *Journal of Islamic Banking and Finance*, 32(3), 9–19.

Kenworthy, L. (1998). *Do Social-Welfare Policies Reduce Poverty? A Cross-National Assessment*, Luxembourg Income Study Working Paper No. 188.

Social aids and willingness to work   105

Social aids and willingness to work   105

Kahf, M. (n.d.). Role of Zakah and Awqaf in Reducing Poverty: A Proposed Institutional Setting within the Spirit of Shari'ah. _Thoughts on Economics_, 18(3), 58–59.

Kurt, İ. (2011). Kredi Kaynağı Olarak Para Vakıfları (Cash Awqaf as Lending Sources). In _İslâm Hukuku Açısından Tarihten Günümüze Kredi ve Finans Yöntemleri_ (pp. 315–339). Istanbul: Ensar Neşriyat.

Lemieux, T., & Milligan, K. (2008). Incentive Effects of Social Assistance: A Regression Discontinuity Approach. _Journal of Econometrics_, 142(2), 807–828.

OECD. (2014). _Society at a Glance 2014: OECD Social Indicators._ Paris: OECD Publishing. Doi:10.1787/soc_glance-2014-en.

Rawlings, L. B. (2004). _A New Approach to Social Assistance: Latin America's Experience with Conditional Cash Transfer Programs._ Washington, DC: World Bank.

Riphahn, R. T. (2001). Rational Poverty or Poor Rationality? The Take-Up of Social Assistance Benefits. _Review of Income and Wealth_, 47(3), 379–398.

Sahih Muslim, Book 013, Hadith 4006. Retrieved from www.searchtruth.com/book_display.php?book=013&translator=2&start=0&number=4006#4006.

Schneider, H., & Uhlendorff, A. (2005). The Transition from Welfare to Work and the Role of Potential Labor Income. _Journal of Applied Social Sciences Studies_, 125(1), 51–61.

Senadjki, A., & Sulaiman, J. (2015). An Empirical Study on the Influence of Islamic Values in Poverty Alleviation. _Journal of Islamic Accounting and Business Research_, 6(2), 222–243.

Sunan Abu-Dawud, Kitab Al-Zakat, Hadith No: 1629-1631. Retrieved from www.searchtruth.com/book_display.php?book=9&translator=3&start=40.

Sunan Ibn Majah, Vol. 3, Book 12, Hadith 2198. Retrieved from http://sunnah.com/urn/1265170.

Surender, R., Noble, M., Wright, G., & Ntshongwana, P. (2010). Social Assistance and Dependency in South Africa: An Analysis of Attitudes to Paid Work and Social Grants. _Journal of Social Policy_, 39(2), 203–221.

The Flashes. (Revised 2009 edition), The Nineteenth Flash, p. 196. Retrieved from www.nur.gen.tr/en.html#.

The Words, Gleams. Retrieved from www.nur.gen.tr/en.html#.

Umar, M. B., Ismail, S., & Abdullahi, M. S. (2015). Sustainable Economic Development through View of Said Nursi: The Challenge of the West. ICIC Conference Paper, 6–7 September, Universiti Sultan Zainal Abidin, Malaysia.

7 The role of *waqfs* in socio-economic life in terms of poverty alleviation

Husnu Tekin

With the emergence of the industrial revaluation in the 18th and 19th century, there have been numerous changes in the economic life due to new production techniques. As is well-known, there are always pros and cons for these kinds of tremendous changes for different parts of societies, while some parts of societies or some countries benefiting from these kinds of substantial changes, some not or some benefit only partially.

Accordingly, one may argue that one of the most critical shortcomings of the new economic system is the fact that the income per capita gap between countries has increased dramatically as well as income inequality inside countries. According to the most recent data, as of 2012, around 13% of the world's population lives at, or below, $1.90 a day and the same figure for low-income countries is around 50%. On the other hand, income inequality is another problem of today's world. Even in developed countries income inequality matters. However, the situation in terms of the poverty headline and income inequality in Muslim countries is quite bad.

Because of this reality, most of the international financial institutions have taken alleviating poverty all around the world as a duty to reduce the negative effects of the economic system.

On the other hand, the *waqf* institutions appeared in the history as charity organizations carrying out various social functions and were encouraged by Islam. Today, numerous local and foreign studies exist on *waqfs* active in during heyday of the Ottoman period. The main objective of this study is to reveal the main functions of *waqfs*, which are the main institutions of Ottoman Empire in the socioeconomic life.

For this aim, in our study, firstly we will try to demonstrate the current situation of world economy in terms of poverty and income inequality, then, we are going to assess the *waqf* institutions as one of the premodern institutions to fight for poverty in those periods by touching upon their roles in providing social justice in the society in the time of Ottoman Empire.

Fighting against poverty: millennium development goals and contemporary efforts of IFIs for reducing poverty

New production techniques emerged in the 18th and 19th century with the help of new inventions such as steam-operated machines lead an increase in capital accumulation and so-called industrial revaluation. (BLUES, 2016) Even if meaning of revaluation implies suddenness as in the case of French revolution, which lasted a few years, the industrial revolution was not a sudden and took too many years since it implies mostly changes to the economic systems.

No doubt that, thanks to the industrial revolution, growth of industrial production increased sharply. These huge changes in the production techniques caused numerous changes in the economic life as well as social life in general. (Charls, 2000) Of course, there are always pros and cons for these kinds of tremendous changes for different parts of societies, while some parts of societies or some countries benefit, some not.

Therefore, some international financial institutions took alleviating poverty all around the world as a duty to reduce the negative effects of the aforementioned economic system. As is well-known, many International Financial Institutions (IFIs) exist whose main goal is to fight against poverty all around the world. The most important ones are the United Nations, the World Bank, the Asia Development Bank and the Islamic Development Bank. If you look at the webpage of these institutions, you can see that the main objective of these institutions is to alleviate poverty in their region or globally. For instance:

> Since its founding in 1966, ADB has been driven by an inspiration and dedication to improving people's lives in Asia and the Pacific. By targeting our investments wisely, in partnership with our developing member countries and other stakeholders, we can alleviate poverty and help create a world in which everyone can share in the benefits of sustained and inclusive growth.
>
> (ADB, 2016)

Accordingly, at the beginning of the new millennium, world leaders gathered and determined eight targets to be achieved at the end of 2016, the so-called Millennium Development Goals (MDGs), to alleviate extreme poverty which is defined by those living on less than $1.25 a day in the world. As of today, when we look at the results of these efforts, even if a significant decline has been achieved in global poverty, 14% of the total population of the developing world which means 836 million people is still living on less than $1.25 a day. Therefore, this shows us that there much more effort is needed to fight against poverty globally. For this reason, world leaders gathered in 2015 again and agreed on the to-do list over the next 15 years to alleviate poverty and set more with the 17 Sustainable Development Goals. (UN, 2016)

Current situation in the world regarding poverty and income inequality, especially in Muslim countries

According to the most recent estimates by the World Bank, in 2012, 12.7% of the world's population lives at or below $1.90 a day. The same ratio was 37% in 1990 and 44% in 1981. When we look at the poverty data deeply, one can easily see that developing counties account for a significant share of the high poverty rate for the world. As seen in graph I, the same ratio is almost 50% in the low-income countries while it is "0" in almost all developed countries. However, it does not mean that there is no problem in developed countries in terms of poverty or inequality issues. The main problem in developed countries is income inequality. As depicted in Figure 7.1, in most countries, while the share of a small part of the population in total income is so high, the large number of the population has to share the rest of the national income.

The GINI coefficient is used as an indicator for understanding the level of income inequality in a country. In general, while Latin American countries have a higher GINI coefficient representing disorder in the income distribution, in terms of a low GINI coefficient, even if some developed countries such as Nordic countries have a lower GINI coefficient, it seems impossible to generalize about countries according to income level. That is, when we look at the Figure 7.2, even in the US, the richest country in the world, the GINI coefficient is relatively higher than, for example, Sri Lanka. Therefore, here we may conclude that even in developed countries income distribution matters. According to news by USA Today, 1 out of 7 US citizens are suffering with hunger and use food bank. (USA Today, 2014)

As for the Muslim countries, the situation is not different from the rest of the world in terms of poverty and income inequality. As seen in Figure 7.3,

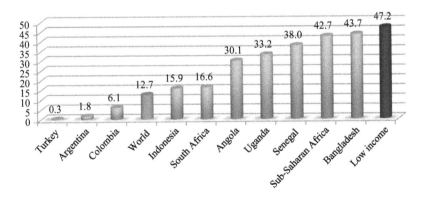

Figure 7.1 Poverty headcount ratio at $1.90 a day (2011 PPP) (% of population)

Note: The latest available data for Senegal, Indonesia and Angola are from 2011.
Source: World Bank Database

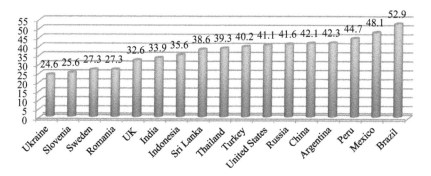

Figure 7.2 GINI coefficient in selected countries, 2012

Note: The latest available data for the selected countries are employed.
Source: The World Bank

most Muslim countries suffer from a poverty issue. Although the Muslim population accounts for approximately 25% of the total world population, half of the global poverty resides in Muslim countries. According to the data, one in five Arabs lives on less than $2 per day. Therefore, the Muslim world seems to be among the poorest in the world.

Economic theory suggests that the main determinant of poverty in an economy is the income level of the economy and this problem mostly emanates from the fact that a large segment of societies have little access to the basic social needs such as education, nutrition and, do not command sufficient material resources to improve their incomes and welfare. Hence, here we may conclude that poverty is very much associated with deprivation. (Zeinelabidin, 1996) However, the poverty and income inequality even in developed countries shows us that there is something wrong with the current economic system or theories in terms of income distribution in the world.

Accordingly, in this study, we are going to try and see if the *waqf* system employed in the Muslim world, especially during the Ottoman Empire, could be part of the solution for fighting poverty in the Muslim world as well as in the rest of the world. For this aim, firstly we will present some information about the *waqf* system in the following.

Premodern institutions for fighting against poverty in Muslim world: *waqfs* as a solution in poverty alleviation

Definition of waqf *and types*

Encouraged by Islamic thought, *waqf* institutions which are a kind of charity institution, have played a significant role by carrying out various social functions in the society such as education, health and income distribution

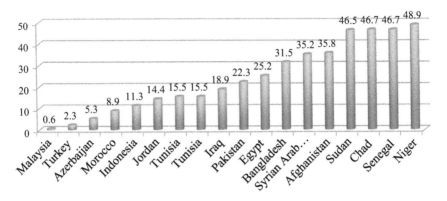

Figure 7.3 Poverty headcount ratio at national poverty lines (% of population)

in the history of Muslim world. Numerous studies exist on *waqfs* especially the ones in time of the Ottoman Empire.

Although there are several different definitions for *waqf*, which literally means hold, confinement, or prohibition in Arabic, we may generally define it as an unconditional and permanent dedication of any property which is possible and lawful according to Islamic Law to benefit from with implied detention in the ownership of God in such a manner that the property of the owner may be extinguished and its profit may revert to, or be applied to, the benefit of mankind except for purposes prohibited by Islam. Imam Muhammad and Imam Abu Yusuf define *waqf* in the context of Islamic law as a property whose benefit is allocated to the public and its property is in the ownership of God. (www.islamahlaki.com, accessed on December 5, 2015) Hence, here the main idea is that an individual, being aware of the fact that he or she is the caliph of God in the world, endows his/her property for God's sake. (Bayartan, 2008; Kudat, 2015; Türkoğlu, 2013). While a person who endowed his/her property is called "*vâkıf*," the endowed property is called as "*mevkuf*." The one who wants to endow his/her property applies to the court and enrolls to an official files named "*vakfiye*" which determines the conditions of *waqf*.

The main aim of the *waqfs* is to make wealth transfer voluntarily, so-called as "philantrophy" in western terminology (Cizakça, 2015).

Taking into consideration the studies on *waqfs*, we can see that there are several classifications related to these institutions. For instance, in his article, Cizakça (2015) classifies *waqfs* as movable and immovable *waqfs* considering the structure of the property endowed and also he argues that it is possible to make another classification by taking into consideration of the its managerial structure. While in some cases, the management of the *waqf* is carried out by its founder, in some cases the government or the guardians of the founder undertake the management of the *waqf*.

Kahf (2013) classifies *waqfs* as religious *waqfs*, family *waqfs* and charity *waqfs*. While the main aim of the religious *waqfs* to meet the religious needs of the society, charity *waqfs* aim to meet the needs of poor. As for the family *waqfs*, they hope to create an income source for the next generations of the founder of *waqf*. According to a research done by Yediyıldız (1982b), only 7% of the *waqfs* in the 18th century served people other than family members. Hence, we may conclude family *waqfs* were accounting for significant part of the total *waqfs* in the last period of Ottoman Empire.

Historical background

Actually, when we look at the historical background of the *waqf* idea, we see that this idea is as old as the history of human beings. It has appeared in every society from past to present, the desire of religious people to doing good is a humanitarian action. Accordingly, numerous records exist that many civilizations have used this kind of institution to meet the various needs of society. For example, there are some evident that from ancient Anatolian People Hittites and Uighurs have used similar institutions like *waqfs*. In addition, despite no direct evidence that there are some signals showing that Babylon and Sumerians have employed this kind of institution. Moreover, it is understood that the *waqf* tradition existed in ancient Greek, Byzantine and in the earlier communities where Buddhist belief prevailed in (Bayartan, 2008).

However, even though *waqfs* have been used in other civilizations, these institutions have been employed in Muslim civilization more commonly and carried out both very important social and economic functions in Muslim communities.

The first known *waqf* in the pre-Islamic period is Ka'bah. As for Islam, the first known *waqfs* are Masjid al-Quba and Al-Masjid al-Nabawi (Kudat, 2015). Having been legalized by Islam *waqf* institutions were established by Caliph Omer according to many scholars (Köprülü, 2012).

However, when mentioned *waqfs*, the first state that comes to mind is the Ottoman Empire. Because, the *waqf* system in the Ottoman Empire became so prevalent that these institutions comprised a significant share of the total Ottoman Economy. *Waqfs* played an important role to meet the main needs of society by stepping in especially during the periods that the government has a weak budget to provide necessary services to the public (Şimşek, 2015).

The first implementations of a *waqf* system occurred during the time of Sultan Orhan, the second ruler of the Ottoman Empire. Sultan Orhan endowed some immovable properties to meet the current expenses of the first madrasah established in Iznik. *Waqfs* in the Ottoman Empire was not only limited religious activities but also in service many social and economic public services (Bayartan, 2008). It is stated that in Istanbul alone there were 2515 *waqfs* in 1546 (Barkan & Ayverdi, 1970). Since 1 out of 3 of the total productive land was under the management of *waqfs*, these institutions were very important an economic sense. According to a research done by Yediyıldız (1982a), the population of Istanbul was 700,000 and 30,000 out of this was being fed by *waqfs* in the 18th Century. On the other hand, according to several studies, *waqfs* were one of the most significant finance sources for Muslim world.

Actually, we know that *waqfs* existed not only in the Ottoman Empire in those times but also in other Muslim countries such as Malaysia, Indonesia, India, Morocco and Algeria places that Muslim communities lived (Cizakça, 2000, pp. 24, 60–69, 167; Hoexter, 1998)

During the last days of the Ottoman Empire, influenced by the western world the *waqfs* were centralized and as a result of this, all properties of money *waqfs* were transferred to the Vakiflar Bank established in 1954 (Cizakça, 2015).

The motivation to establish a waqf

There is no doubt that, the idea of eternity exists in the nature of human beings. Hence, we may state that in general, *waqf* institutions have emerged as a consequence of this idea.

On the other hand, we may argue that there are further reasons emerging of *waqf* system in the Islamic civilizations in addition to the one mentioned above. Even though there are no direct verses in the Holy Qur'an expressing that charities or good works must be done through *waqfs*, some Islamic scholars have deduced that some verses in the Holy Qur'an point out the importance of these institutions. One of the most attributed ones among these verses is Ali Imran 92: "Never will you attain the good (reward) until you spend (in the way of Allah) from that which you love. And whatever you spend—indeed, Allah is knowing of it."[1] On the other hand, Islamic scholars also refer to the *hadith* (Müslim, Vasiyyet 14.,. Ebû Dâvûd, Vasâya 14; Tirmizi, Ahkâm 36; Nesâî, Vasâyâ 8) mentioning that the record of deeds would not close as limited to these three things which are improved children, useful knowledge and s*adaqah-i cariyah* (charity) to emphases the importance the *waqf* institutions. Some Islamic scholars argue that in this *hadith* the term of "*sadaqah-i cariyah*" refers to *waqf* institutions (Kudat, 2015).

Of course, it is possible to count many motives rather than religious motives to establish a *waqf* too. For instance, as mentioned above, the wish to be immortal or gaining a social statue in the society may play a role in establishing a *waqf*. In addition to these motives, especially in the Ottoman Empire we may add one more motive to establish a *waqf*, which is to protect the property rights against some illegal or legal confiscations. As is well-known, in the classical period the Ottoman Elites faced the risk of confiscation and some evident show that they preferred to establish a *waqf* to get out of this situation (Cizakça, 2015). In addition to all these motives, Kuran (2001) asserts that the motive of having a voice in politics was one of the important motives to establish a *waqf* in Ottoman Empire.

Working principle of waqfs

The fundamental characteristic of *waqfs* is their eternity. Hence, the thing endowed must be a real estate etc. However, we see that various entities have been endowed in Muslim communities such as sheep, horses, camels, books, jewels etc. Accordingly, in the classical period there had been comprehensive discussions on what kind of entities could be endowed (Kahf, 2013).

In principal, the founder of the *waqf* appointed the management of the *waqf* so-called "Mutevelli" or "Nazir" which means trustee. The main duty of the board of trustees is to provide continuity to the income of the *waqf*. There were many different types of *waqfs* in terms of purpose of establishing. Even there were *waqfs* aiming to send people to Hajj and getting married young ladies to join (Kahf, 2013). We may state that the goal of the *waqf* might change from region to region and time to time.

When we look at the working principle of *waqfs* in accordance with the types of *waqfs* mentioned in the previous sections, we see that the procedure in real estate *waqfs* is simple: a piece of real estate which can be rented is endowed and the income from the rent is used in charities in accordance with the aim of the *waqf*. Hence, there was continuity in these charities since the property endowed has continuous rent.

Another type of *waqf*, on which there have been serious discussions both in the classical period and Ottoman period if it is lawful, is cash *waqfs*. The working principle of cash *waqfs* were like the following:

A person who wants to give cash establishes a cash *waqf* and he uses this money with various methods such as *Qard-ul Hasan, Mudharabah, Musharakah, Bay-al I'nah* etc. ... to provide credit to the people who need credit. However, in practice the most often used method was *bey' bil istiglal*. In this method, the *waqf* provides credit to the person who needs money by giving his house as a pledge. This pledge continuous until he pays all debt and the borrower can stay in his house provided that he is obliged to pay rent which is the income of *waqf* for staying in the house. This transaction in the cash *waqf* took place in the face of *Quadi* (Judge). Generally, the maturity of these debts was limited to one year but at the end of the maturity it was possible to extend the maturity for three years. If the credit was given as gold it was taken as gold too and silver against silver and so forth. In his article Kurt (2010) mentions that although every kind of class took credit from the money *waqfs*, in general small and medium enterprises used cash *waqfs* to satisfy their medium-sized credit needs.

Even though it was forbidden for non-Muslims to establish a *waqf*, they could benefit from these *waqfs*. There are many records mentioning that European merchants used these *waqfs* during their journeys.

The importance of *waqfs* in economic and social life

In the Ottoman period, the role of *waqfs* in terms of economic development, education and health was very important. According to some researches, when there is a 1% increase in the rate of high school graduates, the poverty rate and income inequality of the society decreases considerably, since it leads to an increase in the share of the bottom income group in total income. Accordingly, taking into consideration the *waqfs* in the education system, we may state that this was not only an educational action but also it played an important role in the socio-economic structure of the societies. Cizakça (2015) in his article states that one considers the success of *waqf* universities; the governments to perform their function properly must support *waqfs*. Actually, when analyzing the *waqf* institutions, one would note that many of them were founded to support education system in Muslim world. Therefore, this shows that education, which improves human capital, was given importance in Muslim worlds. Skillful and intelligent students irrespective of their status and income level were chosen and supported to study in schools which are *waqf*-based education institutions.

Waqfs has played an important role in the Islamic social cooperation mechanism (Saeidi, 2013). *Waqfs* in general have performed important roles in term of meeting the needs of society such as infrastructural needs, charities, education, health and accommodation in the society. Therefore, they have contributed a lot to the socioeconomic life. To give some examples, establishing caravansary for development and easing trade, providing a free curing opportunity for the poor are some of them. At the same time, *waqfs* have contributed to the labor market by creating new employment opportunities for the labor force too. Because, these foundations had to employ labor to manage these organizations. (Bayartan, 2008). According to the data, around 200,000 *waqfs* have been founded during the Ottoman time. *Waqfs* in the Ottoman Empire were so widespread that as of the 19th and 20th century, the share of them in real estate stock and total cultivated lands was around 75% (Cizakça, 2015).

As in the case of cash *waqfs*, these kind of *waqfs* have not only met the needs of infrastructural or poverty-related needs of the society but also they have played a significant role in providing credit needs in local based as one of the first example of banking in the premodern period (Deguilhem, 2004, p. 89). In this regard, some orientalists argue that cash *waqfs* have not turned into banking in the modern sense of the word. Some scholars have pointed out the social benefits of cash *waqfs* state that the main objective of these foundations was to create a source for carrying out social duties such as providing food and health services to the poor rather than making money from money. Moreover, to support their thesis, they assert that these institutions have saved people who need money from falling into the hands of loan sharks (Usurers) and also played a role as a central bank by supplying money to the market so that during the slow times in trade this helped by filling in for a lack of money.

According to the orientalists, the money *waqfs* were dead investments since they could not keep pace with the requirements of the changing times. They further argue that, since this system do not provide elasticity to the management of the *waqf* as in the case of an unexpected situation; the capital endowed to these institutions could not be used efficiently in those times. Furthermore, Kuran (2001) in his article, states that the strict structure of the *waqfs* is one of the most significant factors of high corruption rates in Arabic countries currently. According to another view, since there was a relatively static structure in the economic system in earlier times when the *waqf* system was widespread, these institutions could somehow be interwoven with the existing economic system. However, whenever the economic system turned into a dynamic structure with the industrial revolution, they could not manage to keep up with the changing times due to their strict structure.

Beyond those discussions on cash *waqfs*, in this study, we would like to focus on the role of *waqfs* in fighting poverty and constituting social justice in society. As is well-known, in the literature there are numerous studies on cash *waqfs* suggesting new forms for these *waqfs* to meet the financial needs of Muslim world such as *waqf*-based microfinance suggested by Cizakça (2004), El-Gari (2004), Kahf (2004) etc. It is clear that the Muslim world needs this kind of newly designated financial institutions that are Sharia based to meet financial needs of Muslims. However, in this work, we preferred to focus on *waqfs* rather than cash *waqfs* since those traditional Islamic institutions such as *waqfs, zakah* were able to solve the problem of poverty in the past. Therefore, these institutions are worth of analyzing to develop new solutions for poverty alleviation. Although poverty issue has two dimensions, which are macroeconomic and microeconomics, *waqf* and *zakah* institutions can be considered as possible tools to mitigate poverty at a micro level.

In the case of the *waqf*, as abovementioned, there is a voluntarily income transfer from the rich to poor who are unable to earn a living due to physical/mental inabilities or any other reasons. However, one of the most important issues is to constitute a complete system taking into consideration all necessary Islamic institutions working together. Since even if some scholars argue that there was no existing institutions and system in the past in the Islamic world, yes, there was and what is more there was very strong and well-designated institutions collaborating with each other in, for instance, the Ottoman Empire. That is why they named the state *"Devlet-i Ebed Muddet"* which means endless lifetime state. Because, the founders of the Ottoman Empire believed that the system they established to manage the state was unique and because of this they believed that the Empire would live longer. And when we look at the history of the Ottoman Empire we may state that they were right since no institution or organization can survive for almost 600 years without a well-designated system. Accordingly, a complete system in the Ottoman Empire existed and we think that one should not analyze the institutions in the Ottoman Empire separately. By doing so one could make illogical inferences.

It is obvious that considering their past performance in terms of fighting against poverty and facilitating social justice in the society, that the *waqf* institutions deserve serious consideration for the economic development of a country and poverty alleviation (Ahmad, 2015).

Although *waqf* institutions have many dimensions in terms of socio-economic life, we would like to bring one important aspect of *waqfs* to the forefront in this study, which is quite important for economic development. That is: sustainability.

Sustainability

Even though there is no standard definition the term of "*sustainability,*" became a prominent word in economics at the world's first Earth Summit in Rio, in 1992, in the context of sustainable development. The term sustainability was defined as "Development that meets the needs of the present without compromising the ability of future generations to meet their own needs" in this summit. However, in our study we will would like to highlight this term in the context of alleviating poverty in a sustainable way by taking into consideration *waqf* institutions.

In fact, even in today's world the significance of sustainability has been realized. Therefore, the economics stress the word "sustainability" and economies, governments look for ways, methods to achieve sustainable growth instead of just achieving high-growth rates. Accordingly, sustainability is a really important and far-reaching term in economics. Therefore, when we look at the history of Muslim societies, we can observe that, being aware of this reality, Muslims have employed *waqf* institutions for fighting against poverty by designing them in a sustainable way.

In general, we may mention three kinds of tools for poverty alleviation in Islam, which are *zakah*, *sadaqah* and *waqfs*. While *zakah* is a compulsory charity, the others are not in Islam. In this classification in parallel with our study, it is notable to underline the main characteristic of *waqf*, which is perpetual charity.

We think that the most significant aspect regarding *waqf* institutions is the fact that they have provided sustainability in terms of poverty alleviation as well as in meeting other social needs of society. It seems that there are two main reasons behind this feature of *waqf*, which are their self-sufficient and irrevocable ownership structure.

Because, once *waqf* institutions were founded, they started to create necessary income to finance and realize their objectives. That is, they needed only initial capital. This point has really important aspects for a charity organization. Because, you can provide money, property etc. ... to help poor but this would be a one-time investment, so that you would finance the poor until consuming that money, property. However, in the case of *waqf* institutions, there is a system showing how to endow your money or property to found a *waqf*. Therefore, you have to involve and obey the rules of this system. Once you do this, that money or property is not your property anymore and subject to some certain rules.

As for their irrevocable ownership structure, after it is founded, since it is considered under the heel of God's property, they are nonassignable and inappropriate for repossession any more. That is to say, this system provides sustainability for the charities so they can fight against poverty.

In fact, one can observe how *waqf* institutions were used as a fruitful tool for poverty alleviation by looking at the era of the Ottoman Empire. The Ottoman Empire had successfully adopted these institutions in their economic system both for fighting against poverty and as a decrease in public expenditures. As most of these needs for infrastructural investments and social expenditures such as building mosques, schools and education as well as health expenditures were met by *waqfs*, the government did not have to allocate funds from the government budget to carry out these services. Accordingly, this system also helped reduce government expenditures, which means that it lessened the need for government borrowing. That is to say, the *waqf* system not only play a role for financing the poor in a sustainable way but also lessened the need for the government to borrow. Accordingly, we can conclude that these institutions were helpful for government debt sustainability as well as poverty alleviation (Ambrosa et al., 2015).

From this point of view, there are several studies in the literature that assert that *waqf* institutions could be useful in achieving ultimate goals of the modern economic system with its features reducing the government budget deficit as well as promoting income distribution. For instance, Cizakça (1998) argues that *waqf* institutions may be used as a tool to reduce the government budget deficit in modern economies as in the case of past implications in the Ottoman Empire.

To sum up, we may conclude that the feature of sustainability of *waqf* institutions is very important for not only alleviating poverty but also reducing the need for government borrowing even in today's world if it were redesigned according to the needs of the modern economic system. Because today, governments spend the significant share of their budgets to provide social services to the public that were provided by *waqfs* in the past and since there is generally a gap between income and expenditures of governments, they have to borrow to meet this gap by undertaking extra obligations such as interest. For instance, as of 2015, the share of public investment expenditure in the GDP is around 3% in Turkey and the interest expenditure of the government constitutes around 10% of public expenditure (TURKSTAT, 2016).

Conclusion

Originated from doing good things which comes naturally to human beings, *waqf* institutions have appeared as charity organizations, in both Muslim communities and other societies in history. Although these institutions have been seen in non-Muslim communities, in essence, they have been seen mostly in the Muslim world and came into prominence especially during the Ottoman Empire.

Even if there is no exact verse in the Holy Qur'an regarding these institutions, Islamic scholars have come to an agreement that these institutions were indirectly indicated in the Holy Qur'an. Moreover, there were several examples regarding *waqf* institutions in the time of Prophet Muhammad (*pbuh*).

These institutions were quite widespread in the Ottoman Empire which can explain two situations which took place at the same time or separately. One of them may be the fact that Muslims living in those times were very aware that the property that they owned do not really belong to them and believed that they were only a *khalif* (representative) of God in the world and therefore, they only had the right to use these properties. Therefore, they might think that sacrificing these properties in order to gain the consent of God is the most reasonable way. Regarding this issue, Genç (2013) states that European travelers who visited the Ottoman Empire noticed that there were rarely beggars in those times in Istanbul. Furthermore, he adds that in the same period, the number of beggars in Europe constituted 10% of the population. The second reason for establishing a *waqf* may be so that the Ottoman elites could avoid the aforementioned confiscation implementations. Actually, when we look at studies on the *waqfs* in the Ottoman Empire, we may conclude that both of these motives have been effective in establishing a *waqf*.

The main objective of endowing the property as a *waqf* instead of endowing it directly is to provide sustainability in this charity work. Because, while as is the case of in the first situation there is continuity in this charity, in the later it is endowed only one time. Therefore, we may conclude that these foundations were very important institutions in terms of providing continuous social justice and healthy socioeconomic life.

Regarding the sustainable feature of these institutions, we should also underline the fact that these institutions also helped reducing the borrowing requirement of the government. That is, these institutions were used as a fiscal policy tool as well as a tool for alleviating poverty in the past.

We may state that *waqfs* are actually a kind of non-profit organization in today's sense of the word. Accordingly, it is clear that *waqfs* played an important role in providing social justice by dealing with the issue of poverty issue in history. On the other hand, considering that these kinds of charities were encouraged by Islam, employing these institutions may be a good deal for both poor and rich people. Hence, instead of spending monies or properties to charities only one time, it may be logical to endow these properties or monies under an institution like *waqf* by institutionalizing this charity. So that, there may be provided continuity in charities.

As a result, taking into consideration the current situation of the world economy in terms of poverty and income inequality and the efforts of IFIs in fighting for poverty globally, *waqfs* may be a role model institution by rearranging it according to the new structure of the contemporary economic system to fight against poverty globally as well as fiscal policy tool to reduce the borrowing requirement of governments.

Note

1 عَلِيمٌ بِهِ اللَّهَ شَيْءٍ فَإِنَّ مِن تُنفِقُواْ وَمَا تُحِبُّونَ مِمَّا تُنفِقُواْ حَتَّى الْبِرَّ تَنَالُواْ لَن, Ali-İmran, 92.

References

Ahmad, M. (2015). Role of Waqf in Sustainable Economic Development and Poverty Alleviation: Bangladesh Perspective. Social Science Research Network, September 26.

Ambrosa, A., Aslam, M., & Hanafi, H. (2015). The Possible Role of Waqf in Ensuring a Sustainable Malaysian Federal Government Debt. International Accounting and business Conference 2015, IABC 2015. *Procedia Economics and Finance*, 31, 333–345.

Barkan, O. L., & Ayverdi, E. H. (1970). *İstanbul Vakıfları Tahrir Defteri*. Istanbul: Fetih Cemiyeti.

Bayartan, O. (2008). Osmanlı Şehirlerinde Vakıflar ve Vakıf Sisteminin Şehre Kattığı Değerler. Osmanlı Bilim Araştırmaları X-1.

BLUES Teknoloji ve Yenilik Dönemi. (2016). Sanayi Devrimi. Retrieved from http://my.beykoz.edu.tr/serkang/files/2011/02/sanayi_devrimi.pdf, accessed January 19, 2016.

Charls, M. (2000). *Understanding the Industrial Revaluation*. New York, London: Routledge.

Cizakça, M. (1998). Awqaf in History and Its Implications for Modern Islamic Economies. *Islamic Economic Studies*, 6(1). November 1998.

Cizakça, M. (2000). *A History of Philanrhropic Fundations: The Islamic World from the Seventh Century to the Present*. İstanbul: Boğaziçi Üniversitesi Yayınevi.

Cizakça, M. (2004). Cash Waqf as Alternative to NBFIs Bank. Paper presented in the International Seminar on Nonbanking Financial Institutions: Islamic Alternatives, March 1–3; 2004, Kuala Lumpur Malaysia.

Cizakça, M. (2015). *Osmanlı Dönemi Vakıflarının Tarihsel ve Ekonomik Boyutları*. Istanbul: Bahçeşehir Üniversitesi. Retrieved from www.tusev.org.tr, accessed November 30, 2015.

Deguilhem, R. (2004). The Waqf in the City. Retrieved from https://www.academia.edu/3773781/Deguilhem_Waqf_in_the_City, accessed November 29, 2015.

El-Gari, M.A. (2004). The QardHasan Bank. Paper presented in the International Seminar on Nonbanking Financial Institutions: Islamic Alternatives, March 1–3; 2004, Kuala Lumpur Malaysia.

Genç, M. (2013). *Osmanlı Ekonomisi, Türk Tarih Kurumu.* Youtube Video uploaded August 1, 2013, accessed December 4, 2015.

Hoexter, M. (1998). Waqf Studies in the Twentieth Century: The State of the Art. *Journal of Economic and Social History of the Orient,* 41(4), 474–495.

Kahf, M. (2004). Shariah and Historical Aspects of Zakat and Waqf. Paper presented for Islamic Research and Training institute, Islamic Development Bank.

Kahf, M. (January, 2013). The Role of Waqf in Improving the Ummah Welfare, Presented to the International Seminar on "Waqf as a Private Legal Body", Organized by the Islamic University of North Sumatra, Medan, Indenosia.

Köprülü, B. (2012). Tarihte Vakıflar. Retrieved from http://dergiler.ankara.edu.tr/dergi ler/38/308/3015.pdf, accessed December 1, 2012.

Kudat, A. (2015). Bir Finans Enstrümanı Olarak Nukud Vakfı ve İn'ikad Formülasyonu, II. İslam İktisadı ve Finans Konferansı, İstanbul Zaim Üniversitesi, İstanbul.

Kuran, T. (2001). The Privision of Public Goods under Islamic Law: Origins, Impact, and Limitations of the Waqf System. *Low and Society Association,* 35(4), 841–898, Blackwell Publishing.

Kurt, I. (2010). İslam hukuku Açısından Tarihten Günümüze Kredi ve Finans Yöntemleri. Tartışmalı İlmi İhtisas Toplantısı, Mayıs 8–9, 2010, İstanbul.

Saeidi, A. A. (2013). İslami Sosyal Yardım Sisteminde Vakıfların Rolü. Tahran Üniversitesi, Dünya Vakıflar Konferansı, Eylül.

Şimşek, M. (2015). Osmanlı Cemiyetinde Para Vakıfları Üzerinde Münakaşalar. Retrieved from www.ankara.edu.tr, accessed November 29, 2015.

Türkoğlu, İ. (2013). Osmanlı Devletinde Para Vakıflarının Gelir Dağılımı Üzerindeki Etkileri. Süleyman Demirel Üniversitesi. *The Journal of Faculty of Economics and Administrative Sciencies,* 18(2), 187–196.

Yediyıldız, B. (1982a). Vakıf. *İslam Ansiklöpedisi,* 13, 153–172, Kültür Turizm Bakanlığı, İstanbul.

Yediyıldız, B. (1982b). Müessese- Toplum Münasebetleri Çerçevesinde XVIII Asır Türk Toplumu ve Vakıf Müessesesi. *Vakıflar Dergisi,* 15, 23–53, İstanbul.

Zeinelabidin, A. R. (1996). Poverty in OIC Countries: Status, Determinants and Agenda for Action. *Journal of Economic Cooperation Among Islamic Countries,* 17 (3–4), 1–40.

Retrieved from www.tuik.gov.tr, accessed 04.12.2015

Retrieved from www.islamahlaki.com, accessed 05.12.2015.

Retrieved from www.enfal.de/Fikhi/M/menkullerin_vakfi.htm, accessed 05.12.2015.

Retrieved from www.adb.org/about/main, accessed January 19, 2016.

Retrieved from www.un.org/millenniumgoals/2015_MDG_Report/pdf/MDG% 202015%20rev%20(July%201).pdf, accessed January 19, 2016.

Retrieved from www.usatoday.com/story/news/nation/2014/08/17/hunger-study-food /14195585/.

Retrieved from www.alhudacibe.com/imhd/news22.php, accessed February 5, 2016.

Retrieved from https://themuslimissue.wordpress.com/2012/10/20/islamabad-freelance-columnist-800-million-muslims-out-of-1-4-billion-are-illiterate/, accessed February 5, 2016.

Retrieved from www.globalfootprints.org/sustainability, accessed February 10, 2016.

8   Interest and social justice

In the context of income inequality

Ozan Marasli

Income inequality is a well-known phenomenon, which arises when there is an unequal distribution of assets, income and wealth among society. The unequal distribution of income, generally, leads to a division in society, as the bottom of society suffers from this division, while the top of the society reaps the benefits of it. It makes the poor more vulnerable financially as they have to undertake the burden of the results of it. It varies between societies, different time periods and economic systems. So, when measuring income inequality all the factors should be taken into consideration ranging from demographic and political factors to macroeconomic and cultural factors and even the development level of the country. In this chapter, the relationship between interest and income inequality has been researched using the real interest rate. When income distribution changes in accordance with different income share groups—in general these changes have been in favor of the richest part of the society—the possible reasons for this should be questioned. There are several reasons that lead to an unequal distribution of income. The main aim of this research is to question whether the real interest rate has any impact on income inequality as one of its determinants or not.

Islam places a great emphasis on just distribution of income, especially securing the rights of the poor from irresponsible expenditures and the greed of the rich. Securing the financially least-privileged by which a more equal distribution can be satisfied, and preventing the concentration of wealth and income in the hands of the rich are among the important messages of Islam on the subject of economics, as Allah states that:

مَا أَفَاءَ اللَّهُ عَلَى رَسُولِهِ مِنْ أَهْلِ الْقُرَى فَلِلَّهِ وَلِلرَّسُولِ وَلِذِي الْقُرْبَى وَالْيَتَامَى وَالْمَسَاكِينِ وَابْنِ السَّبِيلِ كَيْ لَا يَكُونَ دُولَةً
بَيْنَ الْأَغْنِيَاءِ مِنكُمْ وَمَا آتَاكُمُ الرَّسُولُ فَخُذُوهُ وَمَا نَهَاكُمْ عَنْهُ فَانتَهُوا وَاتَّقُوا اللَّهَ إِنَّ اللَّهَ شَدِيدُ الْعِقَابِ

And what Allah restored to His Messenger from the people of the towns— it is for Allah and for the Messenger and for [his] near relatives and orphans and the [stranded] traveler—so that it will not be a perpetual distribution among the rich from you. And whatever the Messenger has given you—take; and what he has forbidden you—refrain from. And fear Allah; indeed, Allah is severe in penalty.

(Saheeh International, 1997, 59:7)

In addition, interest has been prohibited and discouraged in several verses in the Holy *Qur'an* (2:275–279, 3:130, 4:160–161, 30:39). One of the most outstanding verses of the *Qur'an*in that sense is:

الَّذِينَ يَأْكُلُونَ الرِّبَا لَا يَقُومُونَ إِلَّا كَمَا يَقُومُ الَّذِي يَتَخَبَّطُهُ الشَّيْطَانُ مِنَ الْمَسِّ ذَلِكَ بِأَنَّهُمْ قَالُواْ إِنَّمَا الْبَيْعُ مِثْلُ الرِّبَا وَأَحَلَّ اللّهُ الْبَيْعَ وَحَرَّمَ الرِّبَا فَمَن جَاءهُ مَوْعِظَةٌ مِّن رَّبِّهِ فَانتَهَىَ فَلَهُ مَا سَلَفَ وَأَمْرُهُ إِلَى اللّهِ وَمَنْ عَادَ فَأُوْلَئِكَ أَصْحَابُ النَّارِ هُمْ فِيهَا خَالِدُونَ

Those who consume interest cannot stand [on the Day of Resurrection] except as one stands who is being beaten by Satan into insanity. That is because they say, "Trade is [just] like interest." But Allah has permitted trade and has forbidden interest. So whoever has received an admonition from his Lord and desists may have what is past, and his affair rests with Allah. But whoever returns to [dealing in interest or usury]—those are the companions of the Fire; they will abide eternally therein.

(Saheeh International, 1997, 2: 275)

Also in the *Last Sermon*, The Messenger of Allah (PBUH) states that interest in all senses is prohibited and relates it to inequity, as he states that:

وَإِنَّ كُلَّ رِبًا مَوْضُوعٌ ، وَلَكِنْ لَكُمْ رُؤُوسَ أَمْوَالِكُمْ لَاتَظْلِمُونَ وَلَا تُظْلَمُونَ. قَضَى اللهُ أَنَّهُ لَا رِبَا، وَأَنَّ رِبَا عَبَّاسِ بْنِ عَبْدُ الْمُطَّلِبِ مَوْضُوعٌ كُلُّهُ

Allah has forbidden you to take usury (interest), therefore all interest obligations shall henceforth be waived. Your capital is yours to keep. You will neither inflict nor suffer any inequity. Allah has Judged that there shall be no interest and that all the interest due to Abbas ibn 'Abd al-Muttalib (Prophet's uncle) be waived.[1]

Justice is an integral component of Islam. The reflection of justice in the social context constitutes one of the outstanding features of Islamic economics. The fundamentals of Islamic economics are characterized by the foundational principles of *Tawhid* and justice. In the Holy *Qur'an*, Allah stated that:

لَقَدْ أَرْسَلْنَا رُسُلَنَا بِالْبَيِّنَاتِ وَأَنزَلْنَا مَعَهُمُ الْكِتَابَ وَالْمِيزَانَ لِيَقُومَ النَّاسُ بِالْقِسْطِ وَأَنزَلْنَا الْحَدِيدَ فِيهِ بَأْسٌ شَدِيدٌ وَمَنَافِعُ لِلنَّاسِ وَلِيَعْلَمَ اللّهُ مَن يَنصُرُهُ وَرُسُلَهُ بِالْغَيْبِ إِنَّ اللّهَ قَوِيٌّ عَزِيزٌ

We have already sent Our messengers with clear evidences and sent down with them the Scripture (Book) and the Balance that the people may maintain [their affairs] in justice. And We sent down iron, wherein is great military might and benefits for the people, and so that Allah may make evident those who support Him and His messengers unseen. Indeed, Allah is Powerful and Exalted in Might.

(Saheeh International, 1997, 57:25)

In relation to social justice, by the narration of Ummul Mumineen Aisha (ra), Rasulullah (saw) states that:

:إِنَّمَا هَلَكَ النَّاسُ قَبْلَكُمْ، أَنَّهُمْ كَانُوا إِذَا سَرَقَ فِيهِمُ الشَّرِيفُ تَرَكُوهُ، وَإِذَا سَرَقَ فِيهِمُ الضَّعِيفُ أَقَامُوا عَلَيْهِ الْحَدَّ، ثُمَّ قَالَ

«وَالَّذِي نَفْسِي بِيَدِهِ، لَوْ أَنَّ فَاطِمَةَ بِنْتَ مُحَمَّدٍ سَرَقَتْ قَطَعْتُ يَدَهَا»

The people who came before you were destroyed because whenever a noble person among them stole, they would let him go. But if one who was weak stole, they would carry out the Hadd punishment on him." Then he said: "By the One in whose hand is my soul, if Fatimah bint Muhammad were to steal, I would cut off her hand.

(Sunan An-Nasai, 2007: 4906)

Leading Islamic economists Chapra (1992, 1996)and Naqvi (1994)point out the importance of justice in economic and social subspaces. Chapra (1996, p. 25) explicitly asserts that:

Islamic economics is based on a paradigm which has socioeconomic justice as its primary objective. This objective takes its roots in the belief that human beings are the vicegerents of the One God, Who is the Creator of the Universe and everything in it.

(Chapra, 1992)

This explains the implications of the principle of justice in an economic sense; as all the basic needs of society should be fulfilled, all of the members may have a respectable source of income, the income and wealth distribution should be equitable and in line with these objectives economic growth and stability can be attained in a more balanced way. On the other hand, Naqvi (1994) explains the role of Islamic ethical axioms in the individual, social and economic contexts, he draws our attention to *Tawhid*, Equilibrium and Beneficence (*al-Adl wal Ihsan*), Free Will (*Ikhtiyar*) and Responsibility (*Fard*). In his classification, *Tawhid* constitutes the vertical dimension which links the finite and imperfect institutions with the Perfect Being, while *al-Adl wal Ihsan* describes the horizontal dimension by which "the various elements of life be (re-)ordered to produce the best economic dispensation" (Naqvi, 1994, p. 28). It also "provides for a complete description of all the virtues of the basic set of social institutions legal, political and economic" (Naqvi, 1994, p. 27). He also adds that:

on the economic plane, the principle desires a first-best configuration of the production, consumption and distribution activities, with the clear understanding that the needs of all the least-privileged members in Muslim society constitute the first charge on the real resources of the society.

(Naqvi, 1994, p. 27)

In that sense, a connection between interest and social justice can be constructed, as Iqbal (2007) indicates that there are "various manifestations of corruption—the prohibited actions—that distort the socioeconomic equilibrium" (Iqbal, 2007, 45). Interest constitutes one of them and it is evaluated as *zulm*/oppression (2:279) which is the converse of justice, as Prophet (saw) equated it with "the absolute darkness in the Day of Judgement."[2] The declaration of "war from Allah and His Messenger" (2:279) is excessively adequate to understand the degree of this oppression.

Interest and social justice in the context of income inequality

Social justice and income inequality

In light of these viewpoints, social justice is a question of equal opportunities, which seeks to establish a fair and just relation between the individual and society. Equitable income and wealth distribution is one of the key indicators for both economic and social justice. In that sense income inequality, which denotes a distortion in the equality of opportunities, is one of the most remarkable phenomenon, which threatens the existence and stability of social justice. So, in this chapter the impact of interest on social justice will be analyzed in the context of income inequality.

Income inequality refers to the extent to which income is distributed in an uneven manner among a population. Income is not just the money received through payment, but all the money received from employment (wages, salaries, bonuses etc.), investments, such as interest on savings accounts and dividends from shares of stock, savings, state benefits, pensions (state, personal, company) and rent. Income inequality has different dimensions, as it can be analyzed through within a country, between country and global levels. Although each level has vital significance, the scope of this study is constrained to global inequality. When the overall state of income inequality in the world is considered, it is recorded that relative global income inequality has declined over the past 35 years, from a relative Gini coefficient of 0.74 in 1975 to 0.63 in 2010, as it is driven by the extraordinary economic growth countries like China and India (UNDP, 2016). However, for absolute income inequality the Gini index has increased from 0.65 to 0.72 between 1975 and 2010. Relative income inequality indicates the proportional inequality level, while absolute inequality shows the exact level. For instance, in a specific country and a certain year, a person earns $1,000 while another person earns $5,000. If this country experiences economic growth, the first person earns $3,000 and the other earns $15,000.

While the relative difference between the two stays constant, the absolute difference has gone up from $4,000 to $10,000. Also the ones who reap the benefits of economic growth are mainly the wealthiest ones, as a UNDP (2016) report claims that 46% of the total increase in income between 1988 and 2011 went to the wealthiest 10%. Even worse, 50% of the increase in global wealth went to the wealthiest 1%, as the poorest 50% received only 1% of the increase. From 2000 to 2010, the wealthiest 1% increased their wealth from 32% to 46% as global wealth has become more concentrated. In general, it can be said that global income and wealth inequality have increased over few decades.

Income inequality, interest and social justice

Interest is seen as one of the most outstanding factors which violates income equality and therefore social justice. Because of its unjust nature, interest leads people to gain an unearned income as it generally occurs at the expense of the vulnerable side. This is a vital point, which should be emphasized, that interest is prohibited because Allah prohibits it. It is not tied to specific reasons, it is just prohibited. Thus, our main thesis is not that the prohibition of interest in Islam is related to income inequality. Also, because of its oppressional nature, it has some detrimental economic impacts in which the vulnerable are hurt In this context, firstly interest and social justice linkages in the literature of Islamic economics will be examined through selected studies. Then, the possible relations of interest and income inequality will try to be revealed from the economic literature through a few selected works.

Interest and income inequality in Islamic economic literature

Interest is supposed to be one of the most outstanding factors which violates income equality and therefore social justice in the literature of Islamic economics as many writers emphasize this point. Siddiqi (2004) points out the interest and income inequality linkage by connecting the increasing level of inequalities and interest-based economic structure and emphasizing the refusal of capital owners to share the uncertainty and risks with others (Siddiqi, 2004, p. 110). Moreover, Chapra (2003) explains how interest has a distorting impact on need fulfilment, full employment, optimal growth, equitable distribution of income and wealth and economic stability; as he remarks that such an "injustice undermines brotherhood and solidarity, accentuates conflict, tensions and crime, aggravates human problems and thus leads ultimately to nothing but misery in this world as well as in the Hereafter."

Ali et al. (2013) also argues that prohibition of interest, elimination of gharar and establishment of *zakah* can "avoid build-up of excessive debt ... provide social insurance against poverty, reduce extreme inequality ... " He emphasizes the role of Islamic finance in development in that sense, also mentioning the interest and inequality relationship. Chapra (2014), in another study he emphasizes the interest and inequality relationship by stating that:

> The financial system does not, however, appear to be attuned to the realization of this goal. It has a built-in tendency towards promoting economic inequality by mobilizing resources from a vast spectrum of society and making them available primarily to a relatively much smaller spectrum.
>
> (Chapra, 2014, p. vii)

As interest is a type of unfair gain which guarantees a fixed rate of return with no risk, the burden should be undertaken by entrepreneurs and workers. Thus the value of participation, labor and risk-taking become less meaningful and access to finance the bottom income groups—by which the income gap may be tighten—cannot be realized, because the wealth and income are more likely to be possessed by top income groups. Zaman and Zaman explain this situation; "banning interest should have the effect of allowing for greater access by population to finance, and hence lead to a better income distribution" (Zaman & Zaman, 2001, p. 10). Furthermore, Al-Suwailem (2008), in his agent-based simulation model which is based on three different financing methods, the interest-free financing is proved to be more equitable than interest-based financing. This study is the unique example in the literature which tries to show the impact of interest and wealth inequality theoretically. However, the supposed relationship between interest and income inequality hasn't been proven through empirical analysis. Thus one of the motivations of this chapter is to prove this supposed relationship in an empirical sense.

Interest and income inequality in economics literature

The role of the real interest rate on income inequality has been questioned in the literature of economics, as few selected works will be taken into consideration in this chapter. Milanovic (2005), Piketty (1997) and Stiglitz (2015) have important findings on the subject. The most outstanding is the study of Milanovic (2005) which tries to explain the impact of globalization on income inequality by analyzing different 10% income percentiles. He uses the real interest rate as an explanatory variable and concludes that the real interest rate is always pro-rich, as he found out an income transfer from the bottom 80% to the top 10%. His results show that only Top 20% reap the benefits of it while the Bottom 80%'s income is reduced by high real interest rates. Even the middle-classes lose when the interest rate is high.

Moreover, Piketty (1997), under the assumption that there is positive relationship between long-run growth and aggregate investment, the countries which have lower real interest rates and in which the capital mobility is higher tend to grow faster than the countries which have higher real interest rates and in which the capital mobility is lower. From this point of view, he argues that in the steady-states characterized by higher real interest rates, wealth inequality will be higher, as these economies tend to grow slower.

On the other hand, Stiglitz (2015), in his recent study, found out that low rate of interest also leads to an inequalizing effect. He analyzes the relationship between credit creation, monetary policy and inequality by developing a theoretical model and concluded that in the short run, "lowering real interest rate leads to an increase in the net income of capitalists by a certain amount and a reduction of income of workers by a corresponding amount. It is, in effect, a direct transfer from workers to capitalists" (Stiglitz, 2015, p. 22). Moreover, recently the "near-zero level interest" policy of FED is also criticized due to its negative externalities on income inequality, as it leads stock prices to be higher—by which the stock owners find more advantageous—and low borrowing costs—by which the large corporations can gain additional capital to boost corporate profits.

Thus, in this study, we aim to reveal whether there is a relationship between income inequality and interest. Our main thesis is that an economic system one of whose fundamental dynamics is interest can lead to distortions in the income distribution. The underlying reason for this statement is that interest may have an income transferor role, by which a specific amount of income of the poor and middle classes flows to the rich. This assumption implies a state of *zulm*, according to Naqvi it "denotes a *social disequilibrium* in the sense that the resources of society flow from the poor to rich" (Naqvi, 1994, p. 28).

Data and methodology

Data

Our data contains the observations from 34 countries, spanning the period 1990–2015. The country list can be seen in Appendix 8.1. For dependent variables the Gini Index and the income share deciles have been taken into consideration, as for the independent variables real interest rate, interest payments in terms of government expenses, inflation (CPI)—which does not lead to multicollinearity problem in the presence of the real interest rate—and GDP growth rate. We used the UNI-WIDER's World Income Inequality Database (WIID) version 3.4 and World Bank's World Development Indicators Database. The WIID3.4 data, which covers 182 countries with 8817 observations, was collected from various sources. This could pose a threat for the validity of the findings, however we try to eliminate any possible risks by using specific datasets for specific country groups such as the Socio-Economic Database for Latin America and Caribbean (SEDLAC) 2016 for Latin American countries, Eurostat 2016 for European countries and World Bank 2016 for the other ones, which constitute the minority in the sample and mainly contains Asian countries.

As it can be seen from Table 8.1, We have 657 Gini Index observations ranging from 21.6 to 60.2 with a mean of 38.55, while we have 642 observations for the deciles. For our sample, the Gini Index has decreased from the beginning of the 1990s to the mid-2010s. Notwithstanding observations of European countries—except Poland—stay almost constant, there has been an outstanding fall in the inequality levels of Latin American countries (see Figure 8.1). Moreover, regarding the income share deciles, total income share of the bottom 70% has risen while for the Eighth 10% rises and falls have almost balanced each other out and the income share of the top 20% has fallen in the sample (see Figure 8.2). As is the case for the Gini Index, the main impact of these changes stem from the equalizing trend of Latin American countries. Also these changes can be evaluated within the relative global income inequality framework rather than an absolute one, as the distinction has been made in the above sections. On average, the Eighth 10% acquires a quadrupled share compared to the Bottom 10%, while the ratio of Top 10% to the Bottom 10% is 12.64. Also, the Ninth 10% takes up roughly half the amount of the Top 10%, as the differences among other deciles can be assumed to be normal. The extent of inequalities between the means of

Table 8.1 Summary statistics

	(1)	(2)	(3)	(4)	(5)
Variables	*N*	*Mean*	*Std. Dev.*	*Min*	*Max*
Real interest rate	764	7.486	14.88	−87.85	93.94
Interest payments (% expenses)	670	9.449	8.043	0.108	79.07
Inflation (CPI)	869	39.69	316.54	−1.418	7481.67
GDP growth (%)	870	3.311	3.969	−14.724	18.287
Gini Index	657	38.55	10.633	21.6	60.2
Bottom 10%	642	2.412	1.08	0.3	5
Second 10%	642	3.969	1.349	0.9	6.3
Third 10%	642	5.024	1.381	2.2	7.4
Fourth 10%	642	6.027	1.356	3.4	8.3
Fifth 10%	642	7.076	1.283	4.6	9.1
Sixth 10%	642	8.268	1.167	5.8	10
Seventh 10%	642	9.75	0.952	7.4	11.1
Eighth 10%	642	11.77	0.594	9.9	13
Ninth 10%	642	15.23	0.959	12.6	17.8
Top 10%	642	30.49	8.029	18.69	46.9

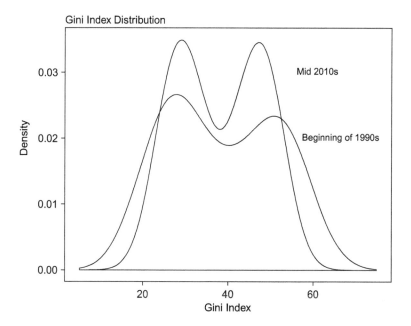

Figure 8.1 Gini index distribution from the beginning of 1990s to the mid-2010s

income share deciles can be seen in Figure 8.3. For mean values, the Top 10% has 14 times more income than the Bottom 10%, while this proportion is roughly 4 of the Fifth 10% and double for the Ninth 10%. In addition, the shares of different income deciles have shown changes in a range between 0.5–1.5, except the Top 10%, which has a standard deviation of 8.029. Despite their decreasing inequality levels Bolivia, Brazil, Chile and Honduras appear to be the most unequal countries, while Austria, Belgium, Czech Republic, Netherlands and Norway are among the most equal ones. Furthermore, regarding the real interest rates, it ranges between –7.5% and 22.5% on average. The negative outliers belong to Belarus and Venezuela, while the positive ones are observed in Bolivia, Brazil, Ecuador and Uruguay. Thus, it is assumed that there are some country-specific reasons behind the very low and very high interest rates. Also, from Figure 8.2, we can say that interest rates have fallen from the 1990s to 2010s.

At first glance, it can be said that the lower real interest rates are associated with lower levels of the Gini Index and with higher levels of most of the income share of the income deciles—except the top 20%. In Figure 8.4, it can be clearly seen that low levels of the income share of the Bottom 10% are associated with high interest rate levels, while for the Top 10% high real interest rate levels are associated with high income shares. Especially, for the

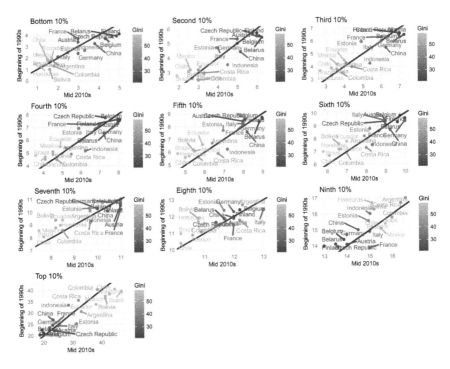

Figure 8.2 Changes in income share deciles from 1990s to the mid-2010s

Bottom 10%, standard deviation of the real interest rate observations is higher for the lower income share levels—between 0% and roughly 2.5%. Approximately between –15% and 0% and between 15% and 70% levels of real interest rate, the Bottom 10% tends to acquire less from the total income.

On the other hand, between these intervals the Top 10% gets more shares, as the Gini Index also tends to be higher. Thus, higher Gini Index levels are also associated with higher real interest rates, as higher interest rates may lead the Gini Index to reach a value ranging from roughly 40% to 60%. Meaning, real interest rate increases may lead to an increase in income inequality. Moreover, higher interest rates have led the Top 10% to acquire a share ranging between 35% and 45% from the total income.

For interest payments in government expenses, as it can be seen from Figure 8.5, lower levels of interest payments are seemed to be related to lower levels of the Gini Index, where the Bottom 10% takes the highest share it can and the Top 10% takes the least. However, the reverse situation is valid for the higher levels of interest payments, as these observations correspond to higher levels of the Gini Index where the Top 10% takes the highest shares and the Bottom 10% takes the lowest ones. Moreover, the

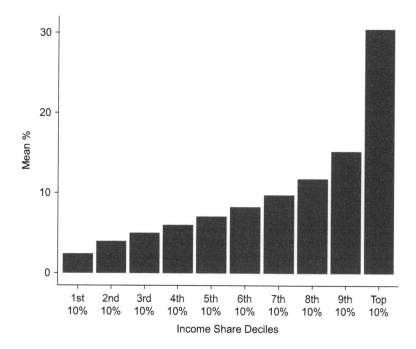

Figure 8.3 Mean values for the income share of the decile groups

Top 10% takes the higher shares for higher levels of interest payments, as the Bottom 10% acquires the lower shares for higher interest payments.

Thus, these interactions may have the potential to explain the changes in the income shares of the deciles, as the real interest rate and interest payments may have an impact on these changes. Consequently, these relationships provide some vital insights about the direction of possible causalities between the relevant variables. We will try to deepen our analysis by examining these relationships empirically.

Methodology and model specifications

For the panel data sample exhibits a random-effects feature and consists of 34 countries and 26 years, we used the Driscoll-Kraay Standard Errors method with pooled OLS (Driscoll & Kraay, 1998) as the sample contains both autocorrelation, heteroskedasticity, cross-sectional dependence problems; while the number of individual observations are greater than the time observations. Driscoll-Kraay Standard Errors are robust when T > N, however this technique does not place any restrictions on the limiting behavior of the number of panels, meaning the size of the cross-sectional dimension in finite samples does not constitute a constraint on feasibility (Hoechle, 2007).

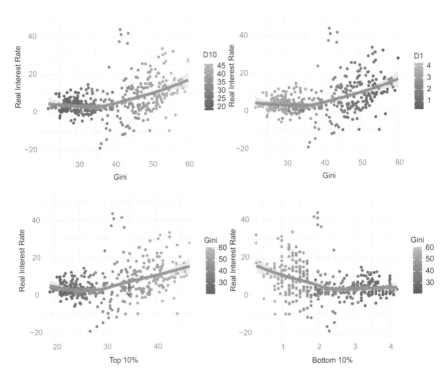

Figure 8.4 Scatterplots of real interest rate, Gini Index, bottom 10% and top 10%

As stated above, in order to see the impact of real interest rate and inter-est payments on income inequality, we use both the Gini Index and income shares of different income deciles. This choice gives us an opportunity to observe the changes in income shares of different income groups and to check whether there is an income transfer from a specific group to the other. By doing this, we benefited from Milanovic (2005), who analyzes the impact of FDI and trade openness on income inequality by using income share deciles. To explain the changes in income deciles and the Gini Index, we use the real interest rate, interest payments, inflation rate—measured by CPI and does not lead to the emergence of multicollinearity problem when used with the real interest rate—and the GDP growth rate. Thus, we can specify the model as follows:

$$y_{it} = \alpha + \beta_1 RealInt_{it} + \beta_2 IntPayments_{it} + \beta_3 Inflation_{it} + \beta_4 GDPgrowth_{it} + \sigma i + \varepsilon it$$

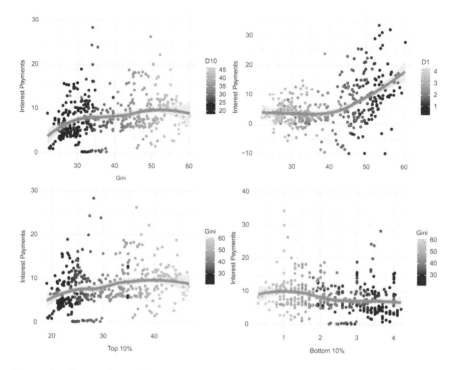

Figure 8.5 Scatterplots of interest payments, Gini Index, bottom 10% and top 10%

where y_{it} equals to represents the Gini Index and income share percent-ages of the income decile groups for $i = 1, \ldots ., 34$ and $t = 1, \ldots , 26$. σi represents the unobserved individual-specific effect, as εit denotes the error term. In accordance with the patterns derived from the graphs above, we expected that increases in the real interest rate would rise the Gini Index, as it can increase the income share of top income deciles while decreasing the share of bottom ones. As is stated above, for the last 20 years the income shares of the Bottom 80% have increased and the Top 20% have decreased while the interest rates have fallen. Also, the real inter-est rate had a positive relationship to the Gini Index and the income share of Top 10%, while it had a negative relationship to the income share of Bottom 10%. These issues will be discussed in detail in the following sections inshaAllah.

Estimation results

By applying the Driscoll-Kraay Standard Errors method, we firstly esti-mate the impact of real interest rate on Gini Index. Also, for eliminating

Table 8.2 Regression results for the Gini Index

Variables	(1) Gini	(2) Gini	(3) Gini	(4) Gini	(5) Gini
Real Interest Rate	0.353*** (0.0308)		0.381*** (0.0268)	0.385*** (0.0403)	0.407*** (0.0333)
Interest Payments		0.692*** (0.0788)		0.353*** (0.0750)	
Inflation (CPI)			0.0220** (0.00834)	0.0231*** (0.00526)	0.0305*** (0.00876)
GDP Growth Rate					0.707*** (0.133)
Constant	36.31*** (0.356)	30.44*** (0.614)	35.86*** (0.337)	30.47*** (0.697)	33.13*** (0.669)
Observations	582	516	580	453	580
R-squared	0.186	0.172	0.196	0.322	0.259
Number of groups	33	30	33	29	33

Notes: standard errors in parentheses.
*** p<0.01,
** p<0.05,
* p<0.1.

possible omitted variable bias we include inflation rate and GDP growth rate. The results can be seen in Table 8.2. With the number of observations ranging between 453 and 580, we found out that real interest rate and interest payments have an inequalizing impact on income distribution, as control variables does not impact the level of significance of the real interest rate. Thus, for this sample, the impact of interest on income inequality does not reflect on the GDP growth rate and inflation rate (CPI), which shows that interest has an effect on inequality by itself, not by two of the possible channels through which it can affect inequality. So, both the real interest rate and interest payments are significant in 1% level of significance for all their regressions. By a percent increase in the real interest rate, the Gini Index can increase by 0.353%–0.411%. Moreover, inflation also has an inequalizing nature regarding income distribution. However, when the magnitude of the impact of a one percent increase in inflation and the real interest rate compared, real interest has roughly 17 times more of an effect on inequality, which provides some insights regarding the unjust nature of interest. For interest payments in terms of government expenses, by a one percent increase in interest payments the Gini Index increases by 0.69 points. This can be an important evidence that the interest payments are being carried out on some specific income groups, mainly on the richest ones who are more likely to buy specific purpose securities and government treasury notes and bonds. Also, it can be said that for our sample, the GDP growth rate has a significant impact on income inequality. Surprisingly, in terms of the magnitude of coefficients, the GDP growth rate has the highest effect on income inequality. This may show that the ones who reap the benefits of the income growth are the richer ones, which can be interpreted as favor arguments about trickle-down economics are not being valid for our sample. Moreover, in terms of the variation in inequality explained by the real interest rate, it can explain the 17%–32%, which sounds like a reasonable amount.

In order to elaborate the scope of analysis, income shares of the deciles are taken as dependent variables in the following regressions. By conducting the analysis with the same independent and explanatory variables, we can see the consequent impact of a change in the real interest rate on income inequality, as we can also check whether there is a transfer of income between some deciles or not.

As can be seen from Table 8.3, first we try to examine the sole effect of the real interest rate on the deciles, without using any control or explanatory variables. In this analysis conducted on roughly 568 observations, we found out that by a percent increase in real interest, income shares of the bottom 80% falls, as income share of the top 20% rises. Through a percent increase in real interest, bottom 80% loses 0.2855% in total, while the top 20% gains 0.2842% *which denotes an explicit income transfer with a welfare loss of 0.0013%.* 92.5% of this income transfer is acquired by the top 10%. These results are significant at 1% level of significance. Most of the loss is borne by the first seven deciles which constitute the bottom 70%, by an amount that ranges between 0.03%–0.04% per decile. Instead, the 8th decile loses 10% 0.0157% respectively. These percentages denote the income shares taken from the total income, which means they do not exhibit percent changes from the relative incomes of different deciles; rather they have the same weight for every decile. Thus, poor, lower-middle and middle classes are the ones who should bear the consequences of the detrimental effects of the real interest rate changes. From the analysis, we can say that the interest rate can explain 14.6%–18.5% of variation in income shares of the income deciles except the 8th 10% and 9th 10%.

For the succeeding regressions, we include the control and explanatory variables—inflation and GDP growth—to reveal the true impact of the real interest rate on income inequality. When the inflation rate is included, the magnitude of the income transfer from the bottom 80% to top 20% increases to 0.3076%, as all of the results are significant at 1%. Moreover, in Table 8.4, inflation has also an inequalizing impact on income distribution, and decreases the income share of the bottom 80% and increases the income share of the top 10%. It just cannot explain

Table 8.3 Regression results for income deciles (I)

Variables	(1) Bottom 10%	(2) 2nd 10%	(3) 3rd 10%	(4) 4th 10%	(5) 5th 10%	(6) 6th 10%	(7) 7th 10%	(8) 8th 10%	(9) 9th 10%	(10) Top 10%
Real Interest Rate	-0.0314***	0.0417***	0.0437***	0.0434***	0.0411***	0.0378***	0.0307***	0.0157***	0.0212***	0.263***
	(0.00222)	(0.00373)	(0.00406)	(0.00412)	(0.00399)	(0.00386)	(0.00352)	(0.00261)	(0.00154)	(0.0270)
Constant	2.609***	4.230***	5.299***	6.300***	7.338***	8.509***	9.950***	11.88***	15.10***	28.80***
	(0.0430)	(0.0522)	(0.0566)	(0.0577)	(0.0564)	(0.0557)	(0.0484)	(0.0354)	(0.0324)	(0.360)
Observations	568	568	568	568	568	568	568	568	568	568
R-squared	0.146	0.165	0.173	0.178	0.178	0.181	0.178	0.117	0.084	0.185
Number of groups	33	33	33	33	33	33	33	33	33	33

Notes:
*** $p<0.01$,
** $p<0.05$,
* $p<0.1$
Standard errors in parentheses

Table 8.4 Regression results for income deciles (II)

Variables	(1) Bottom 10%	(2) 2nd 10%	(3) 3rd 10%	(4) 4th 10%	(5) 5th 10%	(6) 6th 10%	(7) 7th 10%	(8) 8th 10%	(9) 9th 10%	(10) Top 10%
Real Interest Rate	−0.0326***	0.0448***	0.0472***	0.0470***	−0.0447***	−0.0413***	−0.0339***	−0.0176***	0.0226***	0.285***
	(0.00252)	(0.00362)	(0.00381)	(0.00374)	(0.00352)	(0.00322)	(0.00281)	(0.00202)	(0.00167)	(0.0245)
Inflation (CPI)	−0.000914	0.00238**	0.00265**	0.00275**	0.00274***	0.00271***	0.00245***	0.00155***	0.000943	0.0170***
	(0.000675)	(0.00105)	(0.00109)	(0.00105)	(0.000964)	(0.000837)	(0.000619)	(0.000236)	(0.000742)	(0.00572)
Constant	2.626***	4.279***	5.355***	6.358***	7.396***	8.566***	10.00***	11.91***	15.08***	28.45***
	(0.0470)	(0.0558)	(0.0584)	(0.0580)	(0.0553)	(0.0529)	(0.0439)	(0.0288)	(0.0344)	(0.354)
Observations	566	566	566	566	566	566	566	566	566	566
R-squared	0.148	0.174	0.183	0.188	0.189	0.194	0.194	0.131	0.089	0.195
Number of groups	33	33	33	33	33	33	33	33	33	33

Notes: standard errors in parentheses
*** p<0.01,
** p<0.05,
* p<0.1

the income share of 9th 10%. However, its impact is roughly 16 times less than the impact of the real interest in terms of the magnitude of the effect. Thus, we can say that the only pro-rich income share transfer mechanism is not the real interest rate for our sample, inflation also has some role to play in that sense. Lastly, from Table 8.5, it can be said that the presence of the GDP growth exacerbates inequality, by transferring the 0.5348% of the total income from the bottom 80% to the top 20%. It is also significant for each decile at the 1% level. As for the Gini Index, top 20% reaps the benefits of the economic growth while the remaining 80% loses. Furthermore, the presence of control and explanatory variables does not change the significance level of the real interest rate, which strengthens the thesis that the real interest is *prorich*. Thus, income inequality increases in response to an increase in the real interest rate, inflation and GDP growth, as each of them works as income transfer mechanisms in favor of the rich.

The ratio of interest payments to government expenses is also a significant income transfer mechanism, as can be seen from Table 8.6, a percent increase in interest payments leads to 0.5586% of the total income transferring to the Top 20%. Also, 89.4% of this transfer goes to the Top 10%. The results are significant at the 1% level and the R-squared is between 15% and 24%. When the control variables are added, the level of significance does not change for interest payments, while inflation has a surprising effect. Inflation, when it is used with interest payments, increases the income of the Bottom 50% while decreasing the Eighth 10% and the Ninth 10%. The GDP growth rate has a more powerful impact than interest payments—just like for real interest rate. One percent economic growth transfers 0.612% of the total income to the Top 20%, as 91.7% of this transfer goes to the Top 10%. These results can be seen in Table 8.7.

Furthermore, as it can be seen from Table 8.8, the real interest rate and interest payments do not influence the significance level of each other, as both of them are significant for each income decile group—except the Eighth 10% for interest payments. In the presence of both, interest payments transfer the 0.298% of the total income from the Bottom 80% to the Top 20% while the real interest rate transfers 0.283% of the income. When the control variables are added to the regression, as given in Table. 8.9, both variables are supposed to be the income transfer mechanisms which operate at the expense of the poor. The most powerful ones, in order, are the following: GDP growth rate, real interest rate, interest payments in government expenses and inflation. The GDP growth rate transfers a tripled amount of income compared with interest payments, a doubled amount compared with the real interest rate and roughly 25 times more than inflation. In total, a percent change in the real interest rate and interest payments transfers the 0.691% of the total income to the Top 10%. R-squared is between 17.5% and 40%, as the better explained

Table 8.5 Regression results for income deciles (III)

Variables	(1) Bottom 10%	(2) 2nd 10%	(3) 3rd 10%	(4) 4th 10%	(5) 5th 10%	(6) 6th 10%	(7) 7th 10%	(8) 8th 10%	(9) 9th 10%	(10) Top 10%
Real Interest Rate	-0.0324***	0.0432***	0.0454***	0.0451***	0.0428***	0.0393***	0.0319***	0.0163***	0.0220***	0.273***
	(0.00290)	(0.00510)	(0.00554)	(0.00561)	(0.00543)	(0.00512)	(0.00444)	(0.00295)	(0.00227)	(0.0349)
GDP growth rate	-0.0484***	0.0784***	0.0829***	0.0837***	0.0816***	0.0742***	0.0577***	0.0279***	0.0423**	0.494***
	(0.0136)	(0.0206)	(0.0215)	(0.0208)	(0.0191)	(0.0160)	(0.0115)	(0.00580)	(0.0170)	(0.110)
Constant	2.784***	4.513***	5.599***	6.603***	7.633***	8.778***	10.16***	11.98***	14.95***	27.02***
	(0.0648)	(0.106)	(0.113)	(0.113)	(0.107)	(0.0961)	(0.0734)	(0.0443)	(0.0737)	(0.636)
Observations	568	568	568	568	568	568	568	568	568	568
R-squared	0.175	0.216	0.227	0.234	0.238	0.241	0.232	0.148	0.113	0.241
Number of groups	33	33	33	33	33	33	33	33	33	33

Notes: standard errors in parentheses
*** $p<0.01$,
** $p<0.05$,
* $p<0.1$

Table 8.6 Regression results for income deciles (IV)

Variables	(1) Bottom 10%	(2) 2nd 10%	(3) 3rd 10%	(4) 4th 10%	(5) 5th 10%	(6) 6th 10%	(7) 7th 10%	(8) 8th 10%	(9) 9th 10%	(10) Top 10%
Interest payments	−0.0664***	– 0.0866***	– 0.0900***	– 0.0898***	– 0.0831***	– 0.0711***	– 0.0543***	– 0.0173***	– 0.0592***	– 0.500***
	(0.00654)	(0.00971)	(0.0112)	(0.0102)	(0.00926)	(0.00957)	(0.00740)	(0.00607)	(0.00839)	(0.0601)
Constant	3.202***	5.005***	6.089***	7.076***	8.045***	9.098***	10.38***	11.97***	14.54***	24.62***
	(0.0406)	(0.0680)	(0.0773)	(0.0719)	(0.0671)	(0.0651)	(0.0447)	(0.0401)	(0.0686)	(0.390)
Observations	501	501	501	501	501	501	501	501	501	501
R-squared	0.160	0.170	0.173	0.177	0.168	0.148	0.128	0.035	0.156	0.158
Number of groups	30	30	30	30	30	30	30	30	30	30

Notes: standard errors in parentheses
*** p<0.01,
** p<0.05,
* p<0.1

Table 8.7 Regression results for income deciles (V)

Variables	(1) Bottom 10%	(2) 2nd 10%	(3) 3rd 10%	(4) 4th 10%	(5) 5th 10%	(6) 6th 10%	(7) 7th 10%	(8) 8th 10%	(9) 9th 10%	(10) Top 10%
Interest payments	-0.0689***	-0.0885***	-0.0916***	-0.0911***	0.0837***	0.0708***	0.0532***	-0.0152**	0.0623***	0.502***
	(0.00664)	(0.0101)	(0.0117)	(0.0110)	(0.0102)	(0.0104)	(0.00827)	(0.00590)	(0.00813)	(0.0638)
Inflation (CPI)	0.000844***	0.000687***	0.000618**	0.000545**	0.000374*	0.000140	-9.29e-05	0.000440***	-0.000839***	-0.00195
	(0.000117)	(0.000201)	(0.000227)	(0.000217)	(0.000202)	(0.000208)	(0.000172)	(0.000118)	(0.000145)	(0.00129)
GDP growth rate	-0.0538***	-0.0873***	-0.0942***	-0.0964***	0.0944***	0.0862***	0.0673***	-0.0324***	0.0471**	0.566***
	(0.0155)	(0.0242)	(0.0254)	(0.0257)	(0.0245)	(0.0221)	(0.0170)	(0.00765)	(0.0190)	(0.142)
Constant	3.374***	5.279***	6.384***	7.377***	8.336***	9.359***	10.58***	12.06***	14.38***	22.90***
	(0.0805)	(0.129)	(0.134)	(0.130)	(0.124)	(0.115)	(0.0851)	(0.0444)	(0.110)	(0.720)
Observations	499	499	499	499	499	499	499	499	499	499
R-squared	0.200	0.228	0.235	0.243	0.237	0.215	0.189	0.076	0.198	0.222
Number of groups	30	30	30	30	30	30	30	30	30	30

Notes: standard errors in parentheses
*** p<0.01,
** p<0.05,
* p<0.1

Table 8.8 Regression results for income deciles (VI)

Variables	(1) Bottom 10%	(2) 2nd 10%	(3) 3rd 10%	(4) 4th 10%	(5) 5th 10%	(6) 6th 10%	(7) 7th 10%	(8) 8th 10%	(9) 9th 10%	(10) Top 10%
Real interest rate	-0.0322***	0.0430***	0.0446***	0.0433***	0.0407***	0.0373***	0.0295***	0.0141***	0.0240***	0.259***
	(0.00340)	(0.00568)	(0.00602)	(0.00592)	(0.00565)	(0.00559)	(0.00474)	(0.00306)	(0.00319)	(0.0371)
Interest payments	-0.0373***	0.0477***	0.0497***	0.0506***	0.0457***	0.0361***	0.0262***	-0.00225	0.0400***	0.258***
	(0.00685)	(0.00964)	(0.0110)	(0.0102)	(0.00937)	(0.00992)	(0.00747)	(0.00583)	(0.00940)	(0.0573)
Constant	3.174***	4.963***	6.046***	7.031***	7.998***	9.048***	10.33***	11.94***	14.53***	24.95***
	(0.0672)	(0.0850)	(0.0872)	(0.0826)	(0.0761)	(0.0658)	(0.0523)	(0.0390)	(0.0869)	(0.419)
Observations	440	440	440	440	440	440	440	440	440	440
R-squared	0.283	0.309	0.311	0.309	0.296	0.275	0.244	0.106	0.250	0.291
Number of groups	29	29	29	29	29	29	29	29	29	29

Notes: standard errors in parentheses
*** p<0.01,
** p<0.05,
* p<0.1

Table 8.9 Regression results for income deciles (VII)

Variables	(1) Bottom 10%	(2) 2nd 10%	(3) 3rd 10%	(4) 4th 10%	(5) 5th 10%	(6) 6th 10%	(7) 7th 10%	(8) 8th 10%	(9) 9th 10%	(10) Top 10%
Real interest rate	-0.0353***	-0.0498***	-0.0520***	-0.0508***	-0.0481***	-0.0444***	-0.0356***	-0.0176***	0.0274***	0.304***
	(0.00284)	(0.00407)	(0.00405)	(0.00383)	(0.00354)	(0.00321)	(0.00272)	(0.00181)	(0.00267)	(0.0242)
Interest payments	-0.0360***	-0.0448***	-0.0466***	-0.0475***	-0.0427***	-0.0332***	-0.0237***	-0.000857	0.0384***	0.240***
	(0.00750)	(0.0104)	(0.0112)	(0.0106)	(0.00992)	(0.00955)	(0.00747)	(0.00483)	(0.0100)	(0.0572)
Inflation CPI	0.00172***	0.00371***	0.00403***	0.00406***	0.00399***	0.00384***	0.00327***	0.00185***	0.00191***	0.0244***
	(0.000323)	(0.000622)	(0.000645)	(0.000610)	(0.000557)	(0.000505)	(0.000379)	(0.000172)	(0.000541)	(0.00322)
GDP growth rate	-0.0596***	-0.0978***	-0.105***	-0.107***	-0.105***	-0.0961***	-0.0755***	-0.0374***	0.0514***	0.634***
	(0.00914)	(0.0158)	(0.0166)	(0.0172)	(0.0170)	(0.0158)	(0.0131)	(0.00755)	(0.0144)	(0.0976)
Constant	3.391***	5.341***	6.456***	7.448***	8.407***	9.427***	10.64***	12.09***	14.33***	22.48***
	(0.108)	(0.157)	(0.157)	(0.153)	(0.148)	(0.134)	(0.108)	(0.0442)	(0.139)	(0.846)
Observations	439	439	439	439	439	439	439	439	439	439
R-squared	0.326	0.389	0.399	0.402	0.395	0.377	0.341	0.174	0.293	0.385
Number of groups	29	29	29	29	29	29	29	29	29	29

Notes: standard errors in parentheses
*** p<0.01,
** p<0.05,
* p<0.1

deciles are the Bottom 60% and the Top 10%. The significance level of the variables used, and the results derived, show that most of the variables are significant in 1% level.

These results show that many economic variables can exacerbate income inequality, even though they aren't supposed to have such an impact. For instance, economic growth can be seen as a prerequisite to construct a more equal distribution. Naqvi (1994) indicates that:

> distributive justice can be achieved with less tensions when an economy is growing fast ... by greater employment opportunities and raising real wages (of the unskilled labor) economic growth raises real income. It is also a necessary condition for improving the distribution of income and wealth and reducing poverty. An economy wherein everybody gains in absolute terms—with the poor even getting a higher relative share— is clearly superior to the one in which one can gain only at the expense of the other. But growth is not sufficient condition. Thus, income redistribution and anti-poverty programmes must be implemented to make the society more egalitarian.
>
> (Naqvi, 1994, p. 92)

However, a more equal distribution of income can only be attained with economic growth if the existing mechanism and structures are designed to spread wealth to the whole society. The theses about trickle-down economics are not valid in such situations, where the important economic variables do not perform a welfare spreading role. In our sample, the distortive feature of economic growth on income equality can be explained in that sense. For inflation, it is already known that price changes directly reflect on real incomes and inflation leads real incomes to decrease. However, its relatively low magnitude compared to the other variables reveal that the real interest rate and interest payments in government expenses have stronger effects on income. Governments make interest payments to those who can afford to buy government notes, bonds and special purpose securities. These are mostly the rich and foreign investors. These payments transfer some proportion of income to the bond owners without making any productive impact on the economy. Thus, by this mechanism, the rich are getting richer at the expense of the poor. Moreover, the income transfer mechanisms operate in favor of the Top 20% and at the expense of the 80% in our sample. This brings the Pareto principle to mind which implies that roughly 80% of the effects come from 20% of the causes. However, more important than that, it shows the degree of injustice in contemporary economies in which the 20% gains at the expense of 80%. This could be called a chronic disease from our sample. Top 20%—and especially the Top 10%—reaps the benefits of instantaneous changes in an economy. The continuous transfer of income from the poor and middle classes to the rich consistently drones in the time and it leads to the emergence of chronic inequalities in income within a society.

In order to change the existing mechanisms and structures which exacerbate income inequality, the foundational principles and rules of Islam, which infuses *Tawhid* into people's heart and establish justice and order in the economic life, should be implemented. The prohibition of *riba*, establishment of *zakah* and other related injunctions offer a more equal distribution of income and wealth. Thus, the lack of empirical background of the hypothesis which indicates that income inequality is affected from interest which we have strived to fill in for the sample used in this study. The real interest rate, interest payments from government expenses, the GDP growth rate and inflation have a significant impact on the Gini Index and income decile groups, as they operate as income transfer mechanisms in favor of the rich, which decreases the social welfare. In this chapter, we have tried to construct a linkage between interest and social justice in the context of income inequality.

Conclusion

In this study we have tried to examine the relationship between interest and income inequality through the real interest rate, interest payments in government expenses, the Gini Index and income shares of the income deciles. The main motivation of this study is the prohibition of interest and the opposition to the concentration of wealth in the hands of the rich in Islamic texts. Also, it is our aim to reveal the relationship between income inequality and interest which is discussed but not proven empirically in the literature of Islamic economics. For the analyzed sample, low levels of the income share of the Bottom 10% are observed to be associated with high interest rate levels, while for the Top 10% high real interest rate levels are associated with high-income shares. Also, higher Gini Index levels are also associated with higher real interest rates. In the light of these reciprocal relations, we've found that the real interest rate is *pro-rich*, as a percent increase in it leads to a rise in the Gini Index and an income transfer from the bottom 80% to the top 20%. A percent increase in the real interest rate leads to 0.284% of the total income being transferred from the bottom 80% to the top 20%, as for a percent increase in interest payments in government expenses the amount of total income transferred from the bottom 80% to the top 20% is 0.559%. Furthermore, inflation and the GDP growth rate does not change the significance level of the real interest rate and interest payments. Inflation and the GDP growth rate also have an exacerbating effect on inequality. We acknowledge that arguments related to trickle-down economics are not valid for our sample as only the richest ones reap the benefits of economic growth at the expense of the remaining ones. Inflation has also had an increasing impact on inequality, however its impact is really low compared to the other variables. In that sense, this study is

a humble effort to show the detrimental impacts of interest on income distribution, as it verifies the arguments in Islamic economics literature which are
based on the exacerbating effect of interest on income inequality. Further
studies can be conducted to analyze the underlying interactions, links and
mechanisms of this impact.

And only Allah knows best.

Appendix 8.1 Country List

Argentina
Austria
Belarus
Belgium
Bolivia
Brazil
Bulgaria
Chile
China
Colombia
Costa Rica
Czech Republic
Ecuador
El Salvador
Estonia
Finland
France
Germany
Honduras
Hungary
Indonesia
Italy
Mexico
Netherlands
Norway
Panama
Paraguay
Peru
Poland
Romania
Spain
United Kingdom
Uruguay
Venezuela

Notes

1 See Al-Bukhari (1996), Hadith 1623, 1626, 6361.
2 Saheeh al-Muslim (2007), vol. 4, p. 56, Kitab al-Birr wa al-Silah wa al-Adab, Bab Tahrim al-Zulm, from Jabir ibn Abdullah.

References

Al-Bukhari, M. (1996). *Saheeh al-Bukhari (English Translation)*. Riyadh: Darussalam Publishing.
Ali, S. S., Shirazi, N. S., & Nabi, M. S. (2013). *The Role of Islamic Finance in the Development of IDB Member Countries: A Case Study of the Kyrgyz Republic and Tajikistan*. Jeddah: Islamic Research and Training Institute (IRTI), Islamic Development Bank.
Al-Suwailem, S. (2008). *Islamic Economics in a Complex World*. Jeddah: Islamic Development Bank.
An-Nasai, S. (2007). *English Translation of Sunan An-Nasa'i*. Riyadh: Darussalam Publishing.
Chapra, M. U. (1992). *Islam and the Economic Challenge*. Leicester: The Islamic Foundation.
Chapra, M. U. (1996). *What Is Islamic Economics*. Jeddah: Islamic Research and Training Institute (IRTI), Islamic Development Bank.
Chapra, M. U. (2003). Why Has Islam Prohibited Interest: The Rationale Behind the Prohibiton of Interest. In A. Thomas (Eds.), *Interest in Islamic Economics*. New York: Routledge.
Chapra, M. U. (2014). *Morality and Justice in Islamic Economics and Finance*. MA: Edward Elgar Publishing Limited.
Driscoll, J. C., & Kraay, A. C. (1998). Consistent Covariance Matrix Estimation with Spatially Dependent Panel Data. *Review of Economics and Statistics*, 80, 549–560.
Hoechle, D. (2007). Robust Standard Errors for Panel Regressions with Cross-Sectional Dependence. *The Stata Journal*, 7(3), 281–312.
Ibn Al-Hajjaj, M. (2007). *English Translation of Saheeh Muslim*. Riyadh: Darussalam Publishing.
Iqbal, Z. (2007). *Justice: Islamic and Western Perspectives*. Leicester: The Islamic Foundation.
Milanovic, B. (2005). Can We Discern the Effect of Globalization on Income Distribution? Evidence from Household Surveys. *The World Bank Economic Review*, 19(1), 21–44.
Naqvi, S. N. H. (1994). *Islam, Economics and Society*. London: Kegan Paul International.
Piketty, T. (1997). The Dynamics of the Wealth Distribution and the Interest Rate with Credit Rationing. *The Review of Economic Studies*, 64(2), 173–189.
Saheeh International. (1997). *Al-Qur'an: English Meanings*. Riyadh: Abu'l-Qasim Publishing House.
Siddiqi, M. N. (2004). *Riba, Bank Interest and the Rationale of Its Prohibition*. Jeddah: Islamic Research and Training Institute (IRTI), Islamic Development Bank.

Stiglitz, J. (2015). *New Theoretical Perspectives on the Distribution of Income and Wealth among Individuals: Part IV Land and Credit.* Working Paper no: 21192. Massachusetts: National Bureau of Economic Research.

UNDP. (2016). *Human Development Report: Human Development for Everyone.* New York: The United Nations Development Programme.

Zaman, A., & Zaman, A. (2001). Interest and the Modern Economy. *The Lahore Journal of Economics,* 6, 113–127.

9 Productive *Zakat* and social justice

Aimatul Yumna

Background

Poverty is a serious issue acknowledged in Islamic teaching. Poverty reflects the inability of an individual to meet the five basic requirements in life: religion, physical and emotional well-being, education, offspring and wealth (Hassan, 2010). This understanding of poverty as a concept maintains that religion and life can be protected through the provision of basic needs, including safe food and clean water, health services and secure shelter (Ahmed, 2004). Descriptions of poverty that emphasize the importance of tackling poverty by providing food and social security for each individual in the society abound in Islamic narratives and in the practice of the Prophets and Caliphs (Akhtar, 2000). Efforts to alleviate poverty are considered in the same light as fighting for Allah's cause and are equivalent to the efforts required to maintain fasting and prayer (Leaman, 2006). In the verses of the *Qur'an*, the obligation to pay *Zakat* is stated thirty times with many instances associated with the obligation of prayer in the same verses (Qardhawi, 2009).

Islamic charity has great potential to alleviate poverty since in Islam helping the poor is a central tenet of the faith. Islam addresses the issue of poverty by establishing the concept of social justice, solidarity and equality. Islamic charity plays an important role in creating social justice and equality since *Zakat* creates direct links between the haves and the have-nots (Bremer, 2013). Islamic charity allows the poor to gain access to more resources while as the same time it also prevents the wealthy from accumulating excessive assets accumulation by refusing to share some of their wealth to the poor.

The allocation of scarce resources and wealth transfer through Islamic charity in society exemplifies the centrality of equality concerns within Islamic teaching, a most relevant concept, to modern economic development Shepherd (2009). Islamic charities are major funding sources that play central roles in poverty alleviation (Bonner, 2005). In Islam, it is understood that poverty is not effectively addressed, or "solved," by simply handing out money in a charitable way. Rather, Islamic charity emphasizes the need for the underprivileged poor to take the initiative to work hard in utilizing resources in ways that may raise their living standards and alleviate poverty (Akhtar, 2000).

In relation to the *Qur'an*'s principles on poverty, scholars propose several strategies for poverty alleviation. Akhtar (2000) proposes three strategies for use in Islamic teachings on poverty alleviation. These strategies relate to the fulfillment of basic needs, the enhancement of earning opportunities and the equal distribution of income and wealth through Islamic charity distribution. Taking a more pragmatic approach, Obaidullah (2008) proposes three strategies to alleviate poverty. The first strategy involves the utilization of charity to fulfil basic survival needs, the second strategy attempts to empower the poor and the third attempts to facilitate the poor's participation in a commercial trade.

One of the crucial issues is finding effective and efficient charity distribution mechanisms that can optimize the benefits of Islamic charity for society. Research evidence from several Muslim countries shows that currently, Islamic charity is underutilized and cannot generate significant benefits for society and as a consequence, has a limited role to play in poverty alleviation (Mohammad et al., 2012). In some countries, in order to enhance the benefit of the outcomes, Islamic charity is utilized as sources of funding for empowerment programs, including charity-based microfinance.

The use of Islamic charity for empowerment programs generates several advantages. The first advantage, scholars argue, is that Islamic charity funds can provide basic needs as well as training to increase the skills of the poorest of the poor. (Ahmed, 2007). Furthermore, Obaidullah (2008) believes that Islamic charity has a role to play in assisting the economically inactive poor to become economically active and to facilitate their greater involvement as participants in microfinance. Islamic charity can be distributed in the form of noninterest loans that can be accessed by all segments of the poor and as such, in this way could increase financial inclusion in Muslim countries. Further, Mohieldien et al. (2011) also argue that Islamic charity can also be used as source of funds of microfinance programs. The use of charity as a source of funds will reduce the financial costs of microfinance institutions and increase operational efficiencies. It has been argued that one of the main causes of high rates of nonperforming loans in microfinance institutions is due to clients' use of funds for direct consumption purposes rather than for productive income-producing purposes. By using charity for taking care of clients' basic needs, Islamic microfinance can reduce the possibility of asymmetric information and moral hazard problems and as an outcome, may lead to better loan repayment rates and increased financial sustainability (Ismail & Possumah, 2013).

The strategies described above may enhance understanding of the role of Islamic charity in alleviating poverty. Irrespective, the distribution of charitable funds on its own is unlikely to alleviate poverty in any significant or long-term way. Poverty alleviation efforts are more likely to succeed if these are directed towards empowering and encouraging the poor to participate in some form of productive activities. The main goal of poverty alleviation is the transformation of the poor's circumstances such that they may, in the future, become charity donors rather than charity recipients.

Taking into account case studies of Indonesia, the amount of *Zakat* and other Islamic charity collected is significant in Indonesia, making up approximately 3.4% of the national GDP in 2010 (Firdaus et al., 2012). Traditionally, Islamic charity funds in Indonesia are distributed directly to the poor and largely used for more personal consumption purposes. Although direct distribution still occurs, *Zakat* distribution via institutions has been increasing since the 1960s (Abdullah, 1991). The IRTI Social Finance Report (2014) shows that one-third of Islamic charity funds collected by institutions during the period of 2004 to 2008 are distributed through mechanisms that enable the poor to gain long-term benefits from the charity such as improved access to education and training and to economic empowerment programs.

One of the popular *Zakat* empowerment programs in Indonesia is providing a *qard hassan* loan for *Zakat* recipients to start a new microbusiness. This program allows recipients to generate income, accumulate assets and, after a specific period of time, that they will be wealthier and progress to being *Zakat* payers themselves. Studies by Bremer (2013) and Hassan et al. (2012) show that a productive *Zakat* program has greater potency to enhance social justice and welfare. However, other studies such as Wan Ahmad and Mohamad (2012) and Yumna and Clarke (2011) show, productive *Zakat* may suffer with the problems of program sustainability and exclusion of the poor. This study will further explore opportunities and challenges of the use of *Zakat* for productive activities and empowerment programs in Indonesia.

The overarching research methodology selected to explore research queries is a case study methodology. The research process was designed along two pathways. The first takes a quantitative direction through the use of researcher-administered structured questionnaires to collect data from the case study institution clients and through the use of secondary data from the institutions. The second pathway follows a qualitative methodology in that semi-structured interviews are conducted with case study institutions' staff members.

Productive *Zakat*: a literature review

There are three types of Islamic charity known in the literature: *Zakat, shadaqa* and *waqf.* *Zakat* is the most regulated types of charity mentioned in the *Qur'an.* The regulation of *Zakat* includes several issues of the amount of *Zakat*, the recipients of *Zakat*, the payment period and the distribution mechanisms. Islam provides a clear definition of who can be a beneficiary of *Zakat.* As noted in the *Qur'an* (9.60), *Zakat* can only be given to eight categories of people: the poor, the needy, workers in the *Zakat* administration, newly converted Muslims, liberated slaves, those who are in debt, those who work for the sake of God and wayfarers. Among those categories, the poor and the needy are mentioned earlier in the verse of 9:60 indicating that the primary function of *Zakat* is to provide basic resources to meet the basic survival needs of the poor and the needy. According to Kahf (2006) extending relief to the poor and needy is the top priority of *Zakat* disbursement. Specifically, *Zakat* may be distributed to those who have little or no income, orphans, the sick, the disabled and the homeless (Obaidullah, 2008).

In addition, *sharia* also clearly regulates the payment period of *Zakat. Zakat* is an annual compulsory levy that must be paid directly and disbursed to the eligible recipients within one financial year (Hassan, 2010). According to Qardhawi (2009), any investment, or capitalization of *Zakat* funding is prohibited. Many scholars confirm that *Zakat* must be paid directly when accumulated assets reach specific level (*nisab*) (Wan Ahmad & Mohamad, 2012). Consequently, *Zakat* becomes a one-off means of assistance that is most often used to finance the immediate and pressing needs of the recipients. This condition limits the role *Zakat* can play in the provision of funding for longer-term poverty alleviation interventions.

In terms of distribution mechanisms, *Zakat* can be distributed either for direct consumption or income production motives. Traditional direct *Zakat* transfer has a limited impact on the recipients' longer-term welfare. With generally little in the way of resources, the poor may be more likely to use any direct charitable cash payments to meet immediate consumption needs (Sarif & Kamri, 2009). Distributing *Zakat* as productive capital in the form of qard al hasan loans and productive assets is now regarded as a more powerful distribution strategy when seeking to expand the income earning capacity of the poor. Productive *Zakat* is a strategy whereby *Zakat* is distributed in ways that have the potential to assist recipients to develop income generation capabilities. Productive *Zakat* can be distributed using three key mechanisms: *Zakat* as a grant and capital aid, *Zakat* as a source of funding for training provision and *Zakat* as *qard hassan* loans (Ahmed, 2002, Hassan, 2010, Rahman, 1967, Sarif & Kamri, 2009).

Although productive *Zakat* has a great potential to enhance long-term welfare, some aspects of productive *Zakat* implementation may risk compliance obligations to *sharia* (Wan Ahmad & Mohamad, 2012). The risk to *sharia* compliance can occur due to a delay in the disbursement of *Zakat*, the denial of individual rights to *Zakat* and the exposure of *Zakat* funds to risk. As such, much debate surrounds issues to do with the implementation of *Zakat* rules and regulations. Wan Ahmad and Mohamad (2012) examine the viewpoints of the classical Islamic Jurists on this debate and conclude that the allocation of *Zakat* for productive purposes needs to consider two factors: the availability of *Zakat* funds and the types of recipient needs that should be prioritized. Specifically, they argue that the use of *Zakat* in productive activities can be made when there is more than enough *Zakat* available to fulfil the basic needs of the poor.

The most contentious characteristic of *Zakat* is the concept of transfer of ownership (*tamlik*). *Tamlik* can be defined as the transfer of ownership of

Zakat from the wealthy to needy recipients; whereby the recipients have full authority to own and control the use of their *Zakat* funds for their own purposes (Ahmed, 2004, Sarif & Kamri, 2009). *Tamlik* will become an issue in the distribution of productive *Zakat* in the sense that it may not only involve direct distribution but may also involve almost "invisible" indirect distribution (Sarif & Kamri, 2009). For example, recipients may not receive *Zakat* in the form of tangible assets rather as intangible assets such as knowledge and expertise gained through skills training programs. Similarly, distributing productive *Zakat* as a *qard hassan* loan is also contentious in that *Zakat* should be given directly to recipients without any specific conditions imposed on its repayment.

The *Qur'an* does not provide specific guidance on the application of the transfer of ownership for *Zakat* distribution. Thus, the rule of using *Zakat* as a loan are by the scholars' opinion. Kahf (2006) and Qardhawi (2009) share a similar viewpoint in agreeing with the idea that *Zakat* can only be used for interest-free loans in order to assist *al gharimin* (people with difficult debt burdens) to repay their debts. However, neither author mentions the use of *Zakat* for providing financing for productive activities. Similarly, Hassan (2010) suggests that *Zakat* funds can only be used as capital grants for the initial development of a microenterprise without any expectation that the principal be repaid. Zayas (2003) strongly argues that the provision of *Zakat* as a loan can only bring temporary relief and may actually increase the poor's debt burden.

By contrast, the proponents of using *Zakat* in the form of a loan argue that the concept of *tamlik* is not an absolute concept since it is not mentioned in the major Islamic rules. If *Zakat* is distributed as a charitable loan, it is likely to provide many benefits to the society since repaid *Zakat* funds can be distributed to other recipients. Thus, a greater number of poor will benefit from *Zakat* (Hassan et al., 2012). However, *Zakat* is required to be distributed in the form of flexible loans, where repayment of the loan is not compulsory in case borrowers are experiencing repayment difficulties.

Zakat provides for the continual circulation of free funds that have great potential as main sources of social expenditure in Islamic society. *Zakat* can reduce disparities in the economy by discouraging the accumulation of wealth and encouraging the circulation of funds (Suhaib, 2009). The study by Mohieldien et al. (2011) provides an estimate of *Zakat*'s key capability to alleviate poverty in 39 Islamic countries. The researchers found that in 20 out of 39 Islamic countries, the use of *Zakat* has contributed to the alleviation of poverty conditions experienced by those existing on less than $1.25 per day.

The literature review indicated a scarcity of empirical research on the role of *Zakat* in poverty alleviation in the Caliphate period. The review turned up two reports on the effects of *Zakat* during the reign of Umar bin Khatab (13–22H) and Umar bin Abdul Azizz (99–101H) (Ahmed, 2004). Both reports indicated that *Zakat* charity funding may have played a significant role in poverty reduction as indicated by the relatively low numbers of poor people recorded in some regions of Yemen and Egypt. However, the use of

Zakat alone cannot effectively address all of the underlying issues that com-pound the challenges poverty presents (Kahf, 1999). Kahf (1999) noted that at least three factors played into the success of attempts to alleviate poverty in Yemen and Egypt during the Caliphate's era. First, both countries were rich with fertile arable lands that could produce abundant crops; second, the presence of a strong faith and reliance on God; and thirdly, the expanded market conditions and greater financial security of the population. Kahf (1999) argues further that to more effectively address social and economic problems, *Zakat* needs to be complemented with other wealth redistribution strategies.

Similarly, Ahmed (2004) argues that *Zakat* has a limited role in the devel-opment of poverty alleviation strategies. He maintains that *Zakat* is more important for achieving improvements at an individual-needs level rather than at the macroeconomic level. *Zakat* funds can be used to address some of the contributing factors that lead to poverty at the individual level such as a lack of resources in the form of human, physical and financial capital. As such, *Zakat* is expected to provide necessary input to generate income for the productive poor and provide periodic financial assistance for the nonproductive poor. Prior study suggests that there is still only a limited role for *Zakat* in the macroeconomic environment.

Although the issue of productive *Zakat* is debatable, using *Zakat* for *qard hassan* loans has been popular in Indonesia and Malaysia since the 1980s (Abdullah, 1991, Haron et al., 2010). Therefore, by providing some empirical evidence relevant to this debate, this chapter makes a contribution to the scarce literature focused on empirical data related to the appropriate use of Islamic charity as a microfinance funding source.

Case study institutions

Islamic charity in Indonesia is managed by three categories of institutions: Badan Amil Zakat (BAZ) as a state-owned *Zakat* institution, Lembaga Amil Zakat (LAZ) as a private *Zakat* institution, and Unit Pengumpul Zakat (UPZ) as the appointed agents for *Zakat* collection. Currently, BAZ is established in 33 provinces, 277 district level institutions and in 3160 subdis-tricts. In addition, there are approximately 200 LAZ institutions. In this case study, three institutions were selected to represent three categories of *Zakat* institutions: Baitul Qiradh Baznas (BQB) is a state-owned *Zakat* institution (BAZ) and Baitul Maal Muamalat Indonesia (BMMI) is a private *Zakat* insti-tutions (LAZ) and Baitul Maal Beringharjo (BMB) is an appointed agents for collecting *Zakat* (UPZ).

The first institution, BQB is owned by Badan Amil Zakat Nasional (BAZNAS), the government supervisory body of *Zakat* institutions in Indonesia. The BQB microfinance program was developed in February 2010. During 2010, BQB's operations were profit oriented. Using commercial Islamic transaction schemes, BQM distributed its funds from *infaq* and *shadaqa* in the form of microloans for the poor. At that time, BQB was experiencing problems as they were attempting to achieve profitability under the constraint of poor clients who were often facing difficulties with their loan repayments. As a result, the number of nonperforming loans in BQB was very high. Latterly, BAZNAS management considered reorienting BQB's mission from being a commercial microfinance institution towards a voluntary microfinance institution.

The reorientation of BQB began in early 2011. Since then, BQB has taken a position as a mentoring institution that provides *Qard hassan* loans and personal mentoring services (BQB-1, 2011). This program aims to assist *Zakat* recipients raise their income levels, strengthen their work ethos and reduce their dependency on informal money lenders.

The second institution is Baitul Maal Muamalat Indonesia (BMMI). BMMI is a representative of private *Zakat* organizations that was established in 2000 as a social subsidiary of Bank Muamamal Indonesia. BMMI collects Islamic charity from Bank Muamalat's clients and distributes this charity for social purposes. BMMI operations are directly linked to branches of Bank Muamalat Indonesia in most provinces in Indonesia.

BMMI's main program centers on economic empowerment. 70% of its funds are distributed for this purpose through microfinance programs. The programs include three initiatives: Komunitas Usaha Mikro Muamalat Berbasis Masjid (KUMMM), Koperasi Jasa Keuangan Syariah KUMMM (KJKS KUMMM) and Lembaga Keuangan Mikro Syariah (LKMS). These programs have been designed to run as continuous programs that aim to include the poor within the microfinance system by offering different products and services with different periods of interventions and targeting different client profiles.

BMMI KUMMM programs were initially developed in 2007. This program is especially designed for micro entrepreneurs who actively participate in the local mosque. The key objectives of the program are first, to work towards the economic empowerment of the poor and secondly to support religious education for society. This second objective is translated into the institution's mission statement as an intention to develop an individual character with strong religious beliefs, a determined commitment to grow and with the capacity to empathize with others. This mission statement emphasizes the need to enhance participants' well-being and to support growth in their understanding of Islam.

BMMI KUMMM program activities, including client selection, mentoring and loan repayment arrangements are conducted in the mosques. By centralizing these activities in the mosque, the institution believes that it will be able to choose clients who are motivated towards, and committed to, the adoption of positive attitudes and values. These client characteristics may go some way to reducing asymmetric information (Kalifatullah, 2012). This approach is understood to replicate features of the Al Akhuwat microfinance model in Pakistan.

KUMMM offers a continuation program by establishing financial cooperatives for the community surrounding the mosques, named as

Koperasi Jasa Keuangan Syariah (KJKS). This cooperative is registered with the Ministry Cooperative and is regulated as a semiformal organization under cooperative law. The members of the cooperative are successful graduates of the KUMMM program. KUMMM management expects that successful graduates will manage their own cooperatives and begin to participate in commercial microfinance. The role of BMMI is to provide the initial capital and to cover initial operating costs, as well as provide training in KJKS's standard operating procedures. Similar to other financial cooperatives, KJKS also offers various commercial Islamic transaction schemes to cover its operational costs. At this point, continuation program of KUMMM is no longer offering an interest free financing under *qard hassan* scheme.

The third institution, Baitul Maal Beringharjo (BMB) is a social unit of the local financial cooperative in Yogjakarta. The BMB's economic empowerment programs target the poorest level of the poor and have an important role to play in both preparing members of this client group to become more entrepreneurial in their outlook and in expanding opportunities for their financial inclusion. The BMB programs are conducted in three phases. In the first phase, Sahabat Ikhtiyar Mandiri (SIM) is offered for the poorest level of the poor. In the second, Sahabat Mudharabah Kebajikan (SMK) targets graduates of SIM programs, and in the third phase, Mentas Unggul, an advanced empowerment program, selects the best SMK graduates to be coached as entrepreneurs. Each program in each phase targets different clients and is designed to achieve different objectives. After having participated in a series of economic empowerment programs, the graduates of these advanced empowerment programs are expected to be clients of commercial financial instructions.

In addition to the provision of services to the poorest and the poor, BMB also offers some development programs for clients who are mainly new entrepreneurs with a small asset base. One of these programs, BINAR, offers direct assistance in book keeping and professional skills enhancement training. This free service of BMT assists new entrepreneurs to grow and reach their potential. BINAR graduates developed Binar Family (BIFA) as an ambassadorial program that represents and is run by successful participants. BINAR graduates also volunteer to become casual trainers for other BMB empowerment programs.

The case study institutions provide services at different levels of client coverage. Both BMMI and BQB provide services across most parts of Indonesia. BMMI's productive *Zakat* program is a mosque-based program delivered through 185 mosques, in 28 cities and 21 provinces. This mosque-based program includes 4,697 participants with total revolving funds of USD6.46 million and in 2012, employed 202 mentors. By contrast, BQB's productive *Zakat* programs were limited to several areas of Jakarta, Depok, Tangerang, Bekasi and small areas in West and Central Java. The third institution, BMB is a local institution in Yogjakarta has branches in 10 of Yogjakarta's 14 subdistricts with the total clients more than 500 clients.

Case study findings

This section reports the findings of the study by explaining the characteristics of the productive *Zakat* programs, the clients and the opportunity and challenges in distributing productive *Zakat*.

The main product offered by productive *Zakat* program is benevolent loans or qard hassan. This particular loan scheme requires clients to repay the loan financing at a similar amount of the principal within a specific time period.[1] This loan financing strategy is intended to assist *Zakat* recipients to gain access to capital for developing their own microenterprises. The objectives of this loan service are to empower and transform *Zakat* recipients into *Zakat* payers themselves.

Loan financing given to *Zakat* recipient has several unique characteristics. First, the average amount of financing is very low, ranging from 500,000–2,000,000 rupiah per client (around $50–$200). Such low average loan balances indicate that these institutions likely target very poor clients. These loans are short term in nature with full repayment expected within eight months to two years. When clients have repaid their first loan, productive *Zakat* institutions allow clients to obtain a "second round" loan of a higher amount. Interestingly, the institutional reports show that only half of the participants in the first round of loan allocations take up the offer of a second round of financing (Baitul Maal Muamalat Indonesia, 2012). This lower rate of participation may be due to prospective second-round borrowers' hesitancy to take up a loan with requirements similar to commercial loan types. Presumably, they would prefer the same loan conditions as those attached to the initial interest free loan.

Secondly, productive *Zakat* programs provide periodic mentoring supervision services as complementary programs to assist clients to successfully manage their loan funds. Mentoring plays a crucial role in educating clients about the benefits of a disciplined and motivated business approach to the running of their microenterprises. The mentoring process may also encourage some clients to change their mindset about poverty. From the case studies, there are two different mentoring approaches available to ICBMs (Islamic Charity Based Microfinance): direct personal mentoring and group mentoring. Productive *Zakat* institutions have developed training modules that cover several business-related subjects such as entrepreneurship, microenterprise management, financial and marketing management, the Islamic economy, leadership training, and religious education.

Group meetings are conducted in the mosque, or in one of the group member's homes. In 2011, the average weekly attendance for BMMI programs was 69% comparable to the average fortnightly meeting attendance for BMB's programs which was 60–70%. With the meetings beginning at 4 p.m., participants working at this time may not have been able to attend. Attendance at weekly meetings demands a significant time commitment on the part of both clients and mentors, with the meetings themselves incurring additional operating costs. The study's interview data show that the ratio of mentor per client is very high. For example, there are only two fieldworkers employed by BQB to assist approximately 600 clients. Similarly, there are only two mentors serving approximately 300 clients within BMB's empowerment programs. These ratios mean that field workers and mentors are expected to work longer hours and manage their time efficiently and effectively.

Thirdly, case study institutions apply individual lending strategies. The participants are managed in client groups of between five to ten members. Group meetings are intended to promote mentoring activities, and to organize loan installments and savings collections. The productive *Zakat* institutions have not adopted the standard Grameen Bank model of group lending that requires borrowers to select group members by themselves and that stipulates that group members are jointly liable to repay each borrower's loan. Rather, group members are selected by the institutions on the basis of clients' geographical locations in order to more conveniently schedule group meetings and to minimize travel costs. To enforce loan repayments, productive *Zakat* programs have a specific mechanism in place known as the *tanggung renteng* mechanism. The concept of *tangung renteng* is interpreted as a situation that arises when a group member cannot repay their loan and, as a consequence, other group members cannot obtain a second round of loan financing until all the group members' loans are fully repaid. Yet, the enforcement of the *tanggung renteng* mechanism is rarely, if ever enforced as such loan programs are funded by *Zakat*, which is intended to be given directly to the poor. As one management staff argues:

> We are a voluntary practice, this is not a bank... This money is their money that comes from *Zakat*...we treat it as a loan to educate them; so they can grow, from the assets sides, the business side, and religious side. The main purpose of this program is for support the development of mosques, increasing the religious value of the participants as well as developing their business.
>
> (Baitul Maal Muamalat Indonesia, 2012)

Overall, in Indonesia productive *Zakat* programs offer *qard hassan* loans, periodic mentoring and a loan enforcement mechanism. These programs are similar to interest-free (voluntary) microfinance programs.

The clients of productive *Zakat* and challenges to include poor clients' participation

As it is seen in the Table 9.1, on the demographic profiles, the institutions selected mature clients that were older than 45 years old. Most clients have a limited education and did not complete Indonesia's compulsory nine-year education period. On family size, the ICBM clients lived in small family units with two or three children to a family.

Table 9.1 Demographic profiles of the clients of productive *Zakat*

Family characteristics	Mean		
	BMMI	*BQB*	*BMB*
Age of household head (years)	46.77	49.11**	47.36
Formal education: level achieved (years)	7.8	7.48	9.04
Family size	4.3	4.75*	4.06**
Total	48	63	50

Source: constructed by the author from the survey results

As it is seen in the Table 9.2, based on the expenditure and income information, the average monthly per capita expenditure is $1.17 per day and the aver-
age annual per capita income is $987.23 per year or $1–$2.7 per day. This level
of income is higher than the World Bank standard minimal income of
$2 per day. The clients of BMB were reported as having the lowest income and
expenditure than other clients. Using the poverty line on food expenditure, the
study found that that 60% of clients of productive *Zakat* were living above the
national poverty line of Indonesia in 2011. Yet, when the higher benchmark of
the poverty line at $2 was utilized, the study found that the number of clients
living above the $2 per day benchmark is significantly fewer than the number
of clients and nonclients living above the $0.95 per day benchmark. This par-
ticular finding suggests that the clients of productive *Zakat* are not categorized
as poor. However, some clients live marginally above the poverty line and are
highly vulnerable to falling into poverty conditions. This finding also suggests
that when *Zakat* is given for productive activities, the institutions fail to include
the poor clients.

Economic development literature notes several barriers constraining poor
participation in a development program such as basic need problems,

Table 9.2 Clients' income levels

Variable	BMMI	BQB	BMB	Average
Monthly per capita expenditure in Rupiah ($ per day)	260,998.02 ($1.32)	242,757.34 ($1.23)	192,026.32 ($0.97)	231,927.27 ($1.17)
Annual per capita income in Rupiah ($)	7,667,395 ($1,166)	5,990,063 ($911)	5,817,300 ($884.7)	6,491,586 ($987.23)
Percentage of clients living above $0.95 per day	71%	69%	40%	60%
Percentage of clients living above $2 per day	21%	6%	4%	10,33%

Source: constructed by the author from the survey results

cultural barriers, and incompatible institutional policies (Simanowitz & Walter, 2002).

A study by Simanowitz and Walter (2002) suggests that the poor may suffer some basic need problems that may constrain their participation in any development program. Before participating in a development program, the poor may need some interventions to ensure their basic need fulfilment and to protect their health. Additionally, a lack participation by the poor can also be explained by some fundamental cultural factors. A similar story of a lack of participation by the poor in the productive *Zakat* can be evidenced in government-run social assistance programs. Setiawati and Guritno (1997) found that the poor do not want to participate in the government-managed social assistance program of IDT for reasons to do with a lack of resources such as time and skills, a lack of confidence and feelings of anxiety and apathy. Their study painted a distinctive portrait of the poor in Indonesia. Compared to the more financially secure, the Indonesian poor are more introverted, participate less in formal organizations and have children who, as a result of their income-earning responsibilities, experience relatively shorter childhoods and a lack education and work-related skills. These characteristics of the poor are similar to the notion of the culture of poverty introduced by Lewis (1971). Further, Lewis (1971) argued a sense of personal and social efficacy of the poor is highly influenced by the holding, or not of hopeful visions of the future.

In Javanese culture, dominant in this study, the life of many Indonesians, particularly the poor, is driven by the value of "being content" and "being happy" with their existing condition. Several terms acknowledge the importance of *"nrimo"* (being content) and *"sabar"* (being patient) in facing life's obstacles. Life is often symbolized by the wheel of a carriage that can be either in the top position, or in the bottom position. For the poor, being poor is a kind of destiny that has to be faced. These values influence how the poor view the future. For example, BMB's staff member said that clients' conceptualization of profit is very limited. As said by BMB's staff member: "for them profit is when they can still buy the inventory tomorrow" (BMB-1, 2011). The poor are not interested participating in a development program because of their lack of confidence and limited future orientations.

The last factor that may explain limited participation of the poor are the incompatible institutional policies related to client selection which might inadvertently be exclusionary in nature. BMMI, for example, requires prospective clients to have an existing business as a condition of their eligibility to participate in its institutional program. Simanowitz and Walter (2002) argues that for poor individuals and families, having an existing business is near impossible due to a lack of education, inadequate or inappropriate relevant business skills and a fundamental lack, or absence of working capital. As such, the expectation that prospective clients need to have an existing business, by default excludes the participation of the poor and the poorest. Anther institutional policy constraining the poor's participation is the BQB's requirement to create a business proposal for prospective clients. This requirement will limit poor participation since they have very limited knowledge to put together such a proposal.

Opportunities and challenges in achieving programs' sustainability

One of the key success factor of a development program is the ability of the program/institution to continuously provide services to its constituents. This success factor is known as institutional sustainability. Institutional sustainability ensures that a program can provide long-term benefit to the clients and the general society. Program sustainability is influenced by several factors such as the ability of the program to generate continual funding; the ability of the program to comply with regulations, in this case with *sharia* law and the ability to manage the program efficiently and effectively.

In terms of the ability of the institutions to generate funding, the study found that the overall amount of Islamic charity funds collected increased significantly between 2011–2012. The breakdown of funding sources reported in Table 9.3 shows that *Zakat* is the most popular type of charity collected by BMMI and BQB, with more limited funding collected from *shadaqa* and *waqf* sources. A possible reason for disparities between the amounts collected from these charitable funding agencies could be that other types of charitable funds, such as *shadaqa*, are usually voluntarily donated directly to close neighbors and family for more individual personal purposes. While the *waqf* fund is mostly used for building education, health and religious center.

By contrast, BMB collected more funds from *shadaqa* and *infaq* than from *Zakat* such that BMB's funding base is made up of 60% *shadaqa/infaq* funds with 40% derived from *Zakat*-sourced donations (BMB-1, 2011). BMB's *shadaqa* collection amounts to 350–400 million rupiah a year ($53,232 to $60,837). The significant amount of *shadaqa* and *infaq* funding comes predominantly

Table 9.3 Zakat institutions funding sources

	BMMI				BQB			
	December 2011		June 2012		December 2011		June 2012	
	Amount*	%	Amount	%	Amount	%	Amount	%
Zakat	17.59	(77)	24.4	(61)	12.77	(77)	14.069	(84)
Infaq, Shadaqa, Waqf	1.25	(5)	8.87	(24)	3.7	(22)	2.78	(16)
Non-halal income	4.1	(18)	5.6	(14)	0.16	(1)	n.a	n.a
Total	22.94	(100)	39.82	(100)	16.63	(100)	16.85	(100)

Note: *all Amounts are in billion Rp
Source: author's compilation from institutional reports

from private companies' Company Social Responsibility (CSR) funds. BMB has been able to develop and sustain good relationships with these private companies to generate substantial, if at times irregular, contributions from CSR funds. As a consequence, BMB can report that it has sufficient funds to resource all of its programs and still maintain a funding surplus. This surplus allowed BMB to establish four new client groups every month in 2012.

Sharia compliance also becomes a critical aspect to ensure institutional sustainability. Once the society is questionable about the *sharia* compliance of the program, the institution may receive some critical consequences such as reduction of funding collection and society protests. As discussed earlier in the literature review, *Zakat* funding is the most regulated type of Islamic charity. One of the more debatable issues in using *Zakat* for productive economic activities is compliance with the concept of *tamlik*. The analysis of the institutional case studies identified that both BMMI and BQB, institutions primarily funded by *Zakat*, have attempted to comply with the concept of *tamlik*. The findings also brought to light inherent complexities to comply with *tamlik* rulings within *sharia* law.

The first compliance issue relates to the use of *Zakat* to distribute benevolent loans as start-up capital for clients. When *Zakat* is given as a loan, the transfer of ownership of the funds does not take place as the client has to repay the loan. BMMI utilizes *Zakat* to provide revolving loans, which means that loans are never transferred to the borrower to be owned in any way, as might a tangible asset. The repaid loan funds are then used to finance loans to other beneficiaries. In that sense, these loans are described as revolving to other beneficiaries. Such loan-revolving schemes risk contradicting the concept of *tamlik* that stipulates that *Zakat* funds are to be given to the poor as custodians.

One of BMMI's strategies to accommodate the concept of *tamlik* is to establish financial cooperatives that are owned and managed by the poor. A management staff interviewee said that financial cooperatives provide an opportunity to return *Zakat* funding in the form of repaid loan monies to the poor. This practice is also questionable as according to *sharia* law, the poor should have full authority to use their loan funds for their own purposes and interests (Ahmed, 2004; Sarif & Kamri, 2009). Consequently, BMMI needed to seek an agreement from the poor that repaid loan funds would be used to establish financial cooperatives.

The strategy of developing financial cooperatives also carries some limitations, specifically in relation to whether the poor have sufficient skills to manage these. On this issue, BMMI management staff interviewed explained that they would provide technical assistance for one year to support the smooth running of the cooperatives. However, according to some interviewees', one year of technical assistance would not be sufficient as the development of the cooperatives is still sluggish, indicated by their low growth and high staff turnover (Baitul Maal Muamalat Indonesia, 2012).

The second institution, BQB, has taken a different approach to comply with the concept of *tamlik*. BQB states that their financial product is basically a grant rather than a loan. An ordinary grant is supposed to provide one off assistance and is not expected to be repaid. The case is different with the BQB grant in that the grant is explained to clients as a form of *qard hassan* financing that has to be repaid within ten months. One of the reasons management communicates an interpretation of the grants as a *qard hassan* loan is to emphasize the point that *qard hassan* funds are intended to empower the poor. By explaining that the grant is effectively a loan, management expects that grant recipients will work hard to generate sufficient income to repay "the loan." BQB sees this as an effort to educate the poor to be responsible with their grant funds.

Similarly, BMMI claim that its program provides a benevolent loan, not strictly understood as a conventional loan. The case study institutions explained that that repayment of benevolent loans is actually not necessary as *Zakat* is used to fund these. In practice, both BQB and BMMI require clients to repay the "grants" and "benevolent" loans. BQB sends fieldworkers to directly collect repayments from the client's house, while BMMI collects loan repayments during the weekly meetings. In addition, the performance of BQB's staff and fieldworkers is also evaluated based on their ability to collect repayments. Such loan payment collection practices create significant operational inefficiencies as the collection process incurs high operating costs. Interestingly, from the fieldworkers' perspective, they prefer to use the term "loan" rather than "grant" in order to align with the terminology and intent of the programs' success indicators. As one mentor commented:

> I've never said it was a grant since I have a responsibility to collect it back. My work performance is evaluated based on how many clients business survived? How many clients have repaid the loan? How many clients have saving account with BQB?
>
> (Baitul Qiradh Baznas, 2012)

This comment is interesting as it points out some of the complexities inherent in what might be understood as unconventional loan programs and policies. The mentors' performance is evaluated on how well the client is managing their loan repayments, that is, how the loan is performing. This notion of performance seems somewhat contradictory given management has stated that it does not expect participants to repay their loans. Therefore, it is argued that if the institution is highly dependent on *Zakat* funding, the concept of *tamlik* is represents one of the most challenging *sharia* rules to comply with.

The case is slightly different for BMB. Unlike BQB and BMMI that draw only on *Zakat* funds for *qard hassan* loans, the management of BMB said that only a small amount of *Zakat* is used to finance its loan programs. Irrespective of the amount of *Zakat* funding provided, the compliance rule remains. To comply with *sharia* law, BMB has to ensure that funds from different funding sources are kept in separate depositories. *Zakat* funds are intended to be used only to support direct charity programs such as natural disaster assistance, the provision of clean water supplies and mass education. In addition, the funds from *shadaqa* sources are expected to be directed towards empowerment programs through *qard hassan* and other Islamic funding schemes. These funding allocation strategies aim to ensure compliance with *sharia* law (Obaidullah, 2008).

Additionally, the literature discussion section also notes that *Zakat* funds must be disbursed in the same year of collection and are intended to provide short-term assistance to the poor. This relatively short time frame for the disbursement of microfinance funds presents a challenge for institutions. This "time-limit" related rule may severely hinder the achievement of program objectives and consequently weaken their capability to address poverty (Gonzalez-Vega, 1998). These study findings suggest that the rule requiring *Zakat* funds to be used within a year of their donation may significantly constrain the potential of targeted intervention programs to deliver productive outcomes.

The last aspect to consider when evaluating the sustainability of a productive *Zakat* program is financing repayment. In this case study, productive *Zakat* was given as qard al hassan financing. One of the indicators of success stated by the institution is the ability of the clients to repay the financing on time since this type of financing is expected to be distributed to other clients in the future. This study found the average repayment of financing is very low. In BMMI only 56% of the total loan financing distributed in 2010 was repaid; a figure that decreases to 20% of the total financing repaid in 2010. Additionally, for 496 BQB loans distributed in 2011, this study found that only 58% of loans were repaid on time.

In response to the question related to low repayment rates, one of the fieldworker staff interviewed mentioned that there are not enough fieldworkers to monitor all the clients. In 2012, only approximately 15% of BQB's total clients were supervised and monitored by mentors. One fieldworker staff related, "It is not non-performing, it does not perform well because we have never collected the repayment due to the lack of human resources" (BQB-2, 2011). The fieldworker's response supports the claim that one of the major challenges facing ICBMs in achieving institutional sustainability is the lack of human resources. As noted previously, issues around the lack of human resources can often be put down to severe cuts to the institution's operating budget.

Despite human resource-related challenges, one BQB fieldworker indicated that low loan repayment rates may also be due to public perceptions of *Zakat* as social organizations that simply disperse charitable funding directly to those in direct need, without an expectation that this funding be repaid.

Judging from the three factors affecting sustainability described above, this study found some opportunities and challenges in achieving the sustainability of a productive *Zakat* program. The biggest opportunity for productive *Zakat* is an increase in Islamic charity collection. Nowadays, Islamic charity donors placed a greater emphasis on the impact of the program. Productive *Zakat* is more likely to attract donor participation since a productive *Zakat* program is understood as a better mechanism to provide long-term benefits for *Zakat* recipients. However, this study also shows that productive *Zakat* programs experienced some challenges related to *sharia* compliance and financing repayment. These challenges may jeopardize the sustainability of the productive *Zakat* program in the future.

Conclusions

This research discusses the case study of productive *Zakat* in Indonesia exploring questions on opportunities and challenges of productive *Zakat* as mechanisms of social justice. In general, *Zakat* has great potential to foster equality by distributing income from the haves to the have-nots. However, when *Zakat* is distributed for productive activity, the study found that selected productive *Zakat* institutions faced various challenges in achieving high levels of sustainability and outreach. Given its inherent characteristics, *Zakat* funding is most likely suitable in developing poverty intervention initiatives before clients begin to participate in the institution's *qard hassan* program. The previously discussed issues around the negative public perception of *Zakat* as "free money" given directly to the poor, and the challenges inherent in meeting *sharia* compliance may constrain the effectiveness of using *Zakat* funding for *qard hassan* loans.

The study suggested that Islamic charity institutions' roles are to provide sequential services to increase the capacity and capability of the poor, specifically in relation to meeting daily basic needs, developing and encouraging clients' savings routines, providing education and business-related skills training and providing productive assets. Further, *Zakat* funds can be used for providing educational programs designed to prepare the poor in such activities that foster the development of clients' self-confidence and financial literacy (Woolcock, 1999, Wright, 2000). To continue these clients' preparatory programs, *Zakat* institutions should develop partnerships with existing Islamic microfinance institutions in order to provide microloans for participants.

The study grasped the potential for the Islamic charity sector to play a more significant and effective role in setting a more financial inclusive agenda for the poor in Indonesia by enhancing their capabilities to conduct income generation activities; and as a possible consequence, go some way to alleviate poverty. To successfully perform such a role, government supports are certainly needed by creating a regulatory environment around Islamic charity and productive *Zakat*, as well as providing support for the collaboration and integration of Islamic charity organization into existing microfinance providers' operations.

This study provides specific cases of *Zakat* implementation in Indonesia. The study findings provide base study that has a potential to generate further research questions on the impact of the program. This research avenue has great potential to generate high impact findings for both academia and policymakers.

Note

1 From the economist point of view, interest free financing can be seen as negative interest spread due to the inflation rate.

References

Abdullah, T. (1991). Zakat Collection and Distribution in Indonesia. In M. Ariff (Ed.), *The Islamic Voluntary Sector in Southeat Asia* (pp. 50–84). Singapore: Institute of Southeast Asian Studies.

Ahmed, H. (2002). Financing Microenterprises: An Analytical Study of Islamic Microfinance Institution. *Islamic Economic Studies*, 9, 28–64.

Ahmed, H. (2004). *The Role of Zakat and Awqaf in Poverty Alleviation*. Jeddah: IRTI.

Ahmed, H. (2007). Waqf -Based Microfinance Realizing the Social Role of Islamic Finance. In *Seminar on Integrating Awqaf in the Islamic Financial Sector*. Singapore.

Akhtar, M. R. (2000). Poverty Alleviation on a Sustainable Basis in the Islamic Framework. *The Pakistan Development Review*, 39, 631–647.

Baitul Maal Muamalat Indonesia. (2012, December 12). Intreview transcript.

Baitul Qiradh Baznas. (2012, December 8). Intreview transcript.

BMMI. (2011). *Performance Report of KUMMM Program*. Jakarta: Baitul Maal Muamalat Indonesia.

Bonner, M. (2005). Poverty and Economics in the Qur'an. *Journal of Interdisciplinary History*, 35, 391–406.

Bremer, J. (2013). Zakat and Economic Justice: Emerging International Models and their Relevance for Egypt. *Third Annual Conference on Arab Philanthropy and Civic Engagement*, Tunis, Tunisia.

Firdaus, M., Beik, I. S., Irawan, T., & Juanda, B. (2012). *Economic Estimation and Determination of Zakat Potential in Indonesia*. Jakarta: IRTI IDB.

Gonzalez-Vega, C. (1998). Microfinance: Broader Achievements and New Challenges. *The Second Annual Seminar on New Development Finance*. Frankfurt: The Goethe University of Frankfurt.

Haron, N. H., Hassan, H., Jasni, N. S., & Asdul Rahman, R. (2010). Zakat for Asnafs' Business by Lembaga Zakat Selangor. *Malaysian Accounting Review*, 9, 123–138.

Hassan, M. K. (2010). An Integrated Poverty Alleviation Model Combining Zakat, Awqaf and Micri-Finance. *7th International Conference-The Tawhidy Epistemology, Zakat and Waqf Economy*, Bangi, Bangladesh.

Hassan, N. M., Nor, A. H. B. M., & Rom, N. A. M. (2012). Embracing Microfinance: Proposed Collaboration between Zakat Institutions and Microfinance Institutions. *3rd ICBER 2012 Proceeding*.

IRTI. (2014). *Islamic Social Finance Report*. Jeddah, Saudi Arabia: IRTI Islamic Development Bank and Thomson Reuter.

Ismail, A. G., & Possumah, B. T. (2013). Theoretical Model for Zakat Based Islamic Microfinance Institutions in Reducing Poverty. *International Research Journal of Finance and Economics*, 103, 136–150.

Kahf, M. D. (1999). The Performance of the Institution of Zakat in Theory and Practice. *Islamic Economics toward 21st Century*, Kuala Lumpur, Malaysia.

Kahf, M. D. (2006). Role of Zakat and Awqaf in Reducing Poverty: A Proposed Institutional Setting within the Spirit of Syariah. *Thoughts on Economics*, 18(3), 39–67.

Kalifatullah, S. A. (2012). *Mitra Pengelola Zakat BMM pada KJKS/BMT. Bimbingan Teknis Bagi KJKS Dalam Rangka Optimalisasi Pendayagunaan Zakat.* Jakarta: Kementrian Koperasi dan Usaha Kecil dan Menengah Republik Indonesia.

Leaman, O. (2006). Money. In O. Leaman (Ed.), *The Qur'an: An Encyclopaedia* (pp. 411–414). London: Routledge.

Lewis, O. (1971). The Culture of Poverty. In M. Pilisuk & P. Pilisuk (Eds.), *Poor Americans: How the White Poor Live* (pp. 20–6). New York: Transaction Publishers.

Mohammad, M. Z., Chowdhury, M. S. R., & Chowdhury, I. A. (2012). Problems of Waqf Administration and Proposals: A Study in Malaysia. *Journal of Internet Banking and Commerce,* 17(1), 2–8.

Mohieldien, M., Iqbal, Z., Rostom, A., & Fu, X. (2011). *The Role of Islamic Finance in Enhancing Financial Inclusion in Organization of OIC Countries.* Washington, DC: Islamic Economics and Finance Working Group The World Bank.

Obaidullah, M. (2008). *Introduction to Islamic Microfinance.* India: International Institute of Islamic Business and Finance.

Qardhawi, Y. (2009). *Fiqh Al Zakat.* Jeddah, Saudi Arabia: Scientific Publishing Centre.

Rahman, F. (1967). Some Reflections on the Reconstruction of the Muslim Society in Pakistan. *Islamic Studies,* 6(9), 103–120.

Sarif, S., & Kamri, N. A. (2009). A Theoretical Discussion of Zakat for Income Generation and Its Fiqh Issues. *Jurnal Syriah,* 17, 457–500.

Schicks, J. (2007). Developmental Impact and Coexistence of Sustainable and Charitable Microfinance Institutions: Analysing BancoSol and Grameen Bank. *The European Journal of Development Research,* 19, 551–568.

Setiawati, L., & Guritno, S. (1997). *Budaya Kemiskinan di Desa Tertinggal di Jawa Timur: Kasus Desa Tarokan, Kecamatan Banyuanyar, Kabupaten Probolinggo.* Jakarta: Departemen Pendidikan dan Kebudayaan Direktorat Jenderal Kebudayaan.

Shepherd, W. (2009). *Introducing Islam.* London: Reutledge.

Simanowitz, A., & Walter, A. (2002). Ensuring Impact: Reaching the Poorest While Building Financially Self Sufficient Institutions, and Showing Improvement in the Lives of the Poorest Women and Their Families. In S. Daley-Harris (Ed.), *Pathways Out of Poverty: Innovations in Microfinance for the Poorest Families* (pp. 1–74). Bloomfield, CT: Kumarian Press.

Singer, A. (2008). *Charity in Islamic Societies.* Cambridge: Cambridge University Press.

Suhaib, A. Q. (2009). Contribution of Zakat in the Social Development of Pakistan. *Pakistan Journal of Social Sciences,* 29(2), 313–334.

Wan Ahmad, W. M., & Mohamad, S. (2012). Classical Jurist' View on the Allocation of Zakat: Is Zakat Investment Allowed. *Middle East Journal of Scientific Research,* 12, 195–203.

Woolcock, M. J. (1999). Learning from Failures in Microfinance: What Unsuccessful Cases Tell Us about How Group-Based Programs Work. *American Journal of Economics & Sociology,* 58, 17–42.

Wright, G. A. N. (2000). *Microfinance Systems: Designing Quality Financial Services for the Poor.* London: Zed Books.

Yumna, A., & Clarke, M. (2011). Integrating Zakat and Islamic Charities with Microfinance Initiative in the Purpose of Poverty Alleviation in Indonesia. *The 8th International Islamic Economic and Finance Conference,* Doha, Qatar.

Zayas, F. D. (2003). *The Law and Institution of Zakat.* Malaysia: The Other Press.

10 Estimation of potential *Zakat* in OIC

Salman Ahmed Shaikh and Qazi Masood Ahmad

As per the World Bank, an estimated 767 million people were living below the international poverty line of $1.90 per person per day in 2013. In addition to that, there has been an unprecedented change in income inequality between the poor and the rich people during the last half century. According to Oxfam, the 62 richest billionaires own as much wealth as the poorer half of the world's population. In contrast, one in every four people in Africa goes to bed hungry every night, according to Food and Agriculture Organization. Do we really have a scarcity of resources due to which we cannot end poverty, hunger and famine? Nobel Laureate, Sen (1983) did research on famine in Bengal and he argued that famine was not caused by a lack of resources. Strikingly, the world agriculture produces 17% more calories per person today than it did 30 years ago, despite a 70% increase in the population (Pingali, 2002).

The world has enough resources to feed everyone, but the resources are not equally distributed. Inequality in wealth distribution is often a result of income differences arising due to differences in risk tolerance, work effort, productivity and human capital to name a few factors. But, the level of inequality has increased tremendously in post-WWII period as documented by Piketty (2014) even when some of the developed economies had actually faced productivity growth slowdown since the 1980s.

While the developed world needs to find answers for egalitarian distribution of income, the developing world has to achieve both a decline in poverty as well as egalitarian distribution of income. Most of the Organization of Islamic Cooperation (OIC) countries are generally poorer than the other countries on average. Most of the poverty resides in Africa and Asia and the bulk of the OIC countries are located in these continents. Half of the global poverty resides in the Muslim world while the Muslim population is 24% of the total global population. In Pakistan, Naveed and Ali (2012) in a most recent study concluded that as many as 58.7 million people in Pakistan are living in multidimensional poverty with 46% of the rural population and 18% of the urban households falling below the poverty line. Other OIC countries like Bangladesh and Nigeria also have poverty headcount ratio of 43% and 62% respectively. Due to widespread poverty and weak governments, most of the OIC countries are behind in spending on schooling and health services. Hence, the level of human capital, productivity and national income remain at lower levels.

Against this backdrop, we want to empirically analyze the potential of *Zakat* as an institution of wealth redistribution to help in funding the poverty gap in the OIC countries. The chapter is organized as follows. Section 2 provides a review of the literature on socioeconomic effects of *Zakat* and its administration in contemporary economies. Section 3 provides details on the research methodology including sampling methodology and the methods we used to estimate potential *Zakat* collectible. Finally, section 4 presents our analysis. We estimate and compare the potential *Zakat* collectible against the funding gap for alleviating poverty in each of the 17 OIC countries.

Literature review

Wahid (1986) explains that *Zakat* is a compulsory payment on the part of Muslims as a share to the poor. Even though it is a religious obligation, *Zakat* also has a variety of economic and social ramifications. In early empirical literature on welfare potential of *Infaq* (charity) to alleviate poverty in Pakistan, Malik et al. (1994) use microdata to establish that *Infaq* (charity) does have significant impact on reducing the poverty gap. In a recent empirical study for OIC countries, Shirazi and Amin (2009) estimated the resources required for poverty elimination under $1.25 a day and $2.00 a day respectively. Their estimates for Pakistan suggest that Pakistan needs 1% of GDP for poverty elimination under $1.25 a day and needs 6.77% of the GDP for poverty elimination under $2 a day. In another study for Pakistan, Kahf (1989) uses different *Zakat* categories and according to his estimate, *Zakat* collection can be between 1.6% of the GDP to 4.4% of the GDP.

In a more recent study, Azam et al. (2014) in an empirical study for Pakistan established that *Zakat* significantly enhances the welfare of these households. M. Akram and Afzal (2014) in an empirical study for Pakistan argue that *Zakat* disbursement among the poor, needy, destitute, orphans and widows has played a significant role in poverty alleviation. Their results show that there is an inverse relationship between poverty and *Zakat* disbursement both in the short run and in the long run.

Using aggregate data for Malaysia, Suprayitno et al. (2013) find that *Zakat* distribution has a positive, but small impact on aggregate consumption. Hence, *Zakat* distribution should not be limited to the consumption needs, but should also cover other forms of monetary aid that can generate a continuous flow of income for *Zakat* recipients. In another recent study, Abdelmawla (2014) argue based on empirical evidence using aggregated data for Sudan that *Zakat* along with educational attainment significantly reduced poverty in Sudan. However, we note here that using aggregated data for most OIC countries where official the *Zakat* collection is very low does not make a convincing case for poverty alleviation.

In another empirical study for Bangladesh, Hassan and Jauanyed (2007) estimate that *Zakat* funds can replace the government budgetary expenditures ranging from 21% of the Annual Development Plan (ADP) in 1983–1984 to 43% of the ADP in 2004–2005. For Malaysia, Sadeq (1996) finds that about 73% of the estimated potential the *Zakat* collection will be needed annually to change the status of households to the status of nonpoor households in Malaysia. Ibrahim (2006) contends in an empirical study for Malaysia that *Zakat* distribution reduces income inequality. His analysis reveals that *Zakat* distribution reduces poverty incidence and lessens the severity of poverty. Firdaus et al. (2012) estimate the potential of the *Zakat* institution in Indonesia by surveying 345 households. Their results show that the *Zakat* collection could reach 3.4% of Indonesia's GDP.

Some studies also show the comparative potential of *Zakat* as a superior tool for poverty alleviation. Debnath et al. (2013) assessed the effectiveness of *Zakat* as an alternative to microcredit in alleviating poverty in Bangladesh. Through the Propensity Score Matching (PSM) techniques, the study reveals that the impact of the *Zakat* scheme has proven to be greater than the microcredit programs. Besides that, the study also highlights that the *Zakat* scheme significantly increases both the income and expenditure of the recipients in comparison to the microcredit programs.

Other studies like Nadzri et al. (2012) recommend integrating the various poverty alleviation and redistribution tools for creating synergies. The effectiveness of *Zakat* institutions may improve by collaborating with other institutions such as microfinance institutions. Shirazi (2014) suggests that the institutions of *Zakat* and *Waqf* (charitable trust) need to be integrated into the poverty reduction strategy of the Islamic Development Bank (IDB) member countries. The proceeds of these institutions should be made as part of their propoor budgetary expenditures. Hassan (2010) suggests a model which combines Islamic microfinance with two traditional Islamic tools of poverty alleviation such as *Zakat* and *Waqf* in an institutional setup. Hassan (2010) argues that the poor borrowers will have less debt burden as their capital investments will be partly met by funds from *Zakat* that would not require any repayment.

Wahab and Rahman (2011) identify that there are many types of programs that could be funded by *Zakat* such as providing schooling, vocational training and business support by establishing cottage industries and providing fixed assets and equipment to small business projects. In addition to that, *Zakat* could also be used to provide low-cost housing and health care. Abdullah and Suhaib (2011) argue that if *Zakat* is established as an institution, it will create a collective social security scheme for mutual help and the resources can be further utilized for social development.

To achieve such diverse contemporary needs, the institution of *Zakat* is dynamic and flexible. During the Umer (rta) and Abu Bakar (rta) period of government, *Zakat* was collected by the government. But, in the Usman (rta) period, people were allowed to pay *Zakat* privately (Kuran, 2003). Horses were exempted from *Zakat* in the Prophet's time, but, Umer (rta) brought them in the *Zakat* net in his period. Similarly, Mahmud (2001) informs that Umer (rta) levied *Zakat* on horses and skins and at the time when Arabian Peninsula was hit with a drought and famine, he exempted the poor from *Zakat* and suspended *Zakat* from the rich. Usman (rta) also levied *Zakat* on the production in forests which was not the case in the earlier period (Nadvi, 1996). Hence, a policymaker in a modern economy can use this institution flexibly to maximize the welfare benefits of the *Zakat* system.

Nevertheless, *Zakat* is not collected by the government nowadays in most countries and is not considered a compulsory payment to the government (Powell, 2009). Ahmad et al. (2006) examined factors contributing to the dissatisfaction towards formal *Zakat* institutions based on a sample of 753 respondents who paid *Zakat* to six privatized institutions. Their study uses logistic regression to analyze the probability of paying to such *Zakat* institutions. Their results indicate that the satisfaction on the distribution and efficient management of *Zakat* are the main factors influencing *Zakat* payment. About 57% of the respondents were dissatisfied with the distribution of *Zakat* funds which significantly affects payments to the *Zakat* institutions. Wahid et al. (2008) revealed two main factors contributing to dissatisfaction, i.e. the ineffectiveness of *Zakat* distribution and the lack of transparency on information about the distribution of *Zakat*. The lack of confidence in the governance of *Zakat* institutions due to the perceived lack of efficiency and effectiveness may directly undermine the *Zakat* institutions in attaining their desired socioeconomic objectives. Bakar and Rahman (2007) argue that a lack of proper implementation of *Zakat* in OIC countries limits the success of the noble aims of the *Zakat* institution.

To help change this state of affairs, Yusoff (2011) urges that every Muslim country must organize *Zakat* collection and *Zakat* spending in the most effective and efficient manner. Azam et al. (2014) also suggest that there is a need to institutionalize the *Zakat* collection system to increase the overall *Zakat* collection. In another study, Rahman (2003) proposes the introduction of two *Zakat* governance measures, i.e. the promulgation of Islamic accounting standard, and structural and policy reform towards more effective *Zakat* distribution.

One of the other potential reasons for insignificant size of central *Zakat* collection and ineffective disbursement is that the mainstream Islamic scholarship allows taxes to be levied other than *Zakat* for mobilizing public finance. Maududi (1970) argues that *Zakat* is a religious obligation and is not a substitute for tax. Same opinion is held by Siddiqui (1978) and Shaik (1979). Siddiqui (1978) cites prominent Islamic jurists like Ibn-e-Hazm and Imam Shatibi in support of this view. These scholars opine that taxes other than *Zakat* can be imposed in an Islamic economy if these taxes are levied by the legislative council and used for public welfare. He contends that the taxes discouraged in *Ahadith* are those which were imposed by the autocratic kings for their own lavish consumption and this kind of usurpation of public property was discouraged in Islam.

Besides governance, there is a dire need for a standardized approach to the *Zakat* base. Shirazi and Amin (2009) argue that since there is no agreement among the scholars on the new wealth that may be brought into the *Zakat* net, there is an urgent need for the general agreement on the definition of the items, which may be taken as *Zakatable* items. This requires *Ijma* (consensus) of the *ulama* (Islamic scholars) and other contemporary scholars on the issue.

On the need for extending the *Zakat* net by including all forms of wealth and produce, Qaradawi (1999, p. 333) applies the methodology of *Qiyas* (analogical reasoning) and reasons that the emerging and increasing types of wealth in the modern times such as bank deposits and financial securities like shares and bonds are also *Zakatable* (Qaradawi, 1999). Bakar and Rahman (2007) also suggest that the *illah* (basis or reasoning) for *Zakatability* should no longer be productive property, but any property which is in excess of one's personal use. Haneef and Mahmud (2012) also argue that the general directives of the *Qur'an* do not restrict the application of *Zakat* to certain types of wealth to the exclusion of others.

That is why; wealth or assets subject to *Zakat* should include cash in hand or at bank, gold and silver, held-for trade inventory, real estate purchased for the purpose of resale and all types of financial investments in stocks, bonds, debentures, national saving schemes and mutual funds. Likewise, production is not limited to agriculture nowadays. The major part of production comes from industries as well as the services sector. Therefore, income from the industrial production could also be taxed just like agriculture. Similarly, income from the services sector could also be taxed on the same principle.

Lastly, we discuss another important question that whether the investment in financial instruments shall be subject to wealth *Zakat* on total investment value or only the income from such financial investments shall be subject to income *Zakat*. Khan (2005) contends that investment in stocks should be interpreted as any other investment with some means of earning income. Investment in a stock is a means of earning dividend income or capital gains. Just like means of production/income are exempted from *Zakat*, investment in stocks should be exempted from wealth *Zakat*. Therefore, any income arising from investment in stocks must be subject to income *Zakat*. Similarly, this argument could be extended to introduce income *Zakat* on mutual funds, investment in National Savings Schemes (NSS), debentures and bonds. Furthermore, if a real estate is leased, the real estate becomes the means of earning rent for the owner. Hence, income *Zakat* could also be introduced on rental income.

To summarize, we see that on theoretical grounds, *Zakat* is an important redistributive institution. If the governments improve the governance, administration and effective and transparent use of *Zakat* funds, then tremendous gains can be achieved in improving public welfare.

Research methodology

Problem statement

To estimate the potential *Zakat* collectible in selected OIC countries for overcoming the poverty gap as measured by poverty headcount ratio and poverty gap index.

Rationale for the study

Islamic economics literature is rich in describing the economic potential of *Zakat*, but very few empirical studies have undertaken the estimation of potential *Zakat* collectible at the economywide level. The actual *Zakat* collection data reported by various governments is not a true indicator of the total *Zakat* spending since most of the people prefer to pay *Zakat* privately due to the trust deficit between the *Zakat* payers and the government institutions. On the other hand, usually the governments in the OIC countries are weak and rely on easy forms of indirect taxation or natural resources wealth. Both the trust deficit and the lack of intent from the governments to seriously organize and administer the *Zakat* collection and disbursement has resulted in realizing less than potential results from the institution of *Zakat*. Though this study, we make an effort to estimate the potential *Zakat* collectible in the OIC countries and see the potential of the institution of *Zakat* to contribute in alleviating chronic poverty in the OIC countries. The estimate of aggregate *Zakat* collectible is then compared against the funding needs to alleviate poverty. For poverty measures, the study uses poverty headcount ratio as well as poverty gap index, both at $1.25 a day and $2.00 a day respectively.

Sampling methodology

For the estimation of potential *Zakat* collectible at the aggregate level, we had selected 17 members of OIC. The selection is based on the availability of complete data. Due to the nonavailability of data for some variables, we had to drop few OIC countries from the sample. Since the variables are needed to form an aggregate series, any missing value is detrimental in this estimation exercise. It is different in the case of missing observations or variables in a regression analysis where the variables are used to explain changes in a dependent variable rather than to form an aggregate series.

Nature and sources of data

The data is taken from the World Bank's World Development Indicators (WDI) for the period 2008–2013. For official gold holdings in each country, we use the data provided by World Gold Council. In this estimation exercise, we had selected following variables (see Table 10.1).

Table 10.1 List of variables used in *Zakat* estimation

Variable name	Unit of measurement
Total reserves (includes gold)	Current USD
Total reserves minus gold	Current USD
Official gold reserves	Current USD
Broad money	Current USD
Broad money to GDP	Ratio
Market capitalization	Current USD
GDP	Current USD
Changes in inventories	Current USD
Agriculture, value added	Current USD
Industry, value added	Current USD
Services, value added	Current USD
Agricultural irrigated land	Percent of total agricultural land.
Total natural resources rents to GDP	Ratio
Total natural resources rents	Current USD
Population	Total number of people alive in the country
Proportion of Muslim population	Percent of Muslims in total population
Percent income held by top 20%	Percent of total personal income

For measuring poverty, we use following variables (see Table 10.2).

Method for computing aggregate Zakat

For estimating *Zakat* on wealth, we use the following heads:

- Estimated private gold holdings.
- Broad money.
- Market capitalization of stocks.

Table 10.2 List of variables used for poverty measurement

Poverty gap at $1.25 a day (PPP)	Mean shortfall from the poverty line ($1.25 a day) as a percentage of the poverty line.
Poverty headcount ratio at $1.25 a day (PPP)	Percent of total population with below $1.25 a day income.
Poverty gap at $2.00 a day (PPP)	Mean shortfall from the poverty line ($2.00 a day) as a percentage of the poverty line.
Poverty headcount ratio at $2.00 a day (PPP)	Percent of total population with below $2.00 a day income.

• Inventory investment (as proxy for unsold inventory).

To estimate private gold holdings, we use the following formula:

$$Private\ Gold\ Holdings = \frac{Official\ Gold\ Reserves}{Total\ Reserves\ /\ Broad\ Money} \qquad (1)$$

The proxy follows the assumption that the government holds as much official gold reserves as a ratio of private gold holdings as it holds total reserves as a ratio of broad money. For instance, if the ratio of total reserves to broad money is 20%, then we assume that the government's official gold holdings as a ratio of total private gold holdings will also be 20%. Since we know the official reported gold holdings of governments, we can find an estimate of private gold holdings using the above formula. Here, we assume that the government's choice of keeping monetary and gold reserves as a proportion of broad money and total private holdings respectively is the same in the long run.

Since *Zakat* is levied on currency in ownership as well as on money deposited in bank accounts, we use broad money as a proxy for the wealth held as currency and in bank accounts. For *Zakat* on market value of stocks, we use market capitalization. It is calculated as:

$$Market\ Capitalization = \sum_{i=1}^{n} N_i P_i \qquad (2)$$

Where N_i is the number of shares outstanding for company "i" and P_i is the current market price of the stock of company "i".

Lastly, for the estimate of unsold tradable inventory, we use the "inventory investment" figure as reported in the national income accounts. In national income accounting, "inventory investment" represents the value of production in a particular year that remains unsold during that year. It is assumed that the firm has purchased unsold inventory from itself. However, the "inventory investment" figure reported in national income accounts gives an estimate of the tradable inventory for production which took place only in that year. The actual tradable inventory could be much more than the reported "inventory investment" figure.

We are looking to estimate the value of this wealth *Zakat* function:

$$WZ = \sum_{x=1}^{n} 0.025(W_x - MNA) \qquad (3)$$

Here,
  "*WZ*" refers to total Wealth *Zakat*.
  "W_x" refers to wealth in ownership of individual x.

"*MNA*" refers to minimum *Nisaab* amount. It is computed as the market value of 612 grams of silver.

To deduct the *Nisaab* amount at the aggregate level, we have to make an estimate of the number of people whose wealth in ownership exceeds the *Nisaab* amount. We take a conservative route to assume that people in the top income quintile of the population will have the wealth exceeding *Nisaab* amount.

We define "P_{MNA}" as a set of all people belonging to the top income quintile and have wealth exceeding *Nisaab* amount. Mathematically:

$$P_{MNA} = \{x \in P_{top\ 20\%} | W_x \rangle MNA\} \tag{4}$$

If an individual "x" belongs to the top income quintile, he is assumed to have wealth exceeding *Nisaab* amount. From the aggregate value of assets that are subject to wealth *Zakat*, we have to deduct the product: $\{P_{MNA} \times MNA\}$,

In the second part of the estimation, we try to estimate total production value tax that can be collected in individual economies in our sample. The rate of production value tax can be 5%, 10% or 20%. Production processes which use both labor and capital intensive mix of inputs are subject to 5% production value tax. Production processes which majorly use either labor or capital intensive mix of inputs are subject to 10% production value tax. Incomes from sources which neither use labor nor capital intensively are subject to 20% production value tax.

Mathematically, we can represent this principle of levy as in equation (5). Here, $\bar{L}$ and $\bar{K}$ represent very minimal use of the inputs in fixed amount. "*PVT*" refers to the production value tax.

$$PVT = \begin{cases} 10\% & y = f(L, \bar{K}) \\ 10\% & y = f(\bar{L}, K) \\ 5\% & y = f(L, K) \\ 20\% & y = f(\bar{L}, \bar{K}) \end{cases} \tag{5}$$

Hence, we apply 5% of the production value tax to the production arising from irrigated land and the production value of output produced in the industry and services sector. We apply 10% of the production value tax on the production arising from rain-fed lands. Finally, we apply 20% of the production value tax on production arising from rents on natural resources.

Since *Zakat* is only levied on Muslims, we make the adjustment in all variables to account for that. We assume that in the long run, the proportion of Muslims and non-Muslims in the top income quintile will be the same as their proportionate distribution in total population.

For measuring poverty, we use two measures, i.e. the poverty headcount ratio and poverty gap. The poverty headcount ratio is computed as a ratio of the number of people in poverty divided by the total population. The poverty gap index is computed as follows:

$$PGI = \frac{1}{N} \sum_{j=1}^{q} \left(\frac{z-y_j}{z} \right) \tag{6}$$

$$PGI = \frac{1}{N} \sum_{j=1}^{N} \left(\frac{(z-y_j).1_{(y_j<z)}}{z} \right) \tag{7}$$

Here, "N" is the total population of a country, "q" is the total number of poor people in the population with income below the poverty line, "z" is the poverty line defined by a particular threshold of income like \$1.25 or \$2 a day and "y_j" is the income of the poor individual "j". In this index, the poverty gap for individuals whose income is above the poverty line is zero.

Ahmed (2004) uses a conservative crude measure of poverty gap by multiplying the number of poor people with the average minimum annual income of \$365 or dollar a day per nonpoor person. This is a conservative measure since it assumes that poor people have zero annual income (Shirazi & Amin, 2009). Hence, we report both measures for comparative analysis.

Result and analysis

In this section, we present the results of our estimation exercise. We report the results in Table 10.3. In Table 3, "ZGDP" refers to *Zakat* to GDP ratio. "PGI-GDP" refers to the Poverty Gap Index to GDP ratio. It is computed as follows:

$$PGI \ to \ GDP = \frac{PGI * y_p * N}{GDP} \tag{8}$$

Here,

"*PGI*" refers to the Poverty Gap Index value.

"y_p" refers to income at poverty line in current \$.

"N" refers to the total number of people in the country.

"*GDP*" refers to the value of the Gross Domestic Product.

In Table 3, "PHCR-GDP" refers to the Poverty Head Count Ratio to GDP. It is computed as follows:

$$PHCR \ to \ GDP = \frac{PHCR * y_p * N}{GDP} \tag{9}$$

Here,

"*PHCR*" refers to the Poverty Head Count Ratio.

"y_p", "N" and "*GDP*" have the same meaning as defined above.

Table 10.3 Zakat to GDP, poverty gap to GDP and poverty rate to GDP ratio

Country	ZGDP	PGI-GDP ($1.25)	PGI-GDP ($2.00)	PHCR-GDP ($1.25)	PHCR-GDP ($2.00)
Albania	2.60%	0.01%	0.09%	0.05%	0.47%
Azerbaijan	5.83%	0.01%	0.05%	0.02%	0.14%
Bangladesh	2.76%	5.32%	23.13%	20.63%	58.30%
Egypt	3.69%	0.05%	0.62%	0.23%	3.39%
Indonesia	3.53%	0.35%	2.74%	2.13%	9.10%
Jordon	4.30%	0.00%	0.02%	0.01%	0.17%
Kazakhstan	2.69%	0.00%	0.01%	0.00%	0.03%
Kyrgyz Republic	3.13%	0.43%	3.07%	1.84%	12.19%
Malaysia	4.59%	0.02%	0.16%		
Morocco	5.01%	0.08%	0.74%	0.38%	3.30%
Mozambique	0.97%	19.49%	52.67%	45.77%	99.54%
Nigeria	2.20%	4.17%	10.88%	9.41%	19.97%
Pakistan	2.54%	0.69%	7.58%	4.54%	29.02%
Saudi Arabia	8.45%			0.35%	0.70%
Tajikistan	2.36%	0.56%	4.71%	9.11%	19.30%
Tunisia	3.73%	0.02%	0.16%	0.27%	0.76%
Turkey	3.42%	0.00%	0.03%	0.06%	0.17%

Source: author's calculations

We can see that the *Zakat* to GDP ratio exceeds the PGI-GDP ratio except in three countries with the poverty line defined at $1.25 a day. Only in Bangladesh, Mozambique and Nigeria, is the *Zakat* to GDP ratio less than the PGI-GDP ratio with the poverty line defined at $1.25 a day. Mozambique is one of the members of OIC with a very small proportion of Muslims. We can also observe that the *Zakat* to GDP ratio exceeds the PGI-GDP ratio except in 4 countries with the poverty line defined at $2.00 a day. Only in Bangladesh, Mozambique, Nigeria and Pakistan, the *Zakat* to GDP ratio is less than the PGI-GDP ratio with the poverty line defined at $2.00 a day.

We also show the comparison of the *Zakat* to GDP ratio against the poverty headcount ratio. However, one must note that the estimate of funding gap from the poverty headcount ratio assumes that the poor people have zero levels of income. Hence, it exaggerates the true funding needed to alleviate poverty. We can see that the *Zakat* to GDP ratio exceeds the PHCR-GDP ratio except in 5 countries with the poverty line defined at $1.25 a day. The countries in which *Zakat* to GDP ratio is less than the PHCR-GDP ratio with the poverty line defined at $2.00 a day include Bangladesh, Mozambique, Nigeria, Pakistan and Tajikistan. We can also observe that the *Zakat* to GDP ratio exceeds the PHCR-GDP ratio except in seven countries with the poverty line defined at $2.00 a day. The countries in which the *Zakat* to GDP ratio is less than the PHCR-GDP ratio with the poverty line defined at $2.00 a day include Bangladesh, Indonesia, Kyrgyz Republic, Mozambique, Nigeria, Pakistan and Tajikistan.

Therefore, we can see that in most countries, if the potential *Zakat* collection is collected and disbursed effectively, the poverty gap can be funded even in the first round. Since *Zakat* is a combination of the net worth and production value tax, it works effectively irrespective of the phase of the business cycle. Furthermore, it targets the poor and ultra-poor specifically and achieves the redistribution directly.

In Table 10.4, we show the *Zakat* estimation for individual years during the period 2008–2013. It can be seen that the estimates have little variance over the years. Hence, the institution of *Zakat* can provide a stable source of public revenue that can be spent on public welfare directly by a transfer of monetary and nonmonetary assets along with provision of health and educational services through establishing welfare institutions from the *Zakat* fund. Since the institution of *Zakat* only collects *Zakat* from the people who hold at least a prescribed amount of wealth, it ensures that the *Zakat*

Table 10.4 Zakat to GDP ratio during 2008–2013

Country	2008	2009	2010	2011	2012	2013
Albania	2.51%	2.46%	2.58%	2.57%	2.62%	2.60%
Azerbaijan	7.57%	5.92%	6.13%	5.86%	5.41%	5.83%
Bangladesh	3.48%	3.06%	3.01%	2.91%	2.83%	2.76%
Egypt	5.34%	4.02%	3.85%	3.99%	3.72%	3.69%
Indonesia	4.66%	4.03%	3.82%	3.69%	3.52%	3.53%
Jordon	5.84%	5.01%	4.79%	4.67%	4.50%	4.30%
Kazakhstan	3.62%	3.05%	2.97%	2.95%	2.72%	2.69%
Kyrgyz Republic	2.98%	3.02%	3.28%	3.12%	3.20%	3.13%
Malaysia	6.05%	5.99%	5.28%	4.85%	4.65%	4.59%
Morocco	5.61%	4.92%	5.02%	5.10%	5.16%	5.01%
Mozambique	1.21%	1.07%	1.12%	1.03%	0.98%	0.97%
Nigeria	1.80%	3.01%	2.30%	2.39%	2.22%	2.20%
Pakistan	3.06%	2.68%	2.68%	2.64%	2.59%	2.54%
Saudi Arabia	10.58%	8.81%	8.53%	8.85%	8.48%	8.45%
Tajikistan	2.39%	2.37%	2.44%	2.37%	2.36%	2.36%
Tunisia	4.20%	3.59%	3.66%	3.77%	3.77%	3.73%
Turkey	3.48%	3.80%	3.53%	3.55%	3.49%	3.42%

Source: author's calculations

payers are richer than the *Zakat* recipients. This ensures socioeconomic mobility and contributes towards egalitarian income distribution.

In our estimation, we had assumed that only people in the top income quintile are asked to pay *Zakat*. Actual the number of people eligible for the *Zakat* payment may be even more than that especially in the middle-income countries and the emerging economies of South Asia. Since the *Nisaab* value is equivalent to the value of 612 grams of silver, the people who come out of poverty can later on become *Zakat* payers after having previously been *Zakat* recipients.

In Table 10.5, we present the correlation between *Zakat* to GDP ratio and GDP growth rate for the six-year period, i.e. (2008–2013). It can be seen that absolute value of correlation coefficient is more than 0.7 in only 3 out of 17 countries. It is more than 0.8 in only 2 out of 17 countries. In 10 out of 17 countries, the correlation is negative. This suggests the countercyclical stabilization potential of the institution of *Zakat*.

Next, we present how much time it will take to fund the poverty gap through the institution of *Zakat*. The time is shown in the number of years for each of the four poverty measures that we have used in the study. We have assumed that the *Zakat* recipients do not become *Zakat* payers immediately; else the speed of reaching the target will increase as the social mobility sets in. Table 10.6 presents the results.

Table 10.5 Correlation between ZGDP and GDP growth during 2008–2013

Country	Correlation between GDP growth and ZGDP
Albania	–0.58093
Azerbaijan	0.686503
Bangladesh	–0.25932
Egypt	0.785502
Indonesia	–0.22489
Jordon	0.895576
Kazakhstan	–0.42568
Kyrgyz Republic	–0.59264
Malaysia	–0.52276
Morocco	0.40042
Mozambique	–0.80824
Nigeria	0.241723
Pakistan	–0.71059
Saudi Arabia	0.436444
Tajikistan	–0.03663
Tunisia	0.301337
Turkey	–0.57057

Source: author's calculations

Table 10.6 Years required to fund poverty with potential *Zakat* collection for 2013

Country	ZGDP	PGI-GDP ($1.25)	PGI-GDP ($2.00)	PHCR-GDP ($1.25)	PHCR-GDP ($2.00)
Albania	2.60%	0.00	0.04	0.02	0.18
Azerbaijan	5.83%	0.00	0.01	0.00	0.02
Bangladesh	2.76%	1.93	8.38	7.47	21.12
Egypt	3.69%	0.01	0.17	0.06	0.92
Indonesia	3.53%	0.10	0.78	0.60	2.58
Jordon	4.30%	0.00	0.01	0.00	0.04
Kazakhstan	2.69%	0.00	0.00	0.00	0.01
Kyrgyz Republic	3.13%	0.14	0.98	0.59	3.89
Malaysia	4.59%	0.00	0.03	0.00	0.00
Morocco	5.01%	0.02	0.15	0.08	0.66
Mozambique	0.97%	20.09	54.29	47.19	102.62
Nigeria	2.20%	1.89	4.94	4.28	9.08
Pakistan	2.54%	0.27	2.99	1.79	11.43
Saudi Arabia	8.45%	0.00	0.00	0.04	0.08
Tajikistan	2.36%	0.24	2.00	3.86	8.18
Tunisia	3.73%	0.01	0.04	0.07	0.20
Turkey	3.42%	0.00	0.01	0.02	0.05

Source: author's calculations

In Table 10.7, we present the number of people that can be lifted out of poverty with realization of potential collectible *Zakat*. The second and third columns show how much poor people can be lifted out of poverty as the multiple or fraction of the total poor people with poverty line defined at $1.25 and $2.00 a day respectively. It can be seen that in most countries, the value is greater than 1 and which suggests that if the potential *Zakat* collectible is indeed collected by the government and disbursed through direct transfers, these poor people can be adequately helped. However, it is necessary that the poor people are provided with this transfer payment for a necessary number of periods so that they can survive as well as permanently move to the status of nonpoor. In this regard, the public sector educational and health institutions need to provide effective and affordable services with state of the art quality so that the income earning capacity of these poor people can be enhanced along with ensuring their survival and meeting the basic physiological needs of life.

Lastly, we show whether the OIC countries we had selected in our sample collectively have enough resources to overcome poverty from the realization of potential *Zakat* collectible. It can be seen from the Table 10.8 that on most counts of poverty, the aggregate resources pooled together from the

Table 10.7 People lifted out of poverty from potential *Zakat* collection for 2013

Country	People lifted out of poverty (No.)	Multiple of total poor ($1.25/day)	Multiple of total poor ($2.00/day)
Albania	735,046	53.00	21.52
Azerbaijan	8,669,335	306.88	129.95
Bangladesh	9,082,150	0.13	0.00
Egypt	22,000,113	15.77	1.08
Indonesia	67,120,324	1.66	0.04
Jordon	3,171,523	491.02	414.16
Kazakhstan	13,658,865	801.69	1,776.80
Kyrgyz Republic	495,829	1.70	0.09
Malaysia	31,492,916	211.95	150.09
Morocco	11,401,599	13.29	0.94
Mozambique	333,727	0.02	0.00
Nigeria	25,118,087	0.23	0.01
Pakistan	12,921,233	0.56	0.01
Saudi Arabia	138,644,438	24.05	19.24
Tajikistan	440,016	0.26	0.01
Tunisia	3,844,006	88,981,612.33	314.37
Turkey	61,680,905	58.80	22.94

Source: author's calculations

potential *Zakat* collection will be enough to fund resources for poverty alleviation. Hence, there is an important role to be played by OIC to collaborate with member countries and transfer necessary resources from the *Zakat* surplus regions to the *Zakat* deficit regions.

Conclusion and recommendations

In this study, we found that the *Zakat* to GDP ratio exceeds the PGI-GDP ratio in 14 out of 17 countries with the poverty line defined at $1.25 a day. We also discovered that the *Zakat* to GDP ratio exceeds the PGI-GDP ratio in 13 out of 17 countries with the poverty line defined at $2.00 a day. Our empirical analysis also showed that the *Zakat* to GDP ratio exceeds PHCR-GDP ratio in 12 out of 17 countries with the poverty line defined at $1.25 a day. We also found that the *Zakat* to GDP ratio exceeds the PHCR-GDP ratio in 10 out of 17 countries with the poverty line defined at $2.00 a day. Therefore, we conclude that the institution of *Zakat* has ample potential to contribute towards poverty alleviation. Our analysis also revealed that the aggregate resources pooled together from the potential *Zakat* collection in 17 OIC countries will be enough to fund resources for poverty alleviation. Thus, OIC can collaborate with member countries to

Table 10.8 People lifted out of poverty from potential *Zakat* collection for 2013

Country	Potential Zakat collectible (mln$)	PGI ($1.25 per day)	PGI ($2 per day)	PHCR ($1.25 per day)	PHCR ($2 per day)
Albania	335	1	12	6	61
Azerbaijan	3,955	5	37	13	103
Bangladesh	4,144	7,981	34,694	30,936	87,450
Egypt	10,038	139	1,695	636	9,225
Indonesia	30,624	3,055	23,785	18,468	78,980
Jordon	1,447	1	8	3	57
Kazakhstan	6,232	1	15	8	62
Kyrgyz Republic	226	31	222	133	881
Malaysia	14,369	68	499	68	499
Morocco	5,202	83	773	392	3,422
Mozambique	152	3,046	8,232	7,154	15,558
Nigeria	11,460	21,752	56,766	49,111	104,180
Pakistan	5,895	1,612	17,618	10,554	67,413
Saudi Arabia	63,257	2,631	5,261	2,631	5,261
Tajikistan	201	48	401	775	1,642
Tunisia	1,754	10	76	129	358
Turkey	28,142	17	241	479	1,422
Total	187,432	40,478	150,336	121,497	376,573
Surplus/ Shortfall		146,954	37,096	65,935	-189,141

Source: author's calculations

transfer necessary resources from the *Zakat* surplus regions to the *Zakat* deficit regions.

Finally, we outline recommendations at the policy and implementation level so that the institution of *Zakat* can be effectively utilized to contribute in poverty alleviation.

• It is necessary that the poor people are provided with *Zakat* as a transfer payment for a necessary number of periods so that they can survive as well as permanently move to the status of nonpoor. In this regard, the public sector educational and health institutions need to provide effective and affordable services with state of the art quality so that the income earning capacity of these poor people can be enhanced along with ensuring their survival and meeting the basic physiological needs of life.

- It is highly important that the scale and efficiency of public sector institutions in health and education are improved and poor people are provided with education, vocational training and basic health facilities at an affordable cost. In this regard, the institution of *Waqf* (charitable trust) can also be very effective in helping the government to increase its scale of welfare programs and outreach. Social mobility rests on effective income and capacity enhancing support programs rather than just on direct cash transfers.
- The close interaction between the *Zakat* disbursement agency and the Islamic microfinance institutions is also vital. Microfinance institutions can help in identifying targets that require immediate help in meeting consumption expenditure requirements.
- For effective organization and with the objective of maximizing the benefits of *Zakat*, it is appropriate to disburse *Zakat* at the federal level. This way the regional disparities can be reduced more effectively.
- To gain the trust and confidence of people, it is vital to improve the governance and transparency. Collection and disbursement details shall be reported in a standard way periodically.
- Creating synergies between *Zakat* and other welfare programs. Sufficient collection of *Zakat* for filling poverty gap is not enough to end poverty. It is important that *Zakat* funds be disbursed to the right people and through right channels. It is also important to utilize the existing welfare programs for *Zakat* disbursement so that the right targets can be reached more efficiently.
- It is important to modify the accounting standards to achieve transparent computation, assessment and collection.
- It is vital to improve the capacity of the public sector officials to scrutinize accounts for transparent and efficient *Zakat* assessment.
- Pooling resources by transferring surplus *Zakat* funds from the rich countries to the poor countries with lower wealth bases will help in alleviating poverty quickly (Shirazi & Amin, 2009).
- Timing for wealth *Zakat* is especially important. It is better to have equal number of people paying *Zakat* every quarter rather than all paying at a single time of the year. This will help in reducing any possible arbitrage and enable the government to have *Zakat* funds available at all times of the year.
- In direct transfers, it is vital to give enough *Zakat* per person so that the person can come out of poverty and the objective of social mobility can be achieved (Haneef & Mahmud, 2012).
- While there is *Zakat* on assets in personal use, the government in consultation with Islamic scholars has to legislate what comprises regular and ordinary cost of living per person for different income groups. While the government shall not intervene in restraining consumption; at the same time, it shall also not allow people to avoid *Zakat* by maintaining an extra ordinary living standard.

References

Abdelmawla, M. A. (2014). The Impacts of Zakat and Knowledge on Poverty Allevi-
ation in Sudan: An Empirical Investigation (1990–2009). *Journal of Economic
Cooperation and Development*, 35(4), 61–84.
Abdullah, M., & Suhaib, A. Q. (2011). The Impact of Zakat on Social Life of Muslim
Society. *Pakistan Journal of Islamic Research*, 8, 85–91.
Ahmad, S., Wahid, H., & Mohamad, A. (2006). Privatisation of Zakat Institutions in
Malaysia and Its Effect on Formal Payment. *International Journal of Management
Studies*, 13(2), 175–196.
Ahmed, H. (2004). *Role of Zakat and Awqaf in Poverty Alleviation*. Occasional Paper
No. 8. Jeddah: Islamic Research and Training Institute, Islamic Development Bank
Group.
Akram, M. M., & Afzal, M. (2014). *Dynamic Role of Zakat in Alleviating Poverty:
A Case Study of Pakistan*. Munich Personal RePEc Archive. https://mpra.ub.uni-
muenchen.de/56211/1/MPRA_paper_56013.pdf.
Azam, M., Iqbal, N., & Tayyab, M. (2014). Zakat and Economic Development: Micro
and Macro Level Evidence from Pakistan. *Bulletin of Business and Economics*, 3(2),
85–95.
Bakar, N. B. A., & Rahman, A. R. A. (2007). A Comparative Study of Zakat and Modern
Taxation. *Journal of King Abdul Aziz University: Islamic Economics*, 20(1), 25–40.
Debnath, S. C., Islam, M. T., & Mahmud, K. T. (2013). The Potential of Zakat
Scheme as an Alternative of Microcredit to Alleviate Poverty in Bangladesh.
9th International Conference on Islamic Economics and Finance, QFIS, Doha,
Qatar.
Firdaus, M., Beik, I. S., Irawan, T., & Juanda, B. (2012). Economic Estimation and
Determinations of Zakat Potential in Indonesia, IRTI Working Paper Series, WP#
1433-07.
Haneef, S. S. S., & Mahmud, M. W. (2012). *Issues in Contemporary Zakat: A Juristic
Analytical Evaluation*. Kuala Lumpur: IIUM Press.
Hassan, M. K. (2010). An Integrated Poverty Alleviation Model Combining Zakat,
Awqaf and Microfinance. *Seventh International Conference-The Tawhidi Epistemology:
Zakat and Waqf Economy*, Bangi, Malaysia.
Hassan, M. K., & Jauanyed, M. K. (2007). Zakat, External Debt and Poverty Reduction
Strategy in Bangladesh. *Journal of Economic Cooperation*, 28(4), 1–38.
Ibrahim, P. (2006). Economic Role of Zakat in Reducing Income Inequality and Poverty
in Selangor, PhD thesis, Universiti Putra Malaysia.
Kahf, M. (1989). Zakat: Unresolved Issues in Contemporary Fiqh. *Journal of Islamic
Economics*, 2(1), 1–22.
Khan, M. A. (2005). Comments on A. Azim Islahi & M. Obaidullah: Zakat on
Stocks: Some Unsettled Issues. *Journal of King Abdul Aziz University: Islamic Eco-
nomics*, 18(1), 41–42.
Kuran, T. (2003). Islamic Redistribution through Zakat: Historical Record and
Modern Realities. In M. Bonner, M. Ener, & A. Singer (Eds.), *Poverty and Charity
in Middle Eastern Contexts* (pp. 275–293). Albany, NY: SUNY Press.
Mahmud, I. (2001). *Economic System under Umar the Great*. Lahore: Shaikh Muhammad
Ashraf Publishers.
Malik, S. J., Hussain, M., & Shirazi, N. S. (1994). Role of Infaq in Poverty Alleviation
in Pakistan. *The Pakistan Development Review*, 33(4), 935–952.

Maududi, S. A. A. (1970). *Ma'ashiyat-e Islam [Economic System of Islam]*. Lahore: Islamic Publications.

Nadvi, S. M. (1996). *Taareekh-e-Islam [History of Islam]*. Lahore: Maktaba-e-Rehmania.

Nadzri, F. A., Rahman, R. A., & Omar, N. (2012). Zakat and Poverty Alleviation: Roles of Zakat Institutions in Malaysia. *International Journal of Arts and Commerce*, 1(7), 61–72.

Naveed, A., & Ali, N. (2012). *Clustered Deprivation—District Profile of Poverty in Pakistan*. Islamabad: Sustainable Development Policy Institute (SDPI).

Piketty, T. (2014). *Capital in the 21st Century*. New York: Belknap Press.

Pingali, P. (2002). Reducing Poverty and Hunger: The Critical Role of Financing for Rural Development, Food & Agriculture. *International Conference on Financing for Development*, March.

Powell, R. (2009). Zakat: Drawing Insights for Legal Theory and Economic Policy from Islamic Jurisprudence. *Pittsburgh Tax Review*, 7(43), 10–17.

Qaradawi, Y. (1999). *Fiqh az-Zakat: A Comparative Study-The Rules, Regulations and Philosophy of Zakat in the Light of the Qur'an and Sunnah*. London: Dar Al Taqwa Ltd.

Rahman, A. R. A. (2003). Zakat on Business Wealth in Malaysia: Corporate Tax Rebate, Accountability, and Governance. *Journal IKIM*, 11(1), 37–50.

Sadeq, A. H. M. (1996). Ethico-Economic Institution of Zakat: An Instrument of Self Reliance and Sustainable Grassroots Development. *IIUM Journal of Economics and Management*, 12, 2.

Sen, A. (1983). *Poverty and Famines: An Essay on Entitlement and Deprivation*. Oxford: Oxford University Press.

Shaik, A. A. (1979). *Some Aspects of Economics of Zakat*. Indianapolis: American Trust Publication.

Shirazi, N. S. (2014). Integrating Zakat and Waqf into the Poverty Reduction Strategy of the IDB Member Countries. *Islamic Economic Studies*, 22(1), 79–108.

Shirazi, N. S., & Amin, M. F. (2009). Poverty Elimination through Potential Zakat Collection in the OIC-Member Countries: Revisited. *The Pakistan Development Review*, 48(4), 739–754.

Siddiqui, M. N. (1978). *Place of Additional Levies in the Islamic Shari'ah*. New Delhi: Maktaba-i-Islami.

Suprayitno, E., Kader, R. A., & Harun, A. (2013). The Impact of Zakat on Aggregate Consumption in Malaysia. *Journal of Islamic Economics, Banking and Finance*, 9(1), 39–62.

Wahab, N. A., & Rahman, A. R. A. (2011). A Framework to Analyse the Efficiency and Governance of Zakat Institutions. *Journal of Islamic Accounting and Business Research*, 2(1), 43–62.

Wahid, A. N. M. (1986). The Economic Implications of Zakat. *Contemporary Review*, 248(1440), 10.

Wahid, H., Ahmad, S., & Kader, A. R. (2008). Distribution of Zakat in Malaysia: Why Are the Muslims Still Dissatisfied. *Proceedings of Seminar Kebangsaan Ekonomi Malaysia*, Universiti Kebangsaan Malaysia, Bangi.

World Bank Group. Ed. (2012). *World Development Indicators 2012*. New York: World Bank Publications.

Yusoff, M. B. (2011). Zakat Expenditure, School Enrollment, and Economic Growth in Malaysia. *International Journal of Business and Social Science*, 2(6), 175–181.

11 Social justice through Islamic micro-*takaful*

Social capital matter

Yulizar D. Sanrego

The informal economy is defined as a condition where business practices are dominated by low-income rural households including micro, small and medium enterprises (MSMEs), which are excluded for several known reasons from the financial industry-based services market, such as a lack of working capital, low human resources, as well lack of knowledge and technology (Amidzic et al., 2014; Sudaryanto & Hanim, 2002).

It not only happens in the context of financial services in the context of credit or financing facilities but is also associated with the insurance. The injustice condition is indicated pertaining to as rural low-income households does not have a chance to obtain decent financial protection.

In the mitigation of poverty, there is increasing appreciation of the role played by risks in the lives of the poor. It is not sufficient to provide the poor with income alone. For making any meaningful and lasting impact on their lives, there is a need to also protect them from several risks such as the risk of illness, death, loss of assets and so forth. Accordingly, microinsurance, which is basically insurance for low-income households, is gaining importance in most of developing countries (Churchill, 2006). The risk of death, illness, accidents, fires and other disasters could affect anyone, rich or poor. So it is not only rich people who need insurance, but the poor also desperately need it.

Within the context of microcredit, microcredit may increase the vulnerability of recipients when they face shocks that reduce the capacity to repay such loans it is therefore, it has been argued that microinsurance (MI) could improve the effectiveness of microcredit (MC) services. The provision of microinsurance services to communities who already have access to microcredit programs serves to increase the effectiveness of each program respectively (McKinnon, 2004)

However, despite the role of microinsurance in mitigating risk, the demand is relatively low. One of the major issues highlighted in the financial services industry is trust, particularly in the microinsurance market. There is a lot of empirical research that highlights the significance of trust in demand behavior, in both the qualitative and quantitative approach (Basaza et al., 2008; Cai et al., 2009; De Allegri et al., 2006; Dercon et al., 2011;

Dong et al., 2009; Giné et al., 2008). In other words, of all the financial services, insurance is the one which requires the highest trust levels on the consumer side. It is considered to be a crucial factor in the demand for microinsurance as well as the success of microinsurance programs (Maleika & Kuriakose, 2008).

The issue of trust is theoretically very much related to the concept of social capital. Social trust, network and membership and collective action are good proxies for social capital (Coleman, 1990, Ishida & Yokoyama, 2004, Putnam et al., 1993; O'hara, in Nugroho, 2008). With regard to the impact of social capital on the demand for microinsurance, there are some studies that have highlighted this issue. Hsiao reported that people are more willing to pay for Community Based Health Insurance (CBHI) in communities that have sufficient stocks of social capital. Zhang et al. (2006) in their quest for the effect of social capital on the demand for CBHI among farmers in rural China also found that social capital measured by trust and reciprocity had a positive and significant effect on the demand for CBHI. The same finding also reported by Donfouet et al. (2011) in exploring the effect of social capital on the willingness to pay for CBHI in rural Cameroon, whereby he found that the willingness to pay, and demand for, CBHI services were higher among communities with sufficient stocks of social capital than otherwise.

The BMT (*Baitul Mal Wattamwil*) Union of Indonesia (PBMT Indonesia) as Islamic micro-*takaful* provider with its Community-Based Insurance (CBI) is an emerging concept for providing financial protection, particularly for credit life and credit disability against the cost of illness, accidents, fires, and improving access to quality health services for low-income rural households who are excluded from formal insurance (*takaful*).

This chapter is trying to shed light on how this community who are not fortunate enough to be served by the microinsurance program. It is in this context, the issue of social capital is critically matter for the Islamic micro-*takaful* provider. Social capital might allow individuals to cope with the imperfections of a given socioeconomic system (state or market dominated).

To assess the existence of social capital (particularly trust) of members of PBMT Indonesia in this research, a Likert-scale type survey as utilized accordingly. First of all, respondents were asked to indicate their degree of trust in general and towards specific members among the groups. Second, a set of question addressed about the respondents' experience with the willingness to share the risk with *tabarru'*[1] concept.

The concept of microinsurance and social capital

The issues of poverty and inequality continue in the chapter of human life. Those issues are also a concern of many countries and regional-multilateral organizations such as the G20 forum, OECD, the World Bank, IMF, ADB, and ASEAN. A successful development is marked with the establishment of a stable and useful financial system for all people. Within this framework, financial institutions play a vital role through their intermediary function to boost economic growth, equal income distribution, poverty reduction, and achievement of financial system stability. Unfortunately, the rapid development of the financial industry is not always accompanied by adequate financial access. Even though access to financial services is an important prerequisite for community involvement in the economic system.

Indonesia as stated in The World Bank's Survey (2011) shows that only 49% of Indonesian households have access to formal institutions. The Bank of Indonesia revealed the same in a Households Balance Sheet Survey, Indonesia Central Statistics Bureau (2011) showing that 48% of households save their money with formal financial institutions and nonfinancial institutions. Therefore, 52% of people do not have any savings with banks or non-bank financial institutions. Both of these two surveys are in agreement that the access of Indonesian people to formal and nonformal financial institutions is still relatively low, and therefore, the access of Indonesian people to the financial services system must be increased accordingly. Therefore, several policies are formulated in order to overcome these problems. One concept offered by the G20 forum in order to alleviate poverty and reduce income disparity is through financial inclusion system, particularly microcredit/microfinancing.[2]

In recent years, there has been a dramatic increase in the role of microfinance institutions, providing services such as microlending, as a tool for economic development by NGOs and international organizations. It has a significant role in combatting the issue of poverty (Ebimobowei et al., 2012; Idolor & Eriki, 2012; Morduch, 2002). Microcredit has a positive effect for solving the poverty problem. These poor people are particularly vulnerable to risk and negative external shocks (e.g., natural disaster; illness/death of the main breadwinner) due to their low asset bases. In the absence of functioning insurance markets, poor people in developing countries have created a number of formal and informal instruments to manage such risk. These include a risk-pooling scheme (e.g., funeral and burial societies); income support (e.g., credit arrangement, transfer) and consumption smoothing arrangement (e.g., savings, grain bank) (Maleika & Kuriakose, 2008).

Microinsurance is, to some extent, an extension of the microfinance concept into the realm of insurance—to deal explicitly with risk management. Many of the pioneering attempts to provide microinsurance have been closely linked to existing microfinance programs and MFIs, because existing networks make it less costly to deliver new products, and partly because these institutions have started to tie their loans to insurance against the death of the borrower (Rahim et al., 2013). Within this framework, the link between microinsurance and microcredit is like two sides of a coin. Hence, the provision of microinsurance services to communities who already have access to microcredit programs serves to increase the effectiveness of each program respectively (McKinnon, 2004). The idea behind microinsurance programs is that by reducing the amount of money spent on replacing lost capital, disposable income can be increased and therefore economic growth and development is encouraged amongst the poorest communities in developing nations. Microinsurance can also provide these families with much more financial stability, removing the need to constantly maintain finds as a "safety net" against potential shocks or losses (Morduch, 2006).

Microinsurance can be described as "The protection of low-income people against specific threats in exchange for premium payments proportionate to the likelihood and costs of the risks involved." (CGAP, n.d.; Cohen & Sebstad, 2005). There are a number of benefits associated with the use of microinsurance scheme, with many of them addressing the problem which relates to an informal coping mechanism. First is the accessible nature of microinsurance, which is targeted at those most in need of financial services, namely low-income, rural poor involved in the agricultural sector. Microinsurance also provides poor households with the means to stabilize their income in the face of losses, which serves to increase their standard of living. Additionally, the provision of microinsurance services to communities who already have access to microcredit programs serves to increase the effectiveness of each program respectively (McKinnon, 2004). Secondly, microinsurance scheme provide families with the means to increase their standard of living as they no longer have to devote as large a proportion of their income to managing potential risk (Chandhok, 2009). Finally, when low income communities have access to microinsurance services, there is a reduction in the demand for emergency loans as there is now a more cost-effective method for members of the community to manage risk, without having to rely on each other or costly loans. By providing microinsurance services in addition to microcredit, low-income communities are able to choose from a more comprehensive range of financial services (Churchill, 2006).

There are so many research conducted raised the issue of social capital and how it has significance role to the economy as well as financial performance particularly for the informal economy, including microinsurance. Putnam terms social capital as features of social organization, such as trust, norms and networks that can improve the efficiency of society by facilitating coordinated actions and permit cooperation among them (Fukuyama, 1999;). Nugroho (2008) and Yokoyama and Ishida (2006) also argue that social capital through collective actions may improve the quality of life in rural settings through improved productivity in agriculture, diversification of rural economic activities and improved rural resource management, including economic outcomes (efficiency, financial access, information gathering). Social capital through social networks is also assumed to provide the possibilities for the exchange, access and rapid diffusion of the latest technological innovations (Grootaert & Narayan, 2004). Research also suggests that social capital helps to increase the possibilities for collective action among community members which in turn enhance their effectiveness in solving their common problems (Putnam et al., 1993).

In the case of community-based health insurance (CHBI), for example, several studies show that low-income households are willing to pay for CBHI because of the existence of social capital in the community (Donfouet & Mahieu, 2012). Hsiao (2001) reported that people are more willing to pay for Community Based Health Insurance (CBHI) in communities that have sufficient stocks of social capital; the greater the social capital in the community, the more people are willing to prepay for CBHI. As outlined also by Woolcock and Narayan (2000), social capital helps the poor to manage risk and vulnerability. Thus, CBHI which aims at managing risk and vulnerability may be well accepted by a community that possesses a high stock of social capital.

Zhang et al. (2006) in their quest for the effect of social capital on demand for CBHI among farmers in rural China also found that social capital measured by trust and reciprocity had a positive and significant effect on the demand for CBHI. The same finding was also reported by Donfouet et al. (2011) in exploring the effect of social capital on the willingness to pay for CBHI in rural Cameroon, whereby he found that the willingness to pay and demand for CBHI services were higher among communities with sufficient stocks of social capital than otherwise. As outlined by the BIT in Donfouet and Mahieu (2012), one of the key principles of a properly functioning CBHI is solidarity and trust between members. This solidarity and trust stirs up members who are susceptible to risk to pull together their resources for common use. In the same message, Tundui and Macha (2014) revealed that to increase access to health care services in the rural areas and the sustainability of Community Health Fund (CHF) would require building appropriate forms of social capital. Throughout the literature study, it can be concluded that the injustice condition which is indicated as rural low-income households do not have a chance to obtain decent financial protection could be solved by the existence of social capital.

Micro-*takaful* and PBMT At-*Ta'awun*

Takaful and micro-*takaful* are the Islamic alternatives to conventional insurance and microinsurance. The 1985 Fiqh Academy of the Organization of the Islamic Conference (OIC) issued its fatwa declaring that the conventional insurance contract is *haram* due to the presence of the elements of *gharar* (excessive uncertainty), *riba* (interest) and *maisir* (gambling). Insurance is only permissible in Islam when undertaken in the framework of *takaful* (mutual guarantee) and *ta'awun* (mutual cooperation). In order to eliminate the element of *gharar* and *maisir* in the *takaful* contract, the concept of *tabarru'* (donation) is incorporated in it. As with conventional microinsurance, micro-*takaful* is a mechanism to provide *Shari'ah*-based protection to the poor and low-income households at an affordable cost. Table 11.1 illustrates the distinct differences between *takaful* and micro-*takaful* (Hasim, 2014).

Table 11.1 The difference between *Takaful* and Micro-*takaful*

	Takaful	*Micro*-takaful
Market	Policyholders are from middle & high-income households	Policyholders are the poor & low-income households, often working in the informal economy and outside of social insurance coverage with irregular income streams
Market Awareness	Market is largely familiar with insurance	Market is largely unfamiliar with insurance
Contribution (premium)	Based on age or other specific risk characteristics	Low contribution and affordable
Affordability considerations	Contributions are paid by policyholders	Contribution and affordable
Sums insured	Large sums insured	Contribution may be paid in full or partly by a subsidy from Zakat funds, waqf or the government
Policy document	Complex policy document with many exclusions	Simple & easy to understand policy document with a few or no exclusions
Claim handling	Claims process for large sums insured may be quite complicated	Simple & fast procedures to small sums, yet still controls fraud

Source: Hasim (2014)

Theoretically, *takaful* is perceived as cooperative insurance which employs the *tabarru'* concept in its business scheme. The purpose of *takaful* is to uphold the principles of brotherhood and solidarity, which provides mutual financial aid and assistance to its participants in the event of mishaps and difficulties. In microinsurance and micro-*takaful*, profit is not a prime consideration. For example, microinsurance institutions providing health care in developing countries are focusing on service provision and not to make profits. However, any profits are used to build up a reserve, improve the quality of service or to reduce its members' contributions (Hasim, 2014).

Within the framework concept of *takaful* or *tadhamun* (mutual help), The Association of Baitul Mal Wattamwil Indonesia (PBMT Indonesia) has established the program namely PBMT At-*Ta'awun* which literally means *takaful* (mutual help). The scheme or the program of PBMT At-*Ta'awun* (fund manager) has the feature depicted in Figure 11.1.

Figure 11.1 shows the concept of *tabarru'* (donation) is incorporated in it with employing *akad hibah* (*hibah* contract), whereby every single

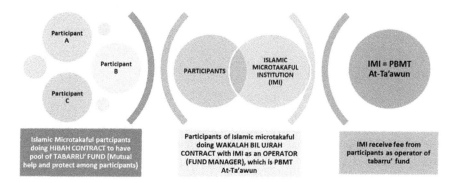

Figure 11.1 Business Scheme of PBMT At-*Ta'awun*

participant donate their money for the sake of mutual help, guarantee and protection. *Hibah* is defined as to give something to another without compensation, whether the thing is wealth or not; a form of a grant either in its physical form (*'ain*) or otherwise (Hammad, 2008). It covers gifts and alms. In fact the scheme depicted in Figure 11.1 is Partner-Agent Model;[3] whereby the insurer utilizes the microfinance institutions' (MFIs) delivery mechanism to provide sales and basic services to the participants. This model often works well in the beginning when MFIs are developing an understanding of insurance and building in-house capacity (Churchill et al., 2012). It is the model that might function as an intermediary for the low-income family to informally seek justice in the form of financial service protection.

As is commonly practiced in microinsurance, profit is not a prime consideration in this model. The model being practiced by PBMT At-*Ta'awun* falls under the principle of mutual help to uphold the principles of brotherhood and solidarity, which provides mutual financial aid and assistance to its participants in the event of mishaps and difficulties. Any profits are used to build up a reserve and to improve the quality of service of PBMT At-*Ta 'awun*.

Finding and discussion: the analysis of social capital existence within the practice of microinsurance

The existence of social capital serves to ensure the participation of the poor in microinsurance program including making the microinsurance program is feasible. Therefore, it is necessary to evaluate by assessing the respond and opinion of the participant members related to the presence of social capital in the implementation of *tabarru'* concept in micro-*takaful* or Islamic micro-insurance. This study was conducted to PBMT At-*Ta'awun* members who have been involved in the implementation of the *tabarru'* concept through questionnaires. The results of the analysis of participants' feedback from the questionnaires using Likert scale are presented as follow:

Level of participation

The level of participation of members PBMT Indonesia in microfinance programs (*ta'awun*) is high with a value scale of 4:32 from 5:00 (see Table 11.2). It shows that in every invitation to a meeting held by PBMT Indonesia there are always many who attend. Most members PBMT Indonesia or as much as 84% (Figure 11.2) will attend meetings related to a microinsurance program.

One of the strategy being practiced by PBMT Indonesia in maintaining the networking (as one of the social capital features) among the members of the microfinance program. Hence, over the course several meetings there will be some sort of information delivered to enhance the knowledge of the members/participants with regard to the microinsurance product as well as strengthening the solidarity among them.

Level of awareness

The level of awareness of the PBMT Indonesia members to perform the *tabarru'* concept and helping each other in the insurance program was found to be high with a scale of 4.9 from 5.00. This level of awareness can be said to be a result of the PBMT Indonesia's effort to build an understanding and level awareness (including trust) of their members in every single meeting regarding the *tabarru'* concept that has the spirit of helping

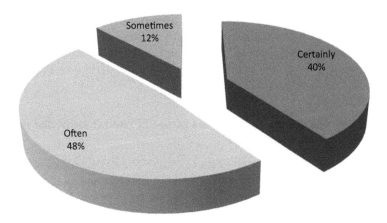

Figure 11.2 Level of participation

Table 11.2 The overall response of PBMT members towards the microfinance program

Respondent	Participation	Awareness	Action	Awareness & cooperation	Satisfaction	Respond
1	4	5	5	5	4	4.6
2	2	5	4	3.5	4	3.7
3	4.5	5	5	4.5	4	4.6
4	3	4.5	4.5	3.5	3	3.7
5	5	5	5	5	4	4.8
6	5	5	5	5	4.33	4.87
7	4.5	5	5	5	4	4.7
8	4	4.5	5	5	4.33	4.57
9	5	5	5	4.5	4	4.7
10	4	5	5	5	4.33	4.67
11	4	4.5	5	4.5	4	4.4
12	4	5	5	4	4.33	4.47
13	5	4	5	4.5	3.33	4.37
14	5	5	5	3.5	4	4.5
15	4	5	5	4.5	4	4.5
16	4.5	5	5	5	4.33	4.77
17	2.5	5	5	4	3.67	4.03
18	4	5	5	5	4	4.6
19	5	5	4.5	3.5	2.67	4.13
20	4.5	5	5	4.5	2.67	4.33
21	5	5	5	5	3.67	4.73
22	4.5	5	5	4	4	4.5
23	5	5	5	5	5	5
24	5	5	5	4.5	3.67	4.63
25	5	5	5	4.5	4	4.7
Average	4.32	4.9	4.92	4.48	3.89	4.50

each other and a strong level of solidarity among the members, especially during the early socialization of the microinsurance program.

Figures 11.3 and 11.4 shows that most members of PBMT Indonesia, as much as 88%, carried through with the sharia contract and 92% of them are aware there is mutual help to become members of the microinsurance program. This high level of awareness is extremely important since the spirit of the *tabarru'* concept is social in nature. The intention to become part of the program is very much influenced by the sense of mutual help or solidarity among the members. This level of awareness has become critical as it is subject to create trust among members or participants to be well fitted with the program proposed by the PBMT Indonesia.

Level of action

The awareness of using the *tabarru'* concept and mutual help behavior among the members is decisively confirmed with the implementation of the contract and the high level of trust towards the fund manager with a scale of 4.92 out of 5.00 (see Figure 11.5). The majority of PBMT Indonesia members are very confident that the microinsurance program managers with a percentage value of 96%. The confirmation of being members of the microfinance program could be considered to be the answer to some obstacles put forward by Patt et al. (2009). Patt et al. asserted that despite the many benefits associated with providing microinsurance to the poor, there are many obstacles facing the poor who demanding microinsurance services, among them is the issue of participant trust. Practitioners need to

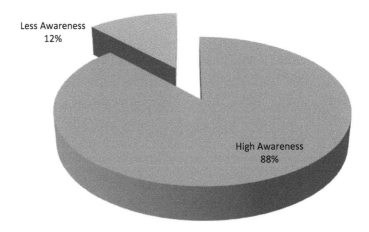

Figure 11.3 The urgency of the *Tabarru'* concept

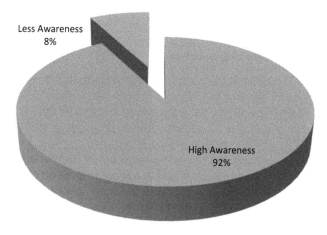

Figure 11.4 The awareness of mutual help

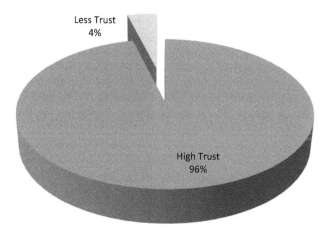

Figure 11.5 Trust to program manager

implement a multidimensional approach to address trust challenges. Patt et al. presented a three-dimensional approach to building trust for practitioners: (1) building trust in the product, (2) building trust in the insurer and other institutions involved in the delivery of the product and (3) leveraging trust that already exists in the communities. Hence, the existence of trust among members of PBMT Indonesia including their trust to the microfinance program manager indicate that social capital has its significant role to the successful of the program.

Level of mutual concern and cooperation

In addition to the element of trust, the level of mutual concern and cooperation among members also has high value with the scale of 4.48 out of 5.00 (see Figure 11.6). This shows the existence of reciprocity between the fellow members in the successful of microinsurance program in **PBMT** Indonesia community.

The high value of scale reinforced by majority of **PBMT** Indonesia members who answered their willingness and readiness to help other members and did not object or feeling a burden to perform the *tabarru'* concept in the microinsurance program(see Figure 11.7). It is reciprocity value within the concept of social capital, along with trust that might affect economic outcomes (e.g., efficiency, financial access, information gathering etc.) (Nugroho, 2008), including the successful of microinsurance program. Social capital contributes to economic performance through their capability to practice and sustain mutual cooperation, mutual trust (reciprocity norms) and reduce transaction costs involved in production and exchange. At the same time, the resulting production and exchange can lead to social capital accumulation, when they are characterized by equal distributions of power and income among community members. Any individual levels or economic agents are willing to sustain long-term cooperation because they care about one another. If each agent is well informed than he/she will take care of each other, he/she will trust one another to carry out their obligation. When each agent behaves honorably toward his/her obligation, monitoring costs are lowered due to the

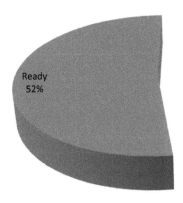

Figure 11.6 Mutual help (reciprocity)

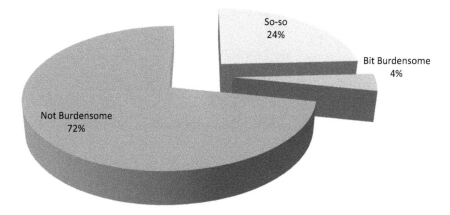

Figure 11.7 Using the *Tabarru'* concept

absence of a moral hazard problem. Groups and associations of households can be used to gather information and reduce transaction costs and make micro clients more attractive to private insurers and/or to allow them to organize as an insurance mutual (Siegel et al., 2011).

Level of satisfaction to the program

Overall, PBMT Indonesia members were satisfied with the performance and the family atmosphere that exists in the PBMT Indonesia community in the implementation of microinsurance (*ta'awun*) programs with the scale value of 3.39 out of 5.00 (see Figure 11.8).

This level of satisfaction indicates that the insurance mutual that happened in this community or association meets the basic feature of the *tabarru'* concept. Hence, the fund managers have performed their job to make sure that there is mutual help and cooperation within the microinsurance program.

The overall response of PBMT Indonesia members or the PBMT At-*Ta'awun* participants to the microfinance program is as depicted in Figure 11.9 and Table 11.2.

Conclusion and policy implication

Through the literature review and by employing a Likert-scale type survey, it was revealed that a higher level of social capital is found within the community members of PBMT Indonesia. The network strategy as a policy of PBMT Indonesia with its Community-Based Insurance (CBI) has shown a significant effect towards the establishment of social capital

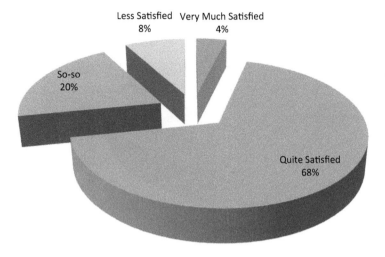

Figure 11.8 Level of satisfaction toward the program

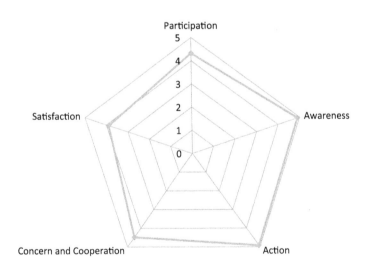

Figure 11.9 The overall response of **PBMT** members toward the microfinance program

within the community or the members, particularly in the form of trust and reciprocity, so that making this social capital matter for the establishment of Islamic micro-*takaful* (insurance mutual) with their *tabarru'* contract (Donfouet & Mahieu, 2012; Donfouet et al., 2011.; Maleika & Kuriakose, 2008; Siegel et al., 2011; Zhang et al., 2006). The *tabarru'* concept is very much accepted among the members or the participant of microfinance program with a high level of trust, networking and reciprocity among the members so that the injustice condition whereby low-income households do not have a chance to obtain decent financial protection could be handled accordingly. Thus, the demand, or the willingness, of the community members to enroll in microinsurance is asserted by the existence of social capital within the community/members. The existence of social capital could be the answer of some obstacles facing the poor on demanding microinsurance services put forwarded by Patt et al. (2009). One important policy implication that might be suggest from this chapter is to create and to enhance insurance service to low-income family, would require appropriate forms of social capital at individual as well as at community levels.

Notes

1 A voluntary act; a gift which is not precede by a request. Grant of an asset ot usufruct by a mature and responsible person, either immediately or at a later time, without compensation with the intention of charity, usually (Hammad, 2008).
2 Microfinance is generally understood as the provision of basic financial services, including savings, credit, money–transfer and even insurance, to the poor—or in a broader sense, those unable to access such services due to exclusion by the mainstream banking industry.
3 The least risky approach to providing micro-*takaful* is by outsourcing the whole business to a regulated or registered *Takaful* insurer known as a partner–agent model by the micro-finance institution (MFI). The MFI acts as *Takaful* agent, selling policies to MFI clients on behalf of the insurer in exchange for a commission (*tsamsarah*).

References

Amidzic, G., Massara, A., & Mialou, A. (2014). Assessing Countries' Financial Inclusion Standing—A New Composite Index. IMF Working Paper, WP/14/36.
Basaza, R., Criel, B., & Van der Stuyft, P. (2008). Community Health Insurance in Uganda: Why Does Enrolment Remain Low? A View from Beneath. *Health Policy*, 87, 172–184.
Cai, H., Chen, Y., Fang, H., & Zhou, L. (2009). Microinsurance, Trust and Economic Development: Evidence from a Randomized Natural Field Experiment. Working Paper 15396, National Bureau of Economic Research.
CGAP. (n.d.). *Consultative Group to Assist the Poor*. Retrieved from What Is Microfinance?: www.cgap.org/p/site/c/template.rc/1.11.947/.
Chandhok, G. A. (2009). Insurance—A Tool to Eradicate and a Vehicle to Economic Development. *International Research Journal of Finance and Economics*, 24, 71–76.

Churchill, C. (2006). What Is Insurance for the Poor? In C. Churchill (Ed.), *Protecting the Poor: A Microinsurance Compendium* (pp. 12–24). Munich: International Labor Organization.

Churchill, C., Dalal, A., & Ling, J. (2012). *Pathways towards Greater Impact: Better Microinsurance Models, Products & Processes for MFIs*. Briefing Note 15. Geneva: International Labour Office (ILO).

Cohen, M., & Sebstad, J. (2005). Reducing Vulnerability: The Demand for Microinsurance. *Journal of International Development*, 17(3), 397–494. Retrieved from http://onlinelibrary.wiley.com/doi/10.1002/jid.1193/.

Cole, S., Giné, X., Tobacman, J., Topalova, P., Townsend, R., & Vickery, J. (2013). Barriers to Household Risk Management: Evidence from India. *American Economic Journal: Applied Economics*, 5(1), 104–135.

Coleman, J. S. (1990). *The Foundation of Social Theory*. Cambridge: Harvard University Press.

De Allegri, M., Sanon, M., Bridges, J., & Sauerborn, R. (2006). Understanding Consumers' Preferences and Decision to Enroll in Community-Based Health Insurance in Rural West Africa. *Health Policy*, 76, 58–71.

Dercon, S., Gunning, J. W., & Zeitlin, A. (2011). The Demand for Insurance under Limited Credibility: Evidence from Kenya. International Development Conference, DIAL.

Donfouet, H. P., Essombè, J. R. E., Mahieu, P. A., & Malin, E. (2011). Social Capital and Willingness-to-Pay for Community-Based Health Insurance in Rural Cameroon. *Global Journal of Health Science*, 3(1), 142–149.

Donfouet, H. P. P., & Mahieu, P. A. (2012). Community-Based Health Insurance and Social Capital: A Review. *Health Economics Review*, 2, 5.

Dong, H., De Allegri, M., Gnawali, D., Souares, A., & Sauerborn, R. (2009). Dropout Analysis of Community-Based Health Insurance Membership at Nouna, Burkina Faso. *Health Policy*, 92, 174–179.

Ebimobowei, A., Sophia, J. M., & Wisdom, S. (2012). An Analysis of Microfinance and Poverty Reduction in Bayelsa State of Nigeria. *Kuwait Chapter of Arabian Journal of Business and Management Review*, 1(7), 38–57.

Eling, M., Shailee, P., & Schmit, J. T. (2014). The Determinant of Microinsurance Demand. *The Geneva Papers*, 39, 224–263.

Fukuyama, F. (1999). *The Great Disruption: Human Nature and the Reconstitution of Social Order*. New York: Free Press.

Giné, X., Townsend, R., & Vickery, J. (2008). Patterns of Rainfall Insurance Participation in Rural India. *The World Bank Economic Review*, 22, 539–566.

Grootaert, C., & Narayan, D. (2004). Local Institutions, Poverty and Household Welfare in Bolivia. *World Development*, 32(7), 1179–1198.

Hammad, N. (2008). *Mu'jam al-Mushthalahat al-Maliyyah wa al-Iqtishadiyyah fi Lughah al-Fuqaha*. Damascus: Dar al-Qalam.

Hasim, H. M. (2014). Microtakaful as an Islamic Financial Instrument, for Poverty Alleviation in Iraq. *Middle-Eastern Journal of Scientific Research*, 21(12), 2315–2325.

Households Balance Sheet Survey, Indonesia Central Statistic Bureau. (2011).

Hsiao, W. C. (2001). *Unmet Health Needs of Two Billion. Is Community Financing a Solution?* Health Nutrition and Population Discussion Paper. Washington, DC: World Bank.

Idolor, J. J., & Eriki, P. O. (2012). Financial Analysis of Assessment of Impact of Microfinancing Institutions towards Poverty Reduction in Nigeria. *Journal of Financial Management & Analysis*, 25, 51–60. Retrieved from www.worldcat.org.

Ishida, A., & Yokoyama, S. (2004). Social Capital and Community Development: Conceptual Framework. *Bulletin of the Faculty of Life and Environmental Science, Shimane University*, 9, 23–31.

Maleika, M., & Kuriakose, A. T. (2008). *Microinsurance: Extending Pro-Poor Risk Management through the Social Fund Platform*. Washington, DC: The World Bank.

McKinnon, R. (2004). Social Risk Management and the World Bank: Resetting the "Standards" for Social Security? *Journal of Risk Research*, 7(3), 297–314.

Morduch, J. (2002). Analysis of the Effect of Microfinance on Poverty Reduction. NYU Wagner Working Paper No. 1014, Issued June 28.

Morduch, J. (2006). Microinsurance: The Next Revolution? In A. V. Banerjee, R. Benabou, & D. Mookherjee (Eds.), *Understanding Poverty* (pp. 337–356). New York: Oxford University Press.

Nugroho, A. E. (2008). A Critical Review of the Link between Social Capital and Microfinance in Indonesia. *Jurnal Ekonomi dan Bisnis Indonesia*, 23(2), 130.

Patt, A., Peterson, N., Carter, M., Velez, M., Hess, U., & Suarez, P. (2009). Making Index Insurance Attractive to Farmers. *Mitigation and Adaptation Strategies for Global Change*, 14, 737–753.

Putnam, R. D., Leonardi, R., & Nanetti, R. Y. (1993). *Making Democracy Work: Civic Traditions in Modern Italy*. Princeton, NJ: Princeton University Press.

Rahim, H., Syachroerodly, D., & Arizal, E. R. (2013). The Role of Microinsurance as a Social Protection. *Jurnal Asuransi & Manajemen Risiko*, 1(1), 1–15.

Siegel, P. B., Alwang, S., & Canagarajah, S. (2011). Viewing Microinsurance as a Social Risk Management Instrument. SP Discussion Paper, No. 0116, pp. 1–18.

Sudaryanto, S., & Hanim, A. (2002). Evaluasi Kesiapan UKM Menyongsong Pasar Bebas Asean (AFTA): Analysis Perspektif dan Tinjauan Teoritis. *Jurnal Ekonomi Akuntansi dan Manajemen*, 1(2), 30–37.

Tundui, C., & Macha, R. (2014). Social Capital and Willingness to Pay for Community Based Health Insurance: Empirical Evidence from Rural Tanzania. *Journal of Finance and Economics*, 2(4), 50–67.

Woolcock, M., & Narayan, D. (2000). Social Capital: Implications for Development Theory, Research, and Policy. *World Bank Research Observer*, 15(2), 225–249.

The World Bank's Survey. (2011).

Yokoyama, S., & Ishida, A. (2006). Social Capital and Community Development: A Review. In S. Yokoyama, & T. Sakurai (Eds.), *Potential of Social Capital for Community Development* (pp. 10–26). Tokyo, Japan: Asian Productivity Organization.

Zhang, L., Wang, H., Wang, L., & Hsiao, W. (2006). Social Capital and Farmer's Willingness-to-Join a Newly Established Community-Based Health Insurance in Rural China. *Health Policy*, 76(2), 233–242.

12 Conclusion

Toseef Azid and Lutfi Sunar

The main focus of this volume was to discuss the issues of social justice, the role of the state, the relationship between the state, market and different Islamic institutions like *Zakat*, interest-free economy and *waqf*. These issued were discussed in two aspects, theoretical and practical. For the first aspect, this volume presented the theoretical background of the different conventional theories with a particular emphasis on the Islamic perspective. For the second aspect, some practical implications of social justice from an Islamic perspective were presented. It was assumed under the Islamic system that every institution that is either market-based on nonmarket-based interacts with each other. The market plays its specific role whereas state and other nonbusiness organizations play their specific roles. It is observed that all the activities under the Islamic system, both market or nonmarket, have their own moral justifications. However, the conventional theories of social justice have their own narrow understanding of social justice. In conventional approaches, only material aspects are discussed whereas its spiritual part is almost ignored in their discussions. Also, these approaches only discussed the worldly affairs whereas the part concerning the life hereafter is completely ignored. However, in the theory of Islamic social justice, both material and spiritual aspects are discussed and simultaneously the interconnection between worldly life and life hereafter is also presented. The theoretical framework of social justice in the Islamic system would be incomplete if it didn't take into consideration the reward from Allah in the life hereafter.

In Islamic political philosophy, social justice has a significant position. Islam places equal importance on individual freedom and social justice and also places equal importance on positive and normative aspects of social justice in the economic framework. The role of the state is not minimal in the functions of Islamic society and acts as a welfare state, on the other hand, the role of the community also has its own significance in establishing social justice. Consequently, reducing inequality among the members of the society, Islam creates an environment which not only automatically corrects the unwanted outcomes of the market but also intervention of the state is required to regulate the market. The concept of the welfare state is part and parcel of establishing the process of social justice. Under this system, both the market and the state work simultaneously to establish social justice in a cooperative way. The norms of Islamic society, and the religious instructions of the Islamic system, are not dependent on any time span or space—these are universal and applicable everywhere and at all times. Islam emphasizes individual freedom and social justice simultaneously. However, Islam also maintains a balance between individual freedom and social justice. In the teaching of Islam, the freedom of the individual has some constraints which are morally and ethically justified. This freedom has no negative connotation. It is also morally acceptable under this system that government can play a role in maintaining justice in the society/community. It is furthermore, worthwhile to note that the market mechanism enforces and supports those regulations which are imposed by the state and played a very significant role in enhancing the redistributive role of the government. It is also appreciable that under this system the role of society, state and market is interconnected. It is not a only static one but also independent from spatial and temporal environment.

All of Islamic injunctions always support efficiency in production and consumption. All of these injunctions have their own moral grounds. Historically, it has been approved that the moral and ethical norms of this system present an optimal solution for all the economic, political and social issues. As we have mentioned above, these norms and ethical values can be incorporated within the framework of modern knowledge without any complications and does not create any overt complexity. Moreover, these ideas become more attractive when these are developed within the Islamic framework. The Islamic social charter, which is presented in chapter Al *Hujra'at* has its own significance and universal character and acceptability. The Islamic concept of overall social utility is also not only based on this world but also interconnected with the life hereafter. Islamic injunctions, moral and ethical values offered an ideal state of social justice where state policies, market mechanism and individual freedom are not in conflict with each other. And due to their complementary features, these institutions collectively solve the issues of social justice. In this system there is well-established mechanism of distributive justice, there is a system of built-in flexibility for the correction of unwanted market outcomes, no room for unfair and unjust activities and there is no conflict among any institutions, individual freedom or social justice.

Any institution, which is free from divine guidance, is not acceptable in the system of Islam. It is perceived that any system without divine guidance cannot be morally justified because it is based on the narrow understanding and self-interest of the human being. Owing to this, it cannot become a universal law and it can be changed with respect to time and space. Moreover, it is completely based on the human knowledge, skills, talents and environment in which they are living. It has also been observed that sometimes manmade laws give more preference to personal interests than to the notion of social justice.

Social justice within the Islamic framework is covering all the aspects of human life, i.e. political, spiritual, material, social and economic. Justice begins with the life of the person himself, then family, then community and so on. Islamic teachings begin with the purification of the heart, without which it is not possible to establish justice in a society. Any human desire or group interests cannot influence it. This is the duty of every Muslim, Islamic state, Islamic society and every institution to establish and maintain social justice.

We feel after reviewing the chapter in this volume, that there is a need to put more efforts in explaining and elaborating the theory of social justice within Islam which should be better understood in this complex world of knowledge. This is the duty of Muslim scholars to fill the gap if they feel there is any. A practical application of this theory in the Muslim countries like Saudi Arabia, Pakistan, Malaysia and Gulf states is also needed.

Index

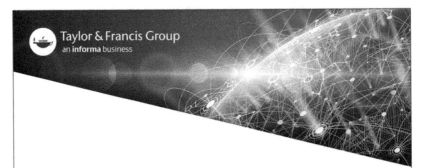

For Product Safety Concerns and Information please contact our EU
representative GPSR@taylorandfrancis.com
Taylor & Francis Verlag GmbH, Kaufingerstraße 24, 80331 München, Germany

www.ingramcontent.com/pod-product-compliance
Ingram Content Group UK Ltd.
Pitfield, Milton Keynes, MK11 3LW, UK
UKHW020957180425
457613UK00019B/730